WHAT EVERY BUSINESS OWNER SHOULD KNOW ABOUT VALUING THEIR BUSINESS

WHAT EVERY BUSINESS OWNER SHOULD KNOW ABOUT VALUING THEIR BUSINESS

Stanley J. Feldman, Ph.D.
Timothy G. Sullivan, Ph.D.
Roger M. Winsby

McGraw-Hill

New York   Chicago   San Francisco
Lisbon   London   Madrid   Mexico City
Milan   New Delhi   San Juan   Seoul
Singapore   Sydney   Toronto

The McGraw·Hill Companies

1 2 3 4 5 6 7 8 9 0 AGM/AGM 0 9 8 7 6 5 4 3 2

ISBN 0-07-140992-0

Valuation GURU is a trademark of bizownerHQ.

This publication is designed to provide accurate and authoritative information
in regard to the subject matter covered. It is sold with the understanding that
neither the author nor the publisher is engaged in rendering legal, accounting,
futures/securities trading, or other professional service. If legal advice or other
expert assistance is required, the services of a competent professional person
should be sought.
>   —*From a Declaration of Principles jointly adopted by a Committee*
>   *of the American Bar Association and a Committee of Publishers*

McGraw-Hill books are available at special quantity discounts to use as
premiums and sales promotions, or for use in corporate training programs.
For more information, please write to the Director of Special Sales,
Professional Publishing, McGraw-Hill, Two Penn Plaza, New York, NY 10121-
2298. Or contact your local bookstore.

 This book is printed on recycled, acid-free paper containing a minimum
of 50% recycled, de-inked fiber.

Library of Congress Cataloging-in-Publication Data

Feldman, Stanley J.
    What every business owner should know about valuing their business / by
Stanley J. Feldman, Timothy G. Sullivan, and Roger M. Winsby.
        p. cm.
    ISBN 0-07-140992-0 (pbk.)
    1. Small business—Valuation.   I. Sullivan, Timothy G.   II. Winsby,
Roger M.   III. Title.
    HG4028.V3 P73 2003
    658.15—dc21
                                                    2002011492

CONTENTS

PREFACE

PURPOSE
The primary purpose of this book is to provide owners of privately held businesses or professional practices with a working understanding of the determinants of the value of their business.

PAYOFF
While knowing the value of a business is typically not essential to successful day-to-day operations, there likely will come a day when this knowledge can make a critical difference in how well an owner will be compensated for the many years of work and the risks taken to build the business. Unless an owner plans simply to close the business on retirement, understanding the ways that potential buyers, the Internal Revenue Service (IRS), and business brokers will determine the value of the business can be one of the best investments of time that an owner can make.

BUSINESS VALUATION IS COMPLEX . . .
Understanding valuation is no small task because the value of any business is related to factors that are complex to determine and generally costly to obtain. The language of finance, and valuation in particular, is arcane, and the process by which most valuations are done takes the form of "black box" calculations. As a general rule, the objective of a business valuation is *not* to educate an owner on what the business is worth; rather, the focus is on developing a valuation estimate that is defensible to other valuation experts.

BUT UNDERSTANDABLE
Most business owners have developed a working knowledge of accounting issues important to their business without fully mastering all aspects of double-entry bookkeeping. Owners know where to go for help, and they have a sense of what the help should cost. They know what questions to ask, and they have a context for evaluating the answers. This should be the starting-point objective for owners in understanding business valuation.

OUR APPROACH

Our approach combines basic information about different methods of business valuation illustrated through case studies set in several different industries. While the valuation issues are different for professional practice firms and for manufacturing firms, for example, the business transition issues are often identical.

The case studies highlight other practical business transition issues facing owners beyond valuation, including

1. The pros and cons of different methods for selling a business
2. Reasons why the sale price of a business may differ from the fair market valuation estimate
3. What skills and experiences owners should look for in advisors to help in planning for the inevitable business transition

WHAT WE ARE

bizownerHQ is an expert valuation services firm. We have reengineered traditional valuation processes to achieve an unbeatable combination of accuracy, consistent high quality, transparency, speed, and cost-effectiveness for our business valuation services. We achieve this through leveraging

1. Internet technology for fast, high-quality, and low-cost information collection and distribution
2. Expanded industry-specific data availability
3. Improvements in industry analysis and modeling capabilities
4. Software for automating the customization of reports
5. Advances in peer-reviewed financial research on business valuation

Valuation is at the center of most business life events facing owners of independent businesses. Business life events include selling a business, making changes in the ownership structure, retirement and estate planning (including the value of a business), and protecting owner income and equity. Business life events, the one thing all small business owners have in common besides being small, are high-stakes issues that have a major impact on an owner's financial success. Managing these events is generally outside an owner's experience. Our research shows that many owners have put off addressing these issues due to a combination of uncertainty about what to do, which advisors to rely on, and concerns about how much the solutions to a business life event will cost.

Our mission is threefold:

1. *Take the Mystery Out of Valuation.* Business owners approaching transition can save significant amounts of time and money by knowing the basics of valuation.
2. *Get Owners Focused on Value Maximization.* Most owners manage based on tax minimization. As they approach transition, those planning to sell will benefit from managing their businesses for value maximization (except for selling within a family).
3. *Make Valuation "Valuable" for Owners.* Most business owners find traditional business valuations to be high cost and low value. We provide high-quality, timely, and affordable alternatives to existing business valuation services.

WHAT WE ARE NOT
bizownerHQ is not a business broker and does not sell any insurance, banking, or other financial services. Our valuation work is completely independent, with neither the company's executives nor investors benefiting from business sales transactions or sales of financial services to owners.

WHAT OWNERS WILL LEARN
For the time invested in reading through the cases in this book, owners will come away with an understanding of the preceding issues and much more:

1. An understanding that they are not alone in having to face business transition issues. The number of owners now beginning to seriously address business transition and related business life events issues is growing rapidly.
2. Practical knowledge of the three primary methods of small business valuation.
3. An understanding of reasons why determining the valuation of a privately held business is so much more difficult than determining the valuation of a publicly traded business.
4. An appreciation of the risks to an owner's retirement portfolio where the dominant asset is the value of the business.
5. An understanding of the valuation methodology used by bizownerHQ to value a business.
6. An appreciation of how the power of the Internet is reducing the barriers and therefore the costs of obtaining a privately held business valuation.

7. An understanding of when an owner should commission a professional valuation of the business and what questions he should ask in the valuation selection process.

8. An understanding of how the information an owner provides to the valuation consultant can influence the valuation result.

INTRODUCTION

THE COMING BUSINESS TRANSITION
TIDAL WAVE ...

The revitalization of the small business economy in America has been a central factor in the economic progress of the last 25 years. Now the entrepreneurs who started this charge have begun to retire. Over the next decade, an unprecedented number of businesses will go through some form of ownership transition. Although the importance of the small business economy to the overall economy has become increasingly recognized over the last 10 years, there has been little recognition of the oncoming business transition tidal wave.

WILL OVERWHELM THE INEFFICIENT SUPPORT NETWORK

The basic professional advisor and financial services support structure for small business owners around what we call *business life events* remains primarily local and highly inefficient. Business life events include selling a business, retirement planning, insuring owner income and equity against risks of disability and death, and estate planning. The costs of many owner-related services, including financing for diversification; insurance coverage for business succession and owner disability; business brokerage; and customized advice for retirement and estate planning are perceived as too high by many business owners. The delivery of customized services to owners of businesses and professional practices have shown little improvement over the last two decades despite remarkable advances in technology elsewhere in the economy. For example, it is generally much easier for business owners to obtain short-term financing through personal credit cards than to apply for loans from their banks.

VALUATION IS KEY TO MANAGING BUSINESS LIFE EVENTS

Determining the value of a privately held business or professional practice is an essential aspect of managing business life events. Valuations also have the potential to assist business owners in deciding on which strategies and tactics to undertake. Value maximization, which has become the key driver of management strategies of publicly held companies, also could have a positive impact on the efficiency, effectiveness, and financial results of privately held businesses. While owners of privately held businesses will never have to worry about tracking their value quarter by quarter as their publicly held counterparts do, setting annual objectives for value maximization is likely to have a significant payback over time. This is especially true as the owner or owners approach their likely time for transitioning out of the business.

DRAWBACKS TO TRADITIONAL VALUATIONS

Business valuation is another area of business owner support that has made little progress in terms of efficiency or turnaround time. Understandably, conducting a business valuation is no small task because the value of any business is related to a set of factors that are complex to determine and costly to obtain. The result is that owners who really do need their businesses valued are loath to reach out to an expert for at least three reasons:

1. *High cost/low benefit.* A traditional business valuation runs anywhere from $5000 to well over $25,000. Ask a business owner who has paid for one whether he got what he paid for, and most will say *No!*

2. *Short shelf life.* The results of a valuation must be "as of" a specific date; thus the results age quickly. In addition, it generally takes between 4 and 6 weeks to complete a valuation. Owners typically need an answer more quickly.

3. *What does it mean?* Probably the most important concern is that the owner is generally perplexed with what a valuation expert often provides even if the valuation is larger than the owner had expected. The language of finance, and valuation in particular, is arcane, and the valuation process is perceived as coming from a "black box" where the output is "managed" by the professional undertaking the exercise.

GOING FORWARD

In the following chapters we have organized the information into multiple sections that allow owners to gain the key messages of each chapter without having to read through all elements of each chapter. In the first two chapters we focus on two basic questions: Who should have their business valued? and What is a business valuation? We also have highlighted key points in bold and italics with the lead-in *"Business owners should know. . . ."* The case study chapters that follow focus on realistic business situations that show different aspects of valuation and business life events across a variety of industry sectors. Following each chapter, we include one or more additional sections. The "Special Focus" section addresses a topic introduced in a particular chapter in more detail. The "Backgrounder" sections address more general issues related to valuing a business. The section entitled "More on Valuation Methods" describes a particular valuation approach and the advantages and disadvantages of its use. For our first "Special Focus" section, we present a summary of the crucial role played by the small business sector in the U.S. economy.

Starting in Chapter 4 we introduce the bizownerHQ Valuation GURU to help the owners in these cases get a reliable business valuation quickly and affordably. We have included examples of the bizownerHQ online summary reports that would be provided in each case. These reports and the company financials, as represented by the business tax return, for each business are placed at the end of each chapter in an appendix.

SPECIAL FOCUS

THE ROLE OF SMALL BUSINESS
The U.S. economy is the largest and, arguably, the most dynamic economy in the history of the world. One aspect of the strength and dynamism of the U.S. economy is its diversity in terms of both the varied types of economic activities and the range of sizes of businesses.

The U.S. Small Business Administration (SBA) defines small businesses as businesses with less than 500 employees. Most small businesses do not sell equity (i.e., ownership shares) to the general public and are also called *privately held businesses*.

bizownerHQ estimates that there are 24.5 million small businesses as of 2001. These are enormously important to our standard of living. According to the SBA,

> Small businesses with fewer than 500 workers employ 53 percent of the private non-farm workforce, contribute 47 percent of all sales in the country, and are responsible for 51 percent of the private gross domestic product. Industries dominated by small firms contributed a major share of the 3.1 million new jobs created in 1998. Over the 1990–1995 period, small firms with fewer than 500 employees created 76 percent of net new jobs.[1]

More women are becoming small business owners. Women-owned businesses are an important part of the growing U.S. economy. Women-owned businesses have expanded at double-digit rates and stand at over 8.5 million firms. These firms have generated well over $3 billion in revenue,

---

[1] The Facts About Small Business 1999, U.S. Small Business Administration, Washington, DC 20416.

and women-dominated firms have increased the fastest in wholesale trade, manufacturing, and construction. In 1992, the latest available data, 3.5 percent of all women-owned firms and 16 percent of those with 20 to 100 employees were franchises.

Small businesses are innovation leaders. Small firms produce 55 percent of innovations. They produce twice as many of both product innovations and significant innovations per employee as large firms. Small firms obtain more patents per dollar of sales than large firms. Estimated rates of return on total research and development (R&D) in firms with a university relationship are 30 percent for large firms and 44 percent for small firms.

WHAT EVERY BUSINESS OWNER SHOULD KNOW ABOUT VALUING THEIR BUSINESS

WHO SHOULD HAVE THEIR BUSINESS VALUED?

VALUATION IS NOT FOR ALL SMALL BUSINESSES

For the 24.5 million small businesses and professional practices, how should the owners determine whether they need a business valuation at some point in the life of the business? To address this question, we have separated the need for a valuation into two categories: required valuations and strategic valuations.

Required Valuations

Many owners of businesses and professional practices will at some point in the life of their business be required to get a valuation as part of a legal proceeding or a tax issue involving the owner. Examples include

1. An owner of a business going through a divorce will need to include the value of her business in the final disposition of the couple's assets.
2. An owner places his ownership of the business into a family trust, and the Internal Revenue Service (IRS) contests the value assigned to the business.
3. The estate of a deceased owner will have to commission a valuation of the business for filing estate tax forms.

4. A business or professional practice with more than one owner generally will need a valuation if one of the owners leaves.

5. An owner facing a court judgment against her net worth may be required to have a business valuation to determine how much the owner can pay toward the judgment.

Owners experiencing these types of business life events or similar ones will have no choice but to pay for a business valuation. The business valuation results in most cases will have a direct impact on their finances. The results will determine an amount they must pay to a spouse, a former partner, a claimant, or the IRS. As a result, owners getting a *required valuation* almost always want the lowest possible value assigned to their businesses.

Strategic Valuations for Managing Business Life Events

For owners who are not required by legal or tax issues to get a business valuation, what should determine whether they choose to have their businesses valued at some point? The simple answer is: If an owner believes that the business is successful enough that it could be sold now or in the future, then getting a business valuation is a crucial step in the strategic management of what we call *business life events*.

What we mean by a business being successful enough is that it has an ongoing value, and therefore, the business entity as it currently exists has a value to a new owner. As a consequence, somebody likely will be willing to pay a price for the right to own the existing business. This ongoing value concept needs to be distinguished from a business's liquidation or termination value. The reason is that a business may have $0 value as an ongoing entity but have a value greater than $0 if the business closed its doors and put its assets up for sale. The proceeds of any asset sale minus any remaining business debts or other liabilities establish the business's liquidation value. In this sense, virtually all businesses have some value; but not all have value as an ongoing enterprise. Unless otherwise noted, throughout this book our use of the term *value* always refers to the value of a firm as an ongoing entity. Therefore, when we say a business has $0 value, we mean that as an ongoing entity it has no value, although it may have value if the business ceased to exist and its assets were sold.

There is somewhat of the "which came first, the chicken or the egg" conundrum in the preceding description. How can an owner know if someone would likely pay her to take over the business without first getting a business valuation. We sympathize with business owners facing this question, since the costs of getting a business valuation traditionally have been in the $5000 to $25,000 range. How much should an owner pay to find out if her business has $0 value? This book will help you determine what the right circumstances are for having a valuation completed for your business.

We also have constructed guidelines that help business and professional practice owners to determine whether their businesses should be considered

- Very Small, that is, not yet of a size or stability likely to have a value greater than $0, or
- Established, that is, worth the time and expense to have a valuation.

CHARACTERISTICS OF VERY SMALL BUSINESSES

Most small businesses will never be sold to another owner. They are simply too small in revenue and profits or too dependent on the current owner(s) for their continuation (especially true in personal services businesses, such as hair cutting). Another factor is that a person looking to enter an industry often can start his own business for less than the cost of buying an existing business. For example, someone wanting to go into lawn care typically can get started with a small investment in equipment. It is simpler and cheaper to compete with existing providers of lawn-care services than to buy the customer list and equipment of an existing provider.

If it is unlikely that a business can be sold as an ongoing entity, then it has $0 value. This is true even if an owner earns a reasonable salary from the business. For example, a person can own a lawn-care business that breaks even after the owner pays himself $65,000 in salary each year. This business would have a value of $0 because it does not produce a return on the owner's investment of time and equipment greater than what is needed to pay the owner's salary. The reason is that any potential buyer of the business would not pay the lawn-care business owner any more than the value of the owner's lawn-care assets, namely, lawn mowers, inventory of fertilizer, and so on. The business name and reputation have no value. If they did, the business would return an income in excess of expenses. Therefore, any potential buyer would be better off simply buying the lawn-care owner's business assets and starting a new lawn-care business.

Roughly 17.1 million of the 24.5 million small businesses and professional practices in the United States are one- or two-person businesses, many of them operating out of a home and often with the owners working part-time on top of a regular job. If the business has any employees, typically the employees are part-time. There are these types of businesses in almost every retail and service sector, for example, child day care, pet grooming, lawn care, business consulting by retired executives, and antique retailers.

These businesses are quite diverse. This category includes businesses that will always stay one- or two-person operations, which we call *Ongoing Very Small businesses*, plus start-up businesses without a demonstrated track record yet, which we call *Emerging businesses*. These start-ups may grow substantially in the future, or they may fail—it is just too soon to tell.

CHARACTERISTICS OF ESTABLISHED BUSINESSES

Only when a business has grown in size and stability to the point where the business generates sufficient income to more than cover all expenses, including a "normal" salary compensation to the owner or owners, does a business have value as an ongoing entity. When a business has value, then the owner should begin planning on how to protect the value of this investment in the case of changes in the business circumstances.

We use the terms *Established* and *Very Small* to separate businesses and professional practices by whether the business is likely to be sold or otherwise continue beyond the current ownership. Ongoing Very Small businesses are almost all sole proprietorships with no full-time employees. Emerging Very Small businesses are generally C- or S-type corporations.[1]

Established businesses tend to be S-type corporations, partnerships, and limited-liability partnerships or corporations; C-type corporations and sole proprietorships also fall into this group. Established businesses generally are not located in the owner's house, have full-time employees, and have been in operation for 3 or more years.

The composition of the U.S. small business market between the Established and Very Small segments is shown in Figure 1-1.

The Established Small business segment is a large and growing market that has been fueled by the entrepreneurial boom over the last 20-plus years. Although only 30 percent of the number of small businesses, they are the dominant generators of the small business engine of growth for the U.S. economy. A more detailed profile of this important segment will be presented in the "Backgrounder" at the end of this chapter. Table 1-1 summarizes the differences between the Established Small and Very Small business segments.

---

[1]More information on legal business forms is presented later as a "Backgrounder."

FIGURE 1-1   Very Small and Established businesses. (*Source:* 2001
bizownerHQ update of 1998 estimates based on SRI, PSI, and
SBA data.)

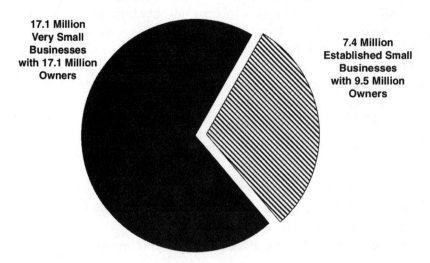

17.1 Million
Very Small
Businesses
with 17.1 Million
Owners

7.4 Million
Established Small
Businesses
with 9.5 Million
Owners

TABLE 1-1   Characteristics of Established and Very Small Businesses

Characteristics	Established Small Businesses	Very Small Businesses
Number of businesses	7.4 million	17.1 million
Number of owners	9.5 million	17.1 million
Number of full-time employees (other than owner)	2–500	0–1
Location	Separate establishment	Owner's home or shared office
Years in business	3 or more years	Emerging companies: Less than 3 Ongoing companies: Varies widely
Corporate form	S Corp, partnership, LLC, C Corp, sole proprietorship	Emerging companies: C or S Corp Ongoing companies: Sole proprietorships

Business Life Events

We have adopted the *business life events* term for use as a catchall descriptor of the critical issues that owners of Established businesses face—outside their day-to-day operational management. Much like personal life events, such as marriage, having children, or buying a house, business life events are major, directional situations for the owner(s). Generally, owners confront these situations only once or a few times during a business's life. As noted earlier, the starting point for an owner encountering business life events is when the business is likely to have a value worth preserving and protecting. The general categories of business life events are

1. Changing the structure of the business ownership
2. Transitioning the current owner out of the business
3. Planning for adequate funding for retirement
4. Planning for the eventual estate-distribution issues and for minimizing estate taxes
5. Protecting owner income and equity through insurance

There are costs to actively managing business life events, and often these costs are significant. Examples include hiring professional advisors to structure ownership changes, retaining a broker to sell the business, buying financial instruments for deferred compensation, and purchasing insurance for estate tax payments, business succession, and owner disability. There is often an even higher cost for not actively managing such events!

THE VALUATION CONNECTION

An accurate estimate of the value of a business is an important first step in the effective management of business life events. Table 1-2 summarizes typical issues that arise in each of the business life event areas where a business valuation is helpful or necessary. It is important to note that in most, but not all, strategic uses of valuation, the owner or owners want the highest possible result for their business. This is in contrast to the situations where owners have to obtain a required valuation.

Let's take the situation where the owner of a well-established insurance agency turns 60 years of age. The prospect of the owner "slowing down" triggers questions like

1. Can I sell an interest in my business to employees, perhaps through an employee stock ownership plan (ESOP)?
2. Can I bring in a partner and sell part of the business to him over time?

TABLE 1-2   Valuation-Centered Business Life Events

Business Life Events	Typical Issues
Ownership structure	Bringing key employees into ownership
	Buyouts of co-owners
	Valuing ownership positions for divorce settlements
Business transition	Selling the business to partners
	Selling the business to a "roll-up" group
	Selling to or buying a competitor
	Establishing an employee stock ownership plan (ESOP)
	Taking the company public
Retirement planning	Choosing the right plan for owners and employees
	Determining the optimal owner portfolio across business and other retirement assets
	Use of deferred compensation plans
Estate planning linkage	Estimating potential estate tax liabilities
	Evaluating alternative tax-minimization strategies
	Picking the right trust vehicle
	Charitable giving options
Income and equity protection	Estimating key-person and regular life insurance needs
	Putting in place owner/key-employee insurance coverage

3. Can I borrow against my equity in the business and use the proceeds to diversify my retirement stock and bond portfolio?
4. Will I have enough money to support my retirement plans after I sell the business?

There are additional questions if the owner has a change in health. For example:

1. If I were to become disabled, who would run the business, and how much money would I continue to receive?
2. If I were to die suddenly, who would run the business? How would my estate pay the estate taxes without selling the business?

Getting owners to consider these issues is a challenge. Once they are ready to confront them, finding reliable answers to these questions can be time-consuming and expensive. Often owners have to seek out professional advisors outside their immediate circle who have specialized expertise in these areas. In the end, most owners are forced to make decisions about their business life events and often at inopportune times. There is a real premium to planning ahead and to understanding the role that business valuations play in the effective management of business life events. This book will help to move owners along this path.

WHO SHOULD HAVE THEIR BUSINESS VALUED?

At the beginning of this chapter we raised the question of which business owners among the 24.5 million U.S. small businesses should have a business valuation done at some point. Our answer in summary is twofold:

1. Owners of Established businesses should have a business valuation done in conjunction with their management of important business life events. This is an example of a strategic valuation, where the owner chooses to have a valuation done as part of the overall owner exit planning.

2. Owners of private businesses who are part of a legal proceeding or tax issue where the value of their businesses is relevant will have to get a business valuation. This is an example of a required valuation.

The valuation techniques are the same whether an owner is required to have one done or chooses to have one done. Owners are well advised to be knowledgeable about valuation regardless of the reason for getting one, since many operational decisions that owners make day to day can have a significant impact on the value of the business. However, in the rest of this book we will focus more on the strategic uses of valuation because these are the issues that will affect almost all the Established business owners at some point in the life of their businesses.

BACKGROUNDER

CHANGING FACES AND ATTITUDES OF BUSINESS OWNERS

In our work researching the American small business community, we often find two completely opposite views of this community from other small business observers. First, there are those who view every small business as unique; in other words, the only issue common to all these businesses is that they are all small. The opposite view is that all small business owners are the same. Common stereotypes are that owners are white, male, over age 50, very independent, skeptical of advisors, tight with their money, and reluctant to plan ahead.

We offer here a summary of our research that presents a different way of thinking about the Established Small business owner community. Our approach recognizes the diversity of the group but also acknowledges important commonalities in attitudes and experiences, especially around the issue of business life events. The need to manage business life events is shared across all owners of Established Small businesses.

For our business owner readers, we offer this information as a way to benchmark their own private feelings on business life events with those of a representative cross section of owners responding to confidential surveys. For professional advisors who serve this community, we recommend this section to help understand important differences within the business owner community on how they want to be served and supported.

A Growing Prosperous Community of Owners

The small business revitalization over the last 20 years has both greatly expanded the numbers of Established Small businesses and significantly increased the wealth of many of these owners. As we saw in Figure 1-1, there are approximately 7.4 million Established Small businesses and professional practices with 9.5 million owners. Figure 1-2 looks at the wealth composition of these Established business owners divided into three segments: Aspiring Affluent, Emerging Affluent, and Affluent. The Affluent segment is defined primarily by having a household net worth of $1 million and above, not including the value of their home. The Emerging Affluent segment earns an income of $100,000 and above and has a household net worth between $300,000 and $1 million. This group is on the track to becoming Affluent if the value of their businesses and other investments continues to grow. The Aspiring Affluent segment covers the remaining owners of Established businesses. The income and net worth dimensions are summarized in Table 1-3.

TABLE 1-3   Income and Net Worth Definitions of Targeted Segments

Segmentation Structure	Net Worth (Not Including Principal Residence, NIPR)		
Annual income	Under $300,000	$300,000–$1 million	Above $1 million
Under $100,000	Aspiring Affluent	Aspiring Affluent	Affluent
$100,000 and above	Aspiring Affluent	Emerging Affluent	Affluent

FIGURE 1-2   The Established business owner community segmented by wealth. (*Source:* 2001 bizownerHQ update of 1998 estimates based on SRI, PSI, and SBA data.)

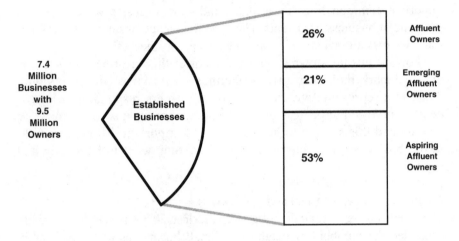

With 2.5 million owners, or 26 percent, in the Affluent segment, owners of Established businesses make up almost 40 percent of the over 6.2 million affluent U.S. households. Contrast this with 1990, when Established business owners made up roughly 25 percent of the 4 million affluent households in the United States. Owning a successful business used to be considered a ticket to the middle class; now it has become a ticket to the upper class.

When we include the Emerging Affluent segment, which tends to be younger, the more financially successful end of the business owner community grows to 4.5 million owners, or 47 percent, of the Established business owner community. As the small business engine continues to chug along, many of the almost 4 million Aspiring Affluent owners also will prosper and become part of the Emerging Affluent or Affluent segments. Looking forward over the next decade, the continuing growth and prosperity of this Established business owner community should lead to even greater political and social influence than the community has exercised to date.

Changing Faces

Since valuation and the management of business life events become more important the more "established" a business is and the older and wealthier the owner is, we will focus our attention on the 47 percent upper end of the segment that comprises the Emerging Affluent and the Affluent owners.

Along with the impressive growth in size and wealth of the upper end of the Established business owner community has come increasing diversity in its demographics. What used to be an almost exclusively white, male, over age 50 group of business owners now has significant percentages of women, people of different ethnic and racial groups, and people under the age of 50. For example, 30 percent of the owners in the upper end of the Established business owner community are women. The percentage of owners who are college educated or beyond also has increased significantly, even after adjusting for professional practices.

However, perceptions of the small business owner market appear to be changing more slowly than the reality of this increasingly diverse group. Research conducted by one of the authors found that professional advisors, business services, and financial services firms that serve this market are still overwhelmingly focused on the white, male, and over age 50 segments.

Changing Attitudes

While these 4.5 million owners of upper-end Established businesses share in common the challenges of managing business life events, their preferences for how to make decisions about business life events and how much they rely on advisors in making those decisions diverge significantly. Interestingly, owners split into different business life events profiles based far more on their attitudinal preferences and perceived needs than along income or business size or other economic-related dimensions. Even more important, the processes that business owners will follow in implementing decisions concerning business life events are generally consistent with the business life events profiles.

These conclusions are based on consistent findings from multiple market research studies of small business owners about business life events. This previous research contributes to bizownerHQ's unique understanding of the needs and requirements of the small business owner marketplace. This segmentation of the Established business owner community provides a bridge between those who see *smallness* as the only shared attribute of business owners and those who think that all business owners are alike.

BUSINESS LIFE EVENTS PROFILES FOR OWNERS

The following are seven profiles that we have defined based on our extensive quantitative and qualitative research on the upper end of the Established business owner community. Owners reading through these profiles are likely to find that one of these profiles matches their current attitudes. It is important to note that these segments are not rigid personality types. Owners can change their business life events profile based on what actions they take and what experiences they have.

Business Life Events Profiles
The share of market is shown for each business life event (BLE) group:

1. *BLE Planners—Expert Dependent (20 percent).* These owners indicated that their needs for solving BLEs were spread evenly across retirement planning, business succession planning, disability protection, and other business life events; hence we call them *balanced needs*. These owners have not done much planning yet but are aware of the need to begin. They are also less confident in their own judgment about these issues and more easily overwhelmed by the number of financial choices they face. They place a high degree of importance on working with an advisor who takes a leadership role; hence the designation *Expert Dependent*.

2. *BLE Planners—Expert Independent (25 percent).* Owners in this segment also report that they are early in their planning and have multiple needs across BLE areas. However, these owners report that they are confident about making the decisions necessary to manage their business and personal finances. They are open to working with an advisor or advisors but only if the owner has close involvement in the BLE solution planning. They expect their financial advisors to provide them with information and options.

3. *Business Succession Focused (10 percent).* This segment places a very high priority on implementing a comprehensive approach to business succession. They have built a business that should continue on for both financial and ego reasons. They want to have a business succession plan in place to ensure that the business has adequate capital through any transition and that the current owner reaps the rewards of building an ongoing business. The payout from the sale of the business will be their primary retirement funding. They also want to have a clear strategy for how the next owner or owners will fill their shoes. However, as of yet, they have not yet made much progress in this area.

4. *Golden Years Focused (20 percent).* In contrast to the Business Succession Focused group, this group is not looking to the sale of their existing business to provide the major source of funding for their retirement. This group wants to maximize the income they can put toward retirement. Over half are sole proprietors, and at least a quarter expects to close their business on retirement. They are looking to put the most money away on a tax-deferred basis rather than to expect some large payout from selling the business.

5. *Needs Being Met—Expert Dependent (17 percent).* This group is the most advanced in already purchasing and/or implementing BLE solutions. Almost half have three or more solutions in place. This group places the highest priority on getting ongoing support from their advisor team.

6. *Limited Needs—Expert Skeptic (8 percent).* This group does not see the need for doing much about BLEs. Half expect to close their business on retirement. These people are generally mistrustful of advisors, business brokers, and consultants.

These segments are shown along with their composition by gender in Table 1-4 and household net worth in Table 1-5.

TABLE 1-4   Affluent and Emerging Affluent Business Owner Segmentation

Segment Name	Segment Description	Market Size	Gender	
			Male	Female
BLE Planners—Expert Dependent	Younger, emerging affluent, and likely to be female	20%	54%	46%
BLE Planners—Expert Independent	High income, very involved in BLE planning	25%	80%	20%
Business Succession Focused	Very high net worth, focused on business succession issues	10%	80%	20%
Golden Years Focused	Lower net worth, focused on building retirement assets	20%	82%	18%
Needs Being Met– Expert Dependent	High net worth, likely female	17%	55%	45%
Limited Needs—Expert Skeptic	Higher net worth, do not trust advisors, mostly sole proprietors	8%	71%	29%
Affluent and Emerging Affluent Market Total		100%	70%	30%

TABLE 1-5   Affluent and Emerging Affluent Business Owner Segmentation

	Net Worth (NIPR)		
Segment Name	$300,000– $1 Million	$1 Million < $2 Million	$2 Million+
BLE Planners—Expert Dependent	64%	32%	5%
BLE Planners—Expert Independent	61%	20%	18%
Business Succession Focused	49%	19%	32%
Golden Years Focused	70%	13%	17%
Needs Being Met—Expert Dependent	46%	31%	23%
Limited Needs—Expert Skeptic	47%	27%	27%
Affluent and Emerging Affluent Market Total	59%	22%	19%

We accompany this information-rich table with the following observations:

1. The one segment that most closely matches the old stereotypes of small business owners, the Limited Needs—Expert Skeptic, today makes up only 8 percent of the upper end of the Established business owner market.

2. Twenty-seven percent of the Limited Needs—Expert Skeptic market has a net worth of $2 million or more. Another 27 percent has net worth between $1 million and $2 million. Their mistrust of advisors and lack of interest in planning for BLEs could be very expensive for their heirs.

3. Women business owners are much more likely to seek out advice from accountants, lawyers, and other professionals. Women comprise close to half the two advisor-focused segments, BLE Planners—Expert Dependent and Needs Being Met—Expert Dependent. These two segments make up 37 percent of the total market.

4. The Business Succession Focused segment, although only 10 percent of the overall market, has the highest percentage (32 percent) of any segment in the $2 million or more net worth category. Their strong concerns for a successful business transition certainly make sense.

5. The Needs Being Met—Expert Dependent segment has the highest percentage of owners (54 percent) in the two top net worth groups. These people recognize the need to plan ahead and have not procrastinated.

2

WHAT IS A BUSINESS VALUATION?

A BUSINESS VALUATION IS AN ESTIMATE OF A SALES PRICE

A business valuation is an analytical process for estimating the price a willing buyer would pay for a specific business and a willing seller would accept—without having to put the business up for sale. This process typically is conducted by a valuation consultant or accountant and is based on the recent financials of the business. The goal of the valuation process is to produce a reasonable estimate of the fair market value of the business. *Fair market value* is defined by the U.S. Internal Revenue Service (IRS) in Revenue Ruling 59-60 as

> The price at which the property would change hands between a willing buyer and a willing seller when the former is not under any compulsion to buy and the latter is not under any compulsion to sell, both parties having reasonable knowledge of relevant facts. Court decisions frequently state in addition that the hypothetical buyer and seller are assumed to be able, as well as willing, to trade and to be well informed about the property and concerning the market for such property.[1]

---

[1] Internal Revenue Service Revenue Rule 59-60, 1959-1, C.B. 237.

The closest analogy to a business valuation that many people have experienced is an appraisal of the value of a house. The same fair market value concept applies to homes as well as businesses.

At the center of this fair market value concept with the willing buyer and seller, there is a fundamental assumption: When faced with an important buying decision, for example, a business or a house, people make economically rational decisions about returns and risks. This means that a person should have a clear idea about the returns, that is, how much income the business could generate in the future, and the risks, that is, a sense of how uncertain that income flow could be. Every valuation method incorporates in some way these fundamental assumptions about returns and risks.

There are two important qualifiers that must be defined in any business valuation: the date of the valuation and the exact description of what is being valued. In the latter case, this is often more complex for a business appraisal than for a home appraisal.

Date

The business valuation process produces a fair market value estimate of the value of a business as of a specific date. Since a valuation is an estimate of an economic activity, the potential sale of a business, the valuation result must be a function of the economic conditions as of the date of the valuation. While this seems to many business owners at first glance to be arbitrary, a simple example can highlight the importance of tying the valuation to a specific date.

Consider the case of a business owner, Emily Ames, who in addition to her business owns 500 shares of stock in Cisco Systems, a publicly held company listed on the Nasdaq. Emily decides to sell her shares to pay off a loan of $10,000. She made the decision to sell on March 19, 2001, when the price was $20.81 per share. Because of a health emergency in her family, she did not get around to selling the Cisco shares until April 4, 2001. By that time, the value of the shares declined 34 percent to $13.69. Her 500 shares are worth only $6845, so she needs an additional $3155 to pay off the personal loan. Figure 2-1 shows what a difference a few weeks can make in value.

Now, for private businesses, valuation swings over such a short period of time may not be as dramatic as it was for Cisco. However, they could be, and here is how. Jill, an owner of a marketing services firm, has been told that her business is worth two times its most current annual revenue of $300,000 or $600,000. The multiple of 2 is based on a comparable public firm as of today, after adjusting for the liquidity discount for private companies (this will be explained later in the book). Assume that Jill decides to sell this business today for $600,000 to Bill. Bill is a financial whiz and expects the Federal Reserve to reduce interest rates some time in the next

FIGURE 2-1   The value of a public company can change rapidly—Cisco
Systems' stock price between March 19, 2001 and April 4, 2001.

several months. The next day the Federal Reserve cuts interest rates by $\frac{1}{2}$ of 1 percent. Jill looks up today's stock prices for comparable firms and notices that the revenue multiple for the comparable firms used to value her business have increased to 2.17. Jill recalculates the value of her firm by multiplying her firm's revenue of $300,000 by the new multiple, that is, 2.17. To Jill's surprise, she finds that if she had waited one more day, she could have sold her business for $651,000, or 8.5 percent more than she did. Bill, on the other hand, feels fortunate. His net worth just increased due only to the timing of the sale and the Federal Reserve policy change.

Business owners should know that a business valuation can still be useful in certain settings well past the "as of" date of the valuation. The key questions that must be examined are

1.   Have there been any significant changes in the financial conditions of the business? For example, has the company lost or gained any major customers?

2. Have there been any significant changes in the U.S. financial markets? For example, have there been any major interest rate changes or have stock market valuations changed significantly?
3. Have there been any significant changes in the industry in which the business operates? For example, have input prices for labor or materials changed, thus making the profit outlook different?
4. Have there been any significant changes in the numbers of businesses in this industry being sold and the prices at which they were sold?

The effort involved in a valuation update (and hence the cost) should be much less than the effort and cost of conducting a valuation for the first time. Business owners who choose to have or are required to have valuations done for their businesses within a space of less than 1 year should consider these factors in negotiating a price for the second valuation.

Finally, the possible timeline for a business valuation is any historical date up to the current date. A business valuation cannot be done as of a date in the future. Valuations done in the past are generally done in cases where an owner has died, and the estate needs a value as of the date of death. Valuations done in the past use the economic and financial factors as of the date of the valuation.

What Is Being Valued?

The second basic condition for a valuation is a description of exactly what is being valued. The "what is being valued" should be obvious in most settings—it is the ongoing operations of a business plus any nonoperating sources of income or value, such as real estate unrelated to the business. However, in cases where there are closely controlled companies owned by the same person or group of people, this description can become very important. For example, there are many business situations in which the office or factory building is owned by a separate company, perhaps a family trust, and the company being valued pays rent to the trust. Determining exactly which entity or entities is being valued in these settings is essential. In addition, the valuation consultant may be required to restate company financials by adjusting transactions between closely controlled companies to reflect current market rents or prices.

Another "what is being valued" issue here is the ownership stake being valued. In the case where there are multiple owners, is the valuation based on owning less than 50 percent of the company or owning a controlling stake (50 percent or more)? In most business valuations, controlling ownership of a business earns a higher value per share than a minority ownership position. This additional value is called the *control premium*, which will be described in more detail later.

For businesses that have been losing money, the "what" of the valuation may change from the value of ongoing operations of the business to its liquidation value, that is, the stand-alone market value of the business assets minus liabilities. For example, a restaurant that is losing money may have $0 value as an operating business but should have a positive value when the kitchen equipment, china, and silverware are auctioned off and the building housing the restaurant is sold.

An Estimate Based on an Analytical Process

Valuation is not an exact science. Valuation experts can and frequently do disagree on the value of a business. This generally occurs when a valuation is presented in an adversarial setting such as a divorce case or an IRS dispute over tax liability related to a transfer of a private business. *Business owners should know how the information they provide in the valuation process could affect the valuation estimates.*

There are several different methods for making valuation estimates for a business. In this book we will explain the most commonly used methods and the strengths and weaknesses of each approach. *Business owners should know the basics of each method and whether the method is likely to produce a reasonable estimate for their particular type of business.*

Valuation Assumptions

Each of these valuation methodologies has its own set of assumptions generated during the analytical process. These assumptions are necessary to develop the estimate of what a willing seller would pay a willing buyer for a business as of that date. While this book is not designed to transform business owners into valuation experts, business owners should be able to apply their knowledge and expertise in their businesses and their industries to determine whether the assumptions made in a valuation are reasonable.

COMPARABLE COMPANIES EXAMPLE

For example, let us examine the business valuation method most similar to the appraisal method for homes, the use of sales of comparable companies. For this approach to produce a valid estimate, the following assumptions must be true:

1. The firm sold and the firm being valued must be in the same industry and similar in their business size and performance.
2. The sale should be very recent to the date of the valuation so that the external conditions that influence valuations are very similar.

Unlike home appraisals, where there are numerous current transactions of equivalent homes, this rarely is true when private firms are being valued. Many private transactions are not reported, so getting the information to verify the similarities of performance may be difficult. In addition, many business sale transactions have seller or third-party financing involved, which complicates measuring the actual price paid. Finally, when data on private business transactions are available, they are often dated, so the conditions of the sale are no longer applicable to developing a current business valuation. In many cases, particularly where the business being valued is unusual, there are no transaction data available of any kind.

Another example illustrates the cost of not using the most current information on business conditions when valuing a private business. Consider an example in which a McDonald's restaurant franchise with sales of $1.5 million sold for two times revenue, that is, $3 million, in January 2000. In September 2001, Alice Watson, the owner of a nearby McDonald's restaurant, wants to have her business valued in preparation for selling it. Jeff Anderson, a business broker, tells Alice that she should save her money on having a valuation done because Jeff knows what the valuation multiple is for McDonald's restaurants in that area. Alice's restaurant has sales of $2 million, so Jeff estimates that it should sell for around $4 million. He offers to list the business for $4.2 million.

A Second Opinion

Alice appreciates this information, but she long ago learned the value of getting multiple opinions. Alice then asked her accountant, Wendy Rosetti, to prepare a valuation. Wendy, who took 1 month and charged Alice $5000 for her valuation analysis, also used the two times revenue comparable for one estimate and then did a discounted cash flow analysis that returned a value of $5 million. This estimate reflected that interest rates in the economy had declined substantially since January 2000, which typically results in higher values for businesses. Wendy averaged the two valuations to come up with a fair market value of $4.5 million. With widely varying valuations for her franchise, how should Alice approach setting a selling price for her franchise?

Businesses Can Sell at Prices Different
from Recent Valuation Results

Remember that a valuation is an estimate based on one or more analytical processes, each with a set of assumptions. ***Business owners should know that, unfortunately, there is no simple process for translating valuation results into the "right" selling price for a business (i.e., the one that will*** *provide the most money for the owner in the least amount of time).* Businesses are often sold at values well above and below the figure set by valuation—primarily because the assumptions that are necessary for the valuation analysis did not apply in the real world. For example, a fair market valuation assumes that the seller does not have to sell quickly, but if the seller has strong reasons to sell in a short period of time, he is likely to get a lower price than the valuation would estimate. Conversely, when a larger company purchases a business, often a premium is paid above the fair market value of the company as a stand-alone entity. In these situations, the typical rationale is that the larger company will be able to generate more cash flow from the acquired company. This could be due to the larger company having lower-cost products or services or a most cost-effective distribution network.

The Most Important Financial Decision of an Owner's Life

Since the selling price that an owner accepts for her business is among the most important financial decisions that a business owner will ever make, we recommend that owners allocate sufficient time and money to this endeavor. In our preceding example, Alice was willing to pay $5000 and wait 4 weeks to get additional information on the value of her business; and Alice should not stop there. She needs to get more information before finalizing the listing price and determining the price and conditions she would be willing to accept. She needs to learn more about the valuation results and about current market conditions, including the available inventory of McDonald's franchises for sale and the expected risk and return of the fast-food restaurant industry.

Business owners should know that only they have the goal of maximizing the value of their business. The valuation consultant's assignment is to estimate the fair market value, not the likely maximum value. While business brokers and investment bankers have their commissions tied to the selling price, they typically focus on making sure that a viable transaction happens quickly. If no sale takes place, they do not get paid or at least do not get full payment.

Thus it is up to the owner to become an instant expert on selling her business. The owner needs to ask lots of questions of her advisors. For example, Alice should ask her accountant, Wendy, why she averaged the values from the two different methods. She should ask which of the two methods is likely to produce results that provide the best insights into how much the asking price for the business should be. She should even try to find out from the buyer of the other McDonald's any information about how the price was determined, how well that franchise is operating, and whether that business is on track to achieve the breakeven period that was projected during the buyer's evaluation of the purchase.

Business owners should know that even after they become instant experts on selling a business, they will still have to make many tough decisions without complete information. For example, in Alice's situation, while there is strong evidence that the discounted cash flow valuation methodology (the method that produced the $5 million value) generally produces the most accurate results, a market-based multiple for a highly similar business (the method that produced the $4 million value) is still important information to consider, even when the sale of this comparable entity took place many months earlier when interest rates were significantly higher.

Averaging Results from Multiple Valuation Methods

The IRS, in its Revenue Ruling 59-60, discourages the use of simple averaging of valuation results to arrive at a composite valuation result. While technically this ruling applies only to valuations used for estate and gift tax filings, it is generally accepted as the standard for valuations in all settings. This ruling recommends that the valuation expert use the valuation results in a weighted-average calculation, where the method or methods that are most appropriate to the circumstances of the business being valued get the highest weights.

Despite this clear statement from the IRS, many in the valuation community have continued to employ the traditional approach of using several valuation methods to estimate a range of values for a business and then to equally weight these values to get a final estimate. Given that valuation is an estimating process and that each method has its own set of assumptions, there is some justification to this averaging approach. When a business valuation is used in a legal setting, there is often the tendency to "split the difference" between two competing proposals by the two parties.

However, the "art" of business valuation is continually evolving, and there is an ongoing effort to improve the methodologies and data sources used to make valuation estimates. There is also a continuing effort to have people conducting business valuations meet a set of professional certification standards.

There is a growing consensus among professional valuation experts that the discounted cash flow method produces the most accurate valuation results for an ongoing, established business if there are no current transactions of very comparable businesses. This is supported by practical experience and peer-reviewed academic research. As this consensus grows, it casts doubt on the value of a simple averaging of the results of other methods. As we saw in the restaurant example, the business comparability was quite high, but the sale timeliness was a serious problem. Averaging a result based on a comparable sale when the prime rate was 10.5 percent with a result when the prime rate is 8.5 percent has a major impact on the final valuation estimate.

Business owners should know that a valuation consultant is likely to use a simple average of the results reached through different valuation methods and should recognize that this averaging may not be in the owner's best interests. Owners should look at how well the underlying assumptions of each valuation method reflect their understanding of how their business and industry operates. If the difference between the highest estimate and the lowest estimate is greater than 10 percent, an owner should ask the valuation consultant to reconsider whether results this divergent are sufficiently reliable to include in the final valuation estimate.

A BUSINESS VALUATION IS BASED ON CURRENT FINANCIALS

An essential step in the analytical process of a valuation is a review of the business's financials. This typically includes a review of unaudited as well as audited financials and the business's tax returns.

Tax Minimization versus Value Maximization

Interestingly, research suggests that rather than having a strategy of maximizing the value of their business, most small business owners have a strategy of minimizing taxes. In fact, some small business owners seem to take minimizing taxes to such extreme levels that it drives most business decisions. To some extent, minimizing taxes makes sense to a small business owner because he pays taxes and sees the forms and payments each year. If the owner adopts a business practice that reduces taxes, he can see the tangible result immediately. Maximizing value is much more difficult to understand and to measure. If a small business owner adopts a business practice, how can he know that this has increased value—and by how much?

Discretionary Expenses

A strategy of minimizing taxes may be very effective at reducing the amount of taxes paid each year but may have a detrimental effect on the value of the business. For many small business owners, this realization only comes when they seriously consider selling their businesses. For example, the desire to minimize taxes may lead the owner to employ family members and pay them well above market for services rendered. Higher reported expenses leads to reduced taxable income. When the business is ready to be sold, the owner can easily treat a portion of these expenses as discretionary and thus add back this discretionary amount to taxable income. This is proper.

However, there are other expenses that cannot be treated in this way as easily. One category of expenses is travel and entertainment. For certain service businesses, this line is large and often contains expenses that are really personal rather than business expenditures. For example, an owner brings her spouse along to an industry event in Florida, Hawaii, or the Caribbean. The owner and spouse spend an additional week relaxing on their own. Backing out what is personal is not that easy. Proving that these expenses are discretionary to a potential buyer presents another level of difficulty. It raises a caution sign to the prospective buyer that the business practices of the seller are questionable and raises the specter that there are skeletons in the closet that even competent due diligence may not pick up.

There are some owners who never intend to sell their businesses, and so they may argue that a focus on minimizing current and future tax liabilities makes the most sense. However, even under this circumstance, it may not be an optimal strategy. Why? If the owner at any point wants to purchase key-person insurance, for example, the amount of coverage will be a direct function of the firm's fair market value. The estimated value of a low-profit and low-tax business is likely to be lower than necessary to a buyout of a deceased owner's share of the business. In a similar way, owners who wish to refinance their businesses will certainly find the process easier if they can demonstrate a direct relationship between their loan request to the fair market value of their businesses to a third party.

Discretionary Expenses Example

Let's take the example of Foster Mortuary, Inc., a business incorporated as an S corporation with one owner. S corporations do not pay any business income tax because the income of the business is "passed through" to the owner's personal tax returns (this will be discussed in detail in Chapter 3). The expense and net income situation for this business are shown in Table 2-1.

TABLE 2-1   Example Financials for Foster and Sons Mortuary

Foster Mortuary, Inc.	2000 as Reported
Total expenses	$1 million
Discretionary expenses	$150,000
Taxable net income	$100,000

Gil Foster has a passion for restoring old hearses, and he displays them at the Foster Hearse Museum, housed in a converted garage next to the mortuary. In a typical year he spends approximately $150,000 on this activity, including travel to find old hearses and vintage parts and the cost of restoration. This spending is at the discretion of the owner. Gil Foster justifies this expense as part of the promotional activities for the mortuary. Let's assume that recent sales of mortuaries in their area have all been completed at four times reported earnings. Consequently, on this basis, we could estimate that the value of this business would be $400,000, that is, four times reported earnings of $100,000. However, Gil knows that any likely buyer of Foster Mortuary would not put any money into the Hearse Museum. Therefore, he adjusts his financials by shifting the $150,000 of discretionary expenses to net income adjusted for valuation purposes.

Using the same rule of thumb of four times earnings, Gil estimates that the true value of Foster Mortuary is $1 million, that is, $400,000 of value attributed to net income as reported and $600,000 attributed to the reclassification of discretionary expenses to net income. These significant differences are summarized in Figure 2-2.

FIGURE 2-2   Expenses, net income, and value for Foster Mortuary.

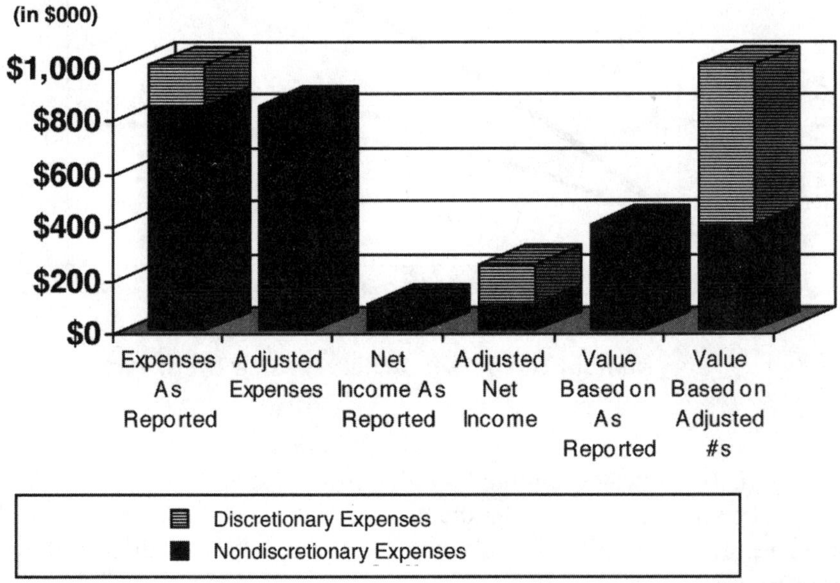

Now, let's examine how long it might take for a tax-minimization strategy to create $600,000 of value? Since discretionary expenses are $150,000, a 40 percent tax rate means that the owner saves $60,000 in taxes each year. We have developed the answer to this question by appealing to a concept known as *present value*, which we describe in more detail in Chapter 5. This concept allows us to calculate how long it will take for the present value of $60,000 of tax savings received each year in the future to cumulate to $600,000, which is the value of the $150,000 in discretionary expenses.

Figure 2-3 shows the sum of the present values of $60,000 payments as of each year. These values are calculated under risk assumptions about the availability of the $60,000 tax benefit. The low-risk assumption means that we are almost 100 percent certain that the $600,000 tax benefit will be available. The medium-risk case assumes that it may be available but not necessarily, and the high-risk assumption means that there is more than a modest chance that the benefit may not be available.

FIGURE 2-3   Advantage of value maximization over tax minimization.

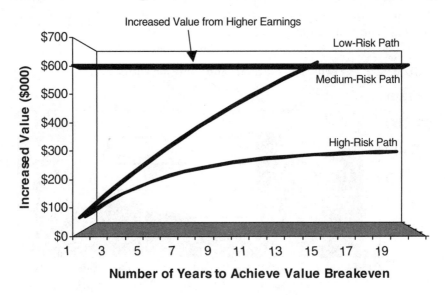

Figure 2-3 indicates that the tax-minimization strategy pays off *only* if one can be virtually certain (i.e., the low-risk path) that the tax benefit will be there. Even in this case it takes 14 years to reach the $600,000 breakeven.

Business owners should know that if they want to maximize the value of their businesses prior to selling, they should start making the strategic change from tax minimization to value maximization at least 3 years in advance of when they plan to list the business for sale. As part of this change, they should carefully review with their accountant the degree to which their personal expenses are intertwined with business expenses. It also makes sense to implement a disentangling of owner and business expenses over a 3- to 5-year transition period.

There are no concrete guidelines as to whether an expense is discretionary or not. A financial planner's country club membership may be a very defensible business expense as a means of meeting wealthy prospects, whereas the cancer surgeon's country club membership likely would be a harder case to make. The more an owner can document that his marketing expenses are effective, the more likely he will be considered legitimate. If the value of Foster Mortuary were to arise in a legal setting, a judge or jury would have to decide whether the Hearse Museum is a reasonable use of company expenses for promotion or whether it is a hobby of the owner.

VALUATION RISKS
The business owner must keep in mind that there are many types of risk that influence the perceived overall riskiness of her business. One risk that often dominates in the case of privately held business is the risk of business operations not being transparent. When this is the case, perspective investors as well as those considering loaning the firm capital tend to view such businesses with some skepticism. They do this because they are not confident that they understand all the critical facets of the business well enough. This translates into the feeling that the business is full of "land mines" that can go off at any time and without sufficient warning. *Transparency*, the feeling that everything is as it appears, results in a firm that is less risky, which translates into higher firm value—a point we demonstrate below.

Lack of Transparency
Lack of transparency for private firms can take several forms. Among the chief concerns are

1. *Underreporting of revenue.* The common stereotype of a small, private business that operates mainly in cash transactions is that only a fraction of the actual business sales are recorded.
2. *Underreporting of income.* As discussed earlier, the line between owner business and personal expenses can be blurred easily, making it difficult to finalize the income stream to be valued.
3. *Customer loyalty after the owner leaves.* Determining how closely tied current customers are to the owner(s) is an important step in understanding the riskiness of buying the company.

4. *Strength of the employee team after the owner leaves.* Determining how well the employees solve customer, supplier, or production problems on their own is another important step to understanding a risk dimension for the firm.

For a public firm, transparency is achieved by providing information about the firm to the public on a regular basis. This will include Security and Exchange Commission (SEC) filings, such as financial statements on quarterly and annual frequencies, and regular press releases. All this information, whether mandated by government agencies or not, is designed to create an openness so that the investing public can have a clear understanding of how the business is managed, how much compensation officers receive, and what the risks and opportunities for the business are from management's perspective. This, and other information, is what investors ordinarily would need to make informed decisions concerning their current or potential future investment in the business.

Creating this transparency is vital to the financial lifeblood of a public firm because without it, even if this were legally possible, the amount of financial capital available to it certainly would decline. Like the public firm, the private firm's access to capital also will be affected adversely by a lack of transparency. All firms need working capital. Without it, it would be very difficult to run a business. However, banks providing the working capital really do need to know that the assets that collateralize the working capital loan are real. Without such confidence, the bank simply would be foolish to make the working capital loan or any loan for that matter.

Like the bank, potential investors would not commit funds if they felt that the firm in question was managed in a way that was not favorable to ownership. Since management and ownership are the same people in privately held small firms, the current business owner/manager generally is unconcerned about the conflict that could lead to loss of transparency. It simply never exists. However, it really does exist; it simply takes a different form if one thinks of the owner not as the current one but as a potential future one. In a sense, the current owner is really the manager of a collection of assets that needs to be managed for maximum value so that the next owner will feel comfortable paying the maximum price when and if the current management is ready to tap into the market for new capital. Again, this does not mean that the business needs to be sold in total, but it may mean that the owner desires to diversify his wealth and sell a portion of the business to an associate, take in a full partner, or sell a controlling interest to employees through an employee stock ownership plan (ESOP).

Managing a Private Firm to Maximize Value

An owner who can show that the value of his privately held firm has grown over time is likely to instill a sense of confidence in any potential buyer or third-party business evaluator that the business is indeed well managed. Achieving transparency takes work and has costs associated with the effort. A well-prepared owner can address the likely concerns mentioned earlier of underreporting of revenue and income by having a comprehensive audit. In addition, the owner can demonstrate his ability to separate from the business through customer retention reports, customer interviews, and presentations by managers and employees describing situations in which they have solved business problems without intervention by the owner. These kinds of efforts should result in the perception that there are no "skeletons in the closet," thus enabling the owner to transfer ownership in the business or refinance the business with a high degree of ease. Owners who have been through these activities attest to the importance of transparency in simplifying the other party's due-diligence efforts. Achieving transparency in business operations should increase value, reduce the time spent on the transaction, reduce professional support costs, and increase the likelihood that a successful transaction will take place. Thus, managing the business to maximize value makes as much sense for owners of private firms in much the same way it makes sense for corporate chiefs.

WHAT OWNERS WILL LEARN IN THE REMAINING CHAPTERS

The remainder of this book will focus on two central and critical areas. First, it will use case studies to highlight the real issues that owners face when they contemplate, develop, and implement any business transition strategy. The second area is helping owners better understand the various components of a business valuation and how each affects the final dollar value that emerges from a valuation analysis.

Through the case studies in Chapters 3 through 7 and the "More on Valuation Methods" addenda to the case studies, we will look at several approaches that are customarily used by business valuation professionals to value a business. These include

1. Value-to-earnings multiple
2. Value-to-revenue multiple
3. Asset-based approach
4. Discounted cash flow approach

For the discounted cash flow approach we will spend time explaining the basic concept of how much should I pay today for cash I expect to receive in the *future*. One need not be a financial professional to come to terms with these concepts. They are easy to understand when presented in an easy-to-understand format.

Starting in Chapter 5 we introduce owners to the approach used by bizownerHQ, the discounted cash flow approach. The focus here is not on the methodology per se but rather on the inputs that are required to undertake the analysis and the meaning of the output received. The bizownerHQ Web site uses the Valuation GURU, a system that incorporates an expert knowledge base about how to value a private firm that allows business owners and their representatives to obtain a private firm valuation.

Our case studies provide a view of the similarities and the unique differences between businesses in different industries. We recognize that not all businesses are the same. Each faces its own unique set of circumstances and operates in industries that are different in a number of important respects. For example, manufacturing firms typically have inventories, whereas professional practices generally do not, or if they do, the dollar values are small. As a result, one may rightfully ask: Should inventories be treated differently when valuing a manufacturing firm as opposed to valuing a dental practice? To better understand how industry differences influence valuation, we review the valuation of the following businesses:

- An insurance brokerage
- A manufacturing firm
- A legal practice
- A consulting practice

In Chapter 8 we integrate the major points from the case studies to focus on ways for owners to maximize the value of their businesses. In this chapter we answer such questions as

- How can I increase the value of my firm through refinancing?
- How can I increase firm value through moving to a higher profit growth path?
- How do I determine the price I should pay for a target firm and ensure that I am maximizing the value of the newly combined entity?

The objective of this book is to empower business owners by making solutions to valuation-based business life problems more understandable and accessible. We seek to help owners move forward in their quests to maximize the value and protect their most important financial asset—their businesses. We want to make clear the factors that determine a business valuation, how a business valuation can be used to improve a firm's operating profit performance, and how this translates into a more valuable business. Most private businesses are valued no more than once in the lifetime of an owner. This is in stark contrast to publicly held firms, which are valued every business day, second by second. Our goal is to create an environment in which owners can afford to value their businesses at least once per year so that they can reap the rewards from managing their businesses for maximum value.

SPECIAL FOCUS

SHOULD OWNERS VALUE THEIR BUSINESSES ANNUALLY?
Setting aside the costs of undertaking this exercise once a year, should an owner do a business valuation annually? To understand why, look at any business magazine and/or the business section of any newspaper. The mantra of most American business leaders is maximizing shareholder wealth. This means that management should do whatever it can within the constraints of legal and ethical guidelines to make the owners of the company wealthier. Who are the shareholders of privately held companies? In most small businesses, the managers and the shareholders are one and the same. Small business owners make plans and business decisions every day. Do they know how much wealthier they expect to become as a result? Put differently, do they know if these actions are going to make their businesses worth more and, if so, by how much? When owners undertake such activities as increasing ad spending, a building expansion, hiring more people, or even buying a computer, do they have any idea whether these actions will add value to the business? Many small business owners do not know the answers to these questions. Most owners do not have a framework for knowing whether they are increasing the value of their most important asset—*their business*.

For example, if asked, most small business owners would conclude that any business that grows revenue and profits year after year must be worth more over time. Unfortunately, this is not always the case. During the energy crisis in the 1970s, the average U.S. business grew profits, but the trend in stock market values failed to keep up. The reason was that profits did indeed grow, but they did not grow fast enough to offset the perception that owning the average business was becoming a riskier activity.

Figure 2-4 shows a hypothetical firm whose profits are growing by 10 percent per year from a base of $1000. Note that firm value actually declines from its peak in year 2 despite the growth in profits. This occurs when investors perceive the firm's future profits to be highly uncertain and becoming more so over time. As a result, the firm's cost of financial capital, the rate of return that investors require to compensate them for this perceived increase in risk, rises.

FIGURE 2-4   Profit growth does not always result in increases in firm value.

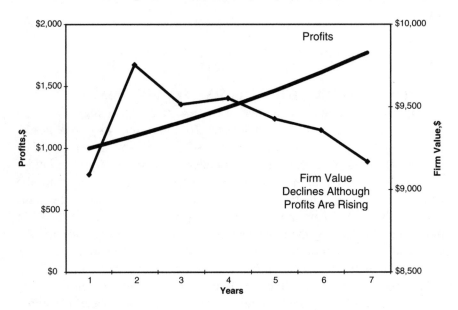

In this example, as shown in Figure 2-5, the cost of financial capital rises from 10 percent to over 20 percent This increase more than offsets the growth in profits, thus preventing the value of the firm rising with profit growth.

We will explain this phenomenon further in Chapter 5. By increasing profits, a business owner is increasing return, but without explicitly taking into account any changes in risk, it is not clear that value will be increased. ***Business owners should know that a valuation must take account of the income potential as well as the risk level of the business.***

The upshot is that when firm value decreases over time, the wealth of the owner, by definition, declines. The opposite is also true; as business value increases, the wealth of the owner increases as well. This increase occurs when the firm's operating cash flows are rising sufficiently to offset the risk associated with obtaining them.

FIGURE 2-5   The cost of financial capital can rise over time.

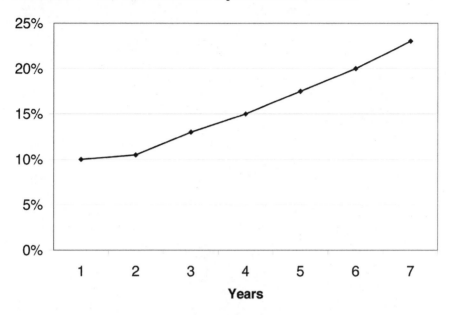

Business owners should know that focusing on building value in their businesses is the right goal regardless of their exit plan. This is so even if the owner does not care to sell the business, because having a firm that is worth more has many financial benefits. One of the more important is the ability to easily refinance the assets of the firm. This means that the owner not only can borrow more money but also can borrow it on more favorable terms than if the firm's value were not increasing. Second, while the owner may not desire to sell the business today, she does not want to give up the option to sell all or part of the business at some future time. Demonstrating that the business is managed for value maximization over time makes the business a more salable entity in the future. This is akin to keeping a single-family home in excellent condition even though the home will not be for sale for a long time. Not keeping the house up, in a manner of speaking, reduces its future value. In a similar fashion, not managing for maximum value today inevitably will reduce the value of a firm in the future.

3

VALUATION FOR
SELLING OR BUYING
A BUSINESS

CASE BACKGROUND

O'TOOLE INSURANCE AGENCY

Brendan O'Toole is an independent insurance broker in Akron, Ohio. Brendan owns the O'Toole Insurance Agency, which offers a full range of insurance products from many major insurance carriers to meet the insurance needs of individuals and small businesses. A number of years ago, on the advice of his friend and attorney, Edward F. Callahan, Brendan incorporated the insurance agency as a Subchapter S Corporation (see "Backgrounder" at the end of this chapter for a discussion of business legal forms). Brendan owns all 600 of the equity shares. The board of directors includes Brendan as chairman plus attorney Callahan and another friend, James Casey, who is a local CPA. The insurance agency is a successful business with over $1.1 million in gross annual premium revenues and employs three full-time people besides Brendan. The agency owns the office building in Akron in which it operates and rents out space to other professional business practices. The business has an additional $225,000 rental income annually before depreciation.

Business Owner Segmentation for Brendan

At this stage of his life, Brendan best fits the Business Succession Focused segment of small business owners. His primary need is to manage the right transition for his business when the time seems right. Success in this transition will secure his dream of the O'Toole Insurance Agency's continuation and should adequately fund the retirement goals for Brendan and his wife, Barbara.

The Owner Officer

Besides being the chairman of the board of directors, Brendan is president and chief operating officer of the O'Toole Insurance Agency. In his capacity as president and chief operating officer, Brendan is an employee of the corporation and entitled to a salary and fringe benefits. When the board of directors discussed his salary, the discussion was rather artificial in nature. After all, Brendan is the chairman of the board and the sole stockholder who elects all board members, who in turn set Brendan's salary as an employee. Jim Casey told Brendan, "It really doesn't matter what you pay yourself. Whatever it is will be taxed as ordinary income. Since this is a Subchapter S Corporation, all the profits will be taxed as ordinary income to you. It really comes down to which of your pockets you want the money to wind up in: wage income or dividend income."

Brendan receives $100,000 as president of the agency. He also receives dividends from his ownership of the stock of the O'Toole Insurance Agency. Last year the business's net income, excluding rental income, was $200,000, which Brendan took as dividend compensation.

DISCRETIONARY EXPENSES

Cars

To perform his duties as chief operating officer of the O'Toole Insurance Agency, Brendan requires the use of a car. Every 3 years the O'Toole Insurance Agency purchases a car for Brendan's use. This year the car the agency purchased was a BMW sedan for $42,000. Brendan has always had a fondness for stylish, expensive vehicles. Brendan keeps a log of the car's use and reimburses the firm for personal use, according to a schedule provided by Jim Casey. At the end of 3 years, Brendan buys the vehicle from the corporation at the *Kelley Blue Book* value (approximately 50 percent of the original cost), and the corporation purchases another vehicle for Brendan's use. The used vehicle is then driven by Barbara or by a member of Brendan's large extended family. Brendan freely admits that the insurance agency probably spends too much money on new automobiles.

Country Club Membership

The O'Toole Insurance Agency bought a membership in the Akron Country Club for Brendan. The board of directors meetings are almost always held on the golf course, followed by dinner at the club, frequently with spouses and other friends in attendance. The O'Toole Insurance Agency picks up the bill for these events. Brendan also frequently conducts insurance business, especially with his larger clients, at the club. The country club offers Brendan a nice place to conduct business while enjoying the personal benefits of sports and exercise.

Employing Family Members

Brendan has five children, and each has worked for the agency during their high school and college years. Each of his children received a salary of $15 per hour, which was considerably more than high school and college students earned in Akron at that time for part-time work. The deal Brendan had with each child was that half their take-home pay was theirs to spend as they saw fit; the other half went into a college expense savings account. Jim Casey explained that when children turned 14 years of age, their income was taxed at a lower rate than that of adults. Brendan enjoyed having his kids around, and they earned part of their college expenses and learned a great deal about the insurance business.

BUSINESS LIFE EVENTS

Exit Strategy

Brendan loved his work and was very proud to be the first in his family to own a business. He also was confident that with the right kind of transition, he would one day pass the business to another owner who would keep the O'Toole Insurance Agency an important player in the Akron business community for years to come.

It had been Brendan's expectation that one or more of his children eventually would take over the agency when he retired. Unfortunately, none wanted to do so because other careers interested each of them. Brendan had just sold 100 shares of General Electric stock to pay off the last of the college education loans he had used to spread out the costs of having five children going through college over the space of 10 years.

Beyond the issue of who would take over the business, Brendan was pretty comfortable with his management of business life events (BLEs). The sale of his business should provide for a comfortable retirement for Brendan and Barbara. With all the kids through college, Brendan's major financial obligations were in the past. Not surprisingly, he had adequate life insurance, although he had never taken the time to put in place a business succession insurance policy or executive disability insurance. He recently purchased a long-term care policy for his wife and himself.

Business Succession Becomes a Reality

Last year Brendan learned that he had prostate cancer, which came as an enormous shock to him and his family. The surgery and chemotherapy were the first time in his life Brendan had experienced significant illness. Although his prognosis is good, the doctors are unable to give him a clean bill of health.

Brendan's illness triggered a series of significant events in his life. He began to get advice about his will and his estate plan. As things stood, his wife Barbara would inherit his entire estate on his death. The major asset in the estate was the insurance agency and the office building, creating a problem for his wife. Barbara was not an insurance professional, and she would not be able to manage the agency. Developing a logical succession plan for Brendan's business became a priority. His earlier daydreams about passing the business along "at the right time" had to quickly become reality. Brendan began to think about what he wanted to do with the rest of his life. He and Barbara enjoyed traveling, but family and business commitments had made this difficult so far. Brendan decided that he wanted to see the world.

Convinced that he would have to sell the insurance agency, Brendan began to ask the questions: To whom, and for how much? Ed Callahan, his attorney, was helpful in outlining some sales options that Brendan might consider. While discussing this issue with a business associates, the name Jill Snyder came up. Jill Snyder is an insurance broker who works out of the Akron office of Taylor and Greenwald. Taylor and Greenwald is a multi-state insurance agency, headquartered in Chicago, that serves the insurance needs of individuals and businesses in the Midwest. Brendan knew Jill from the Chamber of Commerce, the Rotary Club, and professional meetings of insurance brokers. They had also on several occasions made competing bids and presentations to prospective customers. Brendan liked Jill and had no doubt about her professional knowledge and ability. Brendan's friend told him that on occasion Jill Snyder had expressed an interest in going out on her own in the insurance business.

The Negotiations

Brendan called Jill to explain his situation and asked her if she might be interested in buying his insurance agency. Jill said that she had always wanted to own her own business, but a suitable opportunity never seemed to present itself. Before parting, Brendan gave Jill a copy of the agency's financial statement. Jill said she would review it with her financial advisors and get back to Brendan.

Jill remembered reading an article a few years back that gave a rule of thumb for pricing an insurance agency at a multiple of revenue anywhere from 1 to 1.5. She decided to use the midpoint, 1.25, as the basis for planning out the financial details. Using this multiple, the value of the O'Toole Insurance Agency would be approximately $1.375 million (year 2000 revenue of $1.1 million × 1.25). Jill decided to round this up to $1.4 million, since the valuation multiple she had used was at least a few years old.

With this starting point, she and her husband, Tom, went over the possible resources they could use to make a down payment on Brendan's business. They made an assumption that if they could come up with 50 percent ($700,000) of the estimated price of $1.4 million in cash from their resources, they would be able to borrow the rest, either from a bank or from Brendan.

Jill and Tom reviewed their assets, including their savings of $300,000 and the equity in their home. With the decline in interest rates over the last few years, they could refinance their home at a lower mortgage rate, take out $120,000 in equity, and still have the same mortgage payment. This put them more than halfway there for the down payment.

They talked over the opportunity with Jill's family. Jill's father was willing to loan money against Jill's share of his future estate. He cautioned Jill and Tom that they would face advisor and closing costs as well so that they should have extra cash for that. Based on her father's advice, they budgeted an extra 2 percent of the assumed selling price, or $28,000. In total, they needed $728,000, as summarized in Table 3-1. Jill's father would make up the difference of $308,000.

TABLE 3-1   Sources and Uses for Jill's 50 Percent Down Payment

Sources	Amount
Savings	$300,000
Home equity from refinancing	$120,000
Jill's father	$308,000
Total available	$728,000
Uses	**Amount**
Assumed sales price (based on 1.25 revenue multiple)	$1.4 million
50% down payment	$700,000
Estimate of closing costs and advisor expenses (based on 2% of sales price)	$28,000
Total needed	$728,000

Excited that they had come up with $700,000 in cash for a down payment, Jill called Brendan and told him that she had discussed the matter with her family and that she was definitely interested in learning more about the possibility of buying the insurance agency. Brendan suggested that he and Barbara and Jill and Tom, get together for dinner and explore the possibilities. Jill and Tom decided that they would tell Brendan and Barbara that they could raise $700,000 for a down payment as evidence of their serious interest and creditworthiness but not to volunteer their assumption of what the sales price would be.

THE RIGHT TRANSITION

Brendan envisioned a sale and transition to take place over a 3-year period. During the first year, he would sell the buyer one-third (200 shares) of the stock of the O'Toole Insurance Agency. Brendan would work full-time, and the new owner would work full-time, both for a salary of $50,000 each. During the second year, he would sell Jill 200 more shares at an agreed-upon price. Brendan would lend her the money to buy any or all of the 200 shares. The loan would be at 9 percent annual interest and would be paid off in equal annual installments over 10 years. Then, at the end of the third year, Jill would buy the remaining 200 outstanding shares of the agency, again with Brendan offering financing. Brendan would work half-time for $25,000 salary during the second year, and Brendan would work quarter-time at the agency during the third year for $12,500 salary.

The company dividends would be paid out in accordance with the ownership shares over the 3 years. In Table 3-2, the salary and dividend distributions are projected for the next 3 years, assuming that dividends continue at the $200,000 level each year.

TABLE 3-2   Proposed Transition Plan Financials

	Year 1	Year 2	Year 3
Salary: Brendan	$50,000	$25,000 (1/2 time)	$12,500 (1/4 time)
Salary: Jill	$50,000	$75,000	$87,500
Stock: Brendan	400 shares	200 shares	0 shares
Stock: Jill	200 shares	400 shares	600 shares
Dividends: Brendan	$133,400	$66,600	$0
Dividends: Jill	$66,600	$133,400	$200,000

Jill and Tom agreed that the transition plan made sense. It would keep Brendan involved with the agency while Jill came to know the employees and the customers. Customers would slowly begin to deal less with Brendan and more with Jill. Jill and her family would become total owners of the business in 3 years. Of course, they would owe Brendan a loan to be repaid over 10 years. There would be details to work out. Both the buyer and the seller would have to consult with their attorneys and consider tax and other implications. However, the outline of a sale seemed clear. The only major question remaining was the price that would be paid for the O'Toole Insurance Agency.

Brendan gave Jill and Tom the complete set of financial statements and tax returns of the agency. He also told them that he would direct his CPA, Jim Casey, to provide any information or answer any questions that the Snyders or their agents might have.

Brendan remembered and mentioned to Jill that he had purchased a business appraisal of the agency 2 years ago by Continental Appraisers, Inc. At that time, Brendan mistakenly thought that money problems facing his teacher son might lead to a career switch from teaching to insurance. Brendan had wanted to be prepared with all the facts and figures for his son just in case. The report cost Brendan $13,000. He handed a copy of the July 1998 appraisal report to Jill, saying that this report might serve as a basis for setting the value. Brendan told Jill that he had never read beyond the first page but that Jim Casey had said that it looked all right to him. Brendan said that Continental's appraisal came up with a value of $3.75 million and that this was over 2 years ago. Jill, with a brave smile and a strong handshake, thanked Brendan for this information and promised to be back in touch within a week.

The Valuation Conundrum

Jill and Tom were stunned and somewhat depressed on their ride home. They had been so excited about the prospect of buying the business, and Brendan's transition plan seemed sound. They personally liked Brendan and Barbara and thought a business relationship with them would be fine. The $3.75 million price was a shock. Their $700,000 would not even cover a 20 percent down payment on that price. Jill wondered how could this business be worth over three times revenue when her article had said the valuation-to-revenue range was 1 to 1.5.

Jill tried to read the Continental report that night, but the combination of the confusing terminology and her disappointment over Brendan's news made it impossible to understand. She was, however, not giving up. She made plans to meet with her father and with an accountant, Janice Smith, whom she knew from the Akron Women in Business club.

Jill and Tom met 2 days later with Jill's father, Fred, a retired business executive, and Janice Smith. Janice was asked to review the materials that Brendan had provided and to research insurance agency value.

As they were leaving this meeting, Fred took Janice aside to ask for her best guess why the two valuation estimates were so far apart. Janice told Fred that it amazed her how often people buying and selling businesses take seriously the valuation multiples that they hear from a broker or read in a magazine. She added that she had clients who told her every year at tax time how different their businesses were from others in their industry and then turned around and used an industry revenue multiple to estimate the value of their businesses. These people are great businesspeople who can analyze an operational problem down to the last detail, but when it comes to the most important financial decision of their lives, they somehow feel lost. Janice said that this type of owner behavior never ceased to amaze her.

Fred asked Janice again for her best guess, and she responded that Brendan's value number probably included the building the agency occupies. She confirmed that hunch minutes into her review of the valuation report and left voicemails for Jill and Fred, giving them renewed hope that the deal might yet happen.

Valuation Multiples

After a week of late nights trying to fit Jill's last-minute request into her already busy schedule, Janice reported back to Jill, Tom, and Fred on her findings. Janice started with the observation that there is no official source of insurance agency values. There are too few transactions and too much variation across businesses to make that possible. It is not like selling a car, where you can check the *Kelley Blue Book* for the model, year, and mileage.

In her search for information, she was able to find the article that Jill remembered. The article was from 7 years ago. From her discussions with two business brokers who work in Ohio, Indiana, and Illinois, Janice had learned that revenue multiples were not being used anymore for valuing insurance agencies. There was simply too much variation in the earnings across these types of businesses. The rule of thumb the brokers use is that an agency is worth six times net income, although neither has been involved in an agency sale in the last 2 years.

Jill asked what Brendan's agency would be worth at six times net income. Janice said that she did not know yet what the value was. She was just repeating "broker shorthand" when she raised the six times net income figure. "What they really mean is six times *adjusted* net income. Our task is to unbundle or more accurately 'un-Brendan' the O'Toole Insurance Agency financials to see how much cash this business would produce under someone else. The business reports about $200,000 of net income now, so if we use the six times multiple, the business would be worth $1.2 million. There's no way that Brendan will sell it for that."

Fred asked whether the Continental appraisal had made those adjustments, and if so, why should they pay to do it again. Janice read into this question a concern that she was trying to push up her billings. She responded that she agreed with Fred that the Continental report provided useful information to give them a rough guide on what the adjusted income was almost 3 years ago. Summarizing those results was her next topic. However, before doing that, she needed to make a few things clear.

Janice noted that she was a very good accountant but that she was not experienced in conducting a complete business valuation. Therefore, if any updating work to the Continental findings needed to be done, that work should be done by an experienced valuation professional. She offered to help find one and to help Jill and her advisors understand the results.

Janice emphasized that buying this business likely would be the biggest financial decision in Jill's life, involving commitment of the family's savings and taking on hundreds of thousands of dollars of debt. "This is a big decision to make, given that all they have to go on now is a 3-year-old report paid for by the seller and at least 1-year-old estimates from business brokers. A lot has changed in the economy and in the insurance industry since 1998." Janice noted that the Continental report and the broker information should be good enough to see whether Jill is even in the same ballpark with Brendan's asking price. If so, then it will be worth investing more time and money to figure out a more precise answer.

Tom said that Janice had convinced him. He had never heard anybody who charged by the hour admit that they were not an expert in everything. Jill and Fred nodded agreement with Tom's statement, so Janice moved on to the Continental report.

ASSET-BASED VALUATION

The method used by Continental Appraisers was to value the assets of the business. Continental valued each major asset using an asset-appropriate method and then added them up for a total value.

Valuing the Building

One issue that so far had seriously complicated this transaction was that the O'Toole Insurance Agency owned the building in which the business operated and received the rents from other tenants. Continental Appraisers applied a standard valuation rate (developed by the Ohio Realtors' Association) per square foot for commercial real estate in Akron and came up with a value of $1.4 million for the building. One could argue about whether this particular piece of property was in a better or worse location in Akron than an "average" property or was in a higher or lower state of maintenance than an "average" property.

In any case, Janice noted that the building was a solid asset that should be examined. A value of $1.4 million seemed to be in the ballpark. If the building were worth $1.4 million, then the insurance agency itself would be worth $2.35 million ($3.75 million − $1.4 million)—based on Continental's 1998 appraisal.

Jill and Tom exchanged glances at hearing the $2.35 million figure. Jill was optimistic that the number had moved more than halfway toward her initial assumption of $1.4 million. Tom was still concerned that this lower number was almost $1 million more than planned.

Valuing the Ongoing Business

Janice did her best to translate the Continental report language into plain business language as she continued on with her summary. Continental assumed correctly that the O'Toole Insurance Agency was a going concern business. Continental restated the financial statements of the agency, which produced a significantly higher net income by

1. Restating for valuation purposes Brendan's compensation of $100,000 salary and $200,000 of net income paid as dividends; this involves estimating the average salary for insurance managers of similar-sized offices on the basis of a market salary survey; this average salary proxy replaces Brendan's $100,000 in officer's compensation expense; the remainder shows up as net income of the firm that is used in valuation of the firm.
2. Cutting automobile expenses to a national average level.
3. Removing all relatives from the payroll.
4. Eliminating all expenses associated with the Akron Country Club.

The Continental appraiser made the determination that all these expenses were discretionary expenditures reflecting preferences of the current owner. A future owner could avoid them, so Continental was restating the statements to reflect different ownership. With these changes, the restated net income for the O'Toole Insurance Agency was $256,250. Continental's review of comparable sales (not included in their report) found a median value of eight times the adjusted net income rule produced a value of $2.05 million.

Janice noted that there were two possible problems with the Continental assumptions that increased the value of the business. One was Brendan employing his children. Brendan clearly overpaid his kids to work for him, but Janice pointed out that the children probably were doing something useful. It is only the overpayment part of the salaries paid to family and friends that should be considered a discretionary expense. Janice said that she would talk with Jim Casey about what the temporary help situation is like now that Brendan's children are out of the business.

Janice then turned to the second discretionary expense item, the country club and entertainment expenses. She knew that Jill did not plan to spend the company's money in this manner once she was in charge. However, Janice pointed out that the important question is how much advertising and marketing expense does the agency need to maintain its business. Jill noted she had never seen any O'Toole ads or other marketing communications beyond the local Yellow Pages. They all knew that insurance is a relationship business and that Jill would need to spend some money on customer relationships, presumably more in line with her interests. Janice concluded with the observation that Jill should not pay $8 in value for $1 of expense that has mistakenly been reclassified as $1 of net income.

Jill made a quick calculation and then proposed that they consider a price of $1.5 million, based on the Continental adjusted net income, rounded to $250,000, multiplied by the business brokers' valuation rule of six times adjusted earnings. Janice agreed that Jill's calculation should be added to the list but cautioned that she had one more asset to add to the Continental valuation summary.

Valuing the Goodwill
Continental noted that as a going concern, the O'Toole Insurance Agency had an additional asset called *goodwill*. Continental noted that a buyer was getting an established customer base, trained employees, computer systems, and a name that was well established and respected in the Akron community. Continental valued this goodwill at $300,000.

Continental's view was that a buyer of the O'Toole Insurance Agency was buying three assets: A building worth $1.4 million, a generic insurance agency worth $2.05 million, and unique goodwill worth $300,000. Put it all together, and the total package is worth $3.75 million.

Janice concluded with the observation that she believed that Jill and Brendan were "in the same ballpark" in their assessments of the agency's value if Brendan was willing to separate the building from the sale of the agency. Janice encouraged Jill and her team to discuss whether they were comfortable moving forward given Janice's analysis. Janice's summary of estimates is shown in Table 3-3.

TABLE 3-3   Summary of Initial Valuation Estimates for the O'Toole
             Insurance Agency

	Revenue Multiple	Earnings Multiple	Asset-Based Valuation
Source	Jill's 7-year-old article citing 1–1.5 times revenue	Business brokers interviewed by Janice citing 6 times adjusted earnings	Continental report from July 1998 using an 8 times adjusted earnings + goodwill
Company value	$1.4 million	$1.5 million (using a rough estimate of the Continental earnings adjusted for discretionary expenses)	$2.35 million ($2.05 million − earnings adjusted for discretionary expenses + $300,000 goodwill)
Building value	Not included	Not included	$1.4 million
Total value	$1.4 million	$1.5 million	$3.75 million

Jill's Dilemma

After considerable discussion, Jill and her family were anxious and frustrated about what to do. Jill very much wanted to have her own insurance business, and members of her immediate family were very supportive of her in this effort. Unfortunately, Jill and her family were concerned by the wide range of valuation estimates generated for the O'Toole Insurance Agency. Equally important was the fact that the valuation estimates were generated by a range of valuation methodologies. To Jill, it just seemed that valuation must be more of an art than a science if it could support such a wide range of values for the same business. Most of all, she was troubled by not having a logical process for her and Brendan to reach a mutually agreeable solution.

After going round these issues for a few days, Jill spoke again with Janice Smith. Jill described her thought process to Janice, concluding that this whole thing felt like playing a stupid game. Jill had no basis for deciding which multiple, six or eight, was the right one, if either. She was not sure what the right adjustments were for the company earnings number. She noted that these may be interesting questions to a broker or to valuation people, but for her, this involved real money. If she paid too much, she could end up going bankrupt and losing everything. If she did not offer enough, she would not get the business.

Janice responded that there was good news. She had run into Ed Callahan, Brendan's attorney, at a local function, and Ed volunteered that Brendan was open to selling the building and the agency separately. Janice asked Jill if she was ready to take the next step, which was to get an updated valuation of the agency business. Janice noted that a valuation likely would cost between $10,000 and $15,000, but it would provide a current framework from which to negotiate over discretionary expenses. Janice had been asking other professionals in the area about recommending a valuation firm. Two people recommended David Simon and Associates, Inc., a firm of business appraisers and brokers based in Cleveland. Jill quickly agreed to Janice's recommendations.

Another Valuation Exercise

Jill contacted Simon and Associates, and the company agreed to conduct an appraisal of value of the O'Toole Insurance Agency. Jill pressed Simon and Associates to complete the assignment in 1 month's time. Simon agreed to do the appraisal on this "accelerated basis," but it was contingent on Simon having access to all records of the business, as well as access to Brendan O'Toole and his CPA, Jim Casey. The cost of the appraisal normally would be $10,000, but Simon told Jill that the charge would be $14,000 due to the rush. Jill called Brendan, and he reluctantly agreed to the valuation process, his role in it, and the delay it would introduce in the negotiations.

Thirty days later, David Simon and Associates delivered its appraisal report on the O'Toole Insurance Agency. Simon and Associates basically concluded that the agency consisted of two assets—the agency itself and the building in which it and other businesses operated. The real estate was, in their judgment, worth $1.375 million, not that different from the $1.4 million figure that had been discussed previously.

Simon and Associates, with the assistance of Jim Casey, restated the income of the O'Toole Insurance Agency by removing discretionary expenses from the most recent financial statements. Although the reported net income for 2000 was about $16,000 higher than for 1998, the discretionary expenses recognized by Simon and Associates in 2000 were $60,000 lower than those recognized by Continental Appraisers in 1998. The year 2000 adjusted net income came to $212,000, according to Simon and Associates, in contrast to the $256,050 found by Continental Appraisers in 1998. The discretionary expense adjustments from the two valuations are shown in Table 3-4.

TABLE 3-4   Discretionary Expense Adjustments for the O'Toole Agency

Discretionary Expense Adjustments	Continental Appraisers (1998)	Simon and Associates (2000)	Difference
The "dividend" portion of Brendan's $100,000 salary	$50,000	$30,000 (Market salaries increased, and Simon correctly included nonmandatory benefits for Brendan in this estimate.)	$20,000
Temporary help by family members in 1998 and by others in 2000	$6,000	$3,000 (O'Toole continued to use students in the summers and over holidays for temporary help.)	$3,000
Country club membership and client entertainment expenses	$37,000	$0 (The $37,000 spent by Brendan on these activities in 2000 is his only marketing expense. This amount is consistent with the marketing expenditures of similarly sized companies in this industry, so Simon kept these expenses in as ongoing marketing expenses.)	$37,000
Total discretionary expense adjustments	$93,000	$33,000	$60,000
Net income	$163,050	$179,000	$15,950
Adjusted net income	$256,050	$212,000	$44,050

Simon and Associates followed the Continental approach of using an adjusted earnings multiple of eight based on data from the recent sale of comparable firms, even though conditions in the industry and economy had changed significantly since 1998. The multiple was determined to be eight, and the resulting value of the O'Toole Insurance Agency was $1.696 million. Jill inquired about the value of goodwill, which Continental Appraisers placed at $300,000. Simon and Associates said that comparable firms also were going concerns with established employees and customer bases so that goodwill was already priced into the eight times net income multiple.

Jill sent a copy of the Simon and Associates appraisal to Brendan. Jill asked Brendan if he would be willing to continue negotiations based on the appraisal by Simon and Associates. Brendan said that he would need to think it over.

Brendan's Dilemma

Brendan and Barbara went through the appraisal report carefully, but neither was convinced that these results were more credible than the Continental report. Barbara observed that the appraiser spent a lot of time looking at the agency expenses and trying to determine which expenses were discretionary and which were necessary. And then, it seemed like the appraiser spent less than a minute multiplying the earnings by this magic number of eight. Where did that multiple come from, she wondered. Brendan agreed that this final calculation seemed almost like an afterthought but noted that Continental had done much the same.

At the end of the week, Brendan and Barbara were at a loss about what to do next. Brendan asked both Ed and Jim, his two oldest and closest advisors, to meet with him and Barbara and to make their recommendations.

Unfortunately, the meeting did not shed much light on the subject. As contemporaries of Brendan, Ed and Jim had built up their clientele primarily with people their age or younger. Neither Ed nor Jim had yet been deeply involved in the sale of a client's business. Moreover, they felt very close to Brendan and Barbara as friends.

First, Ed stated that this was a business decision, not a legal one. He noted that once Brendan and Barbara decided which was the right path, then he could help draft the documents, manage the closing of the sale, and help redraft wills and revise estate plans. Jim agreed that this was not a question of how to split up the beans, which would be his strength. It was a question of how many beans did Brendan want for his business. Jim noted that the experts had provided two very different numbers, making it hard to accept a simple solution of just splitting the difference. Given this dilemma, Jim raised the possibility of whether Brendan should place his business with a broker to see what other offers might come in.

The next morning Brendan called Sam Andolini, a business broker in Chicago. Brendan had met Sam at an independent insurance agents' conference and had kept his card just in case. After Brendan described his situation, Sam assured Brendan that he could arrange a much better deal. Sam said that there was no need for seller financing. Brendan could get all cash, no phased buy-in, and the building, all as one package by selling to one of the big regional banks. Sam noted that these banks have been picking up "plum" insurance brokerages for the last few years. Brendan interrupted to say that he really wanted the O'Toole Insurance Agency and its current employees to stay intact and independent. Sam thought to himself, "That's what all owners say until they come face to face with two very different offers for their businesses." Sam assured Brendan that he would get Brendan whatever he wanted. Sam immediately sent off an exclusive listing agreement to Brendan.

Brendan related his conversation to Barbara. She wondered what Sam got for helping to sell the business. Brendan said that he thought there was a commission like you pay a real estate agent but that he was not sure. He would look over the agreement the next day. However, already Sam's confidence that the business could be sold for more than the Simon appraisal was worming its way into his thoughts. Brendan knew that he needed experienced help to navigate this unfamiliar territory of selling his business. His attorney and CPA buddies had already washed their hands of this deal. Brendan decided right then that he would go with the "pro." He started rehearsing in his mind how he would break the news to Jill that he would be listing the business with Sam.

Jill's Disappointment
Despite Brendan's considerable skill in breaking bad news to people, Jill nonetheless was very upset about his decision. Jill knew that there was a clear risk the deal would not get done, but she was quite surprised that the deal was over now without any further negotiations. Her dream of owning her own agency in her hometown now seemed dashed. In addition, she had just spent $14,000 for a valuation report that was now worthless to her. This felt like real money going down the drain. She also wondered when the news of her extracurricular activities would reach her manager at Taylor & Greenwald and what the consequences were likely to be.

THE NEXT SIX MONTHS
It turned out that Sam was a better salesman of his services than of Brendan's company. Sam wanted to keep the office building in the deal to maximize his commission. Sam also believed that Brendan would change his mind about keeping the business independent, but so far, he was wrong about that.

Over this period, Brendan had a hard time keeping his mind on his business, given his health concerns. He also found that competing agencies were using the "selling out to the banks" line against him in sales situations. His renewals fell from 88 to 75 percent, a worrisome decline.

Jill also was having a difficult time. Although no one said anything at work, she sensed that she was no longer considered on the "A list." Her clients and prospects also got the news that Jill was looking to get out.

We are going to put this case on hold for now and move on to some of the lessons learned from this example. We will revisit the O'Toole Insurance Agency later in the book.

LESSONS LEARNED

The preceding example demonstrates, in realistic terms, the major issues of valuing and selling a privately held business. The example business is relatively straightforward, with only one owner in one line of a business plus a building. The wide range of values of this business contributed to the difficulty of making this sale happen. Both Brendan and Jill spent time and money and lost focus on their ongoing activities.

Brendan found out that his $13,000 Continental appraisal report was far enough out of date to be useless. He also paid fees to his CPA ($7450) and his attorney ($5450) in connection with the effort. Jill paid David Simon and Associates $14,000 for an appraisal of value, CPA fees ($3280), and attorney fees ($1700). In total, Brendan paid $25,900 in fees, and Jill paid $18,980. Together they spent $44,880 in fees associated with the failed effort to sell the business.

Business owners should know that

1. *Selling a privately held business is typically an expensive and time-consuming activity and that success is often not achieved.* There are the direct costs of paying for valuations and for time from advisors. There also can be substantial indirect costs, such as lost business because the owner withdraws from operational activities to focus on the sales transaction. There is also the danger of information about the potential sale of the business being used by a business's competitors in their sales pitches.

2. *The long-time advisors of the business may not have enough experience to play a critical role in business sales transactions.* When making such important financial decisions, sellers and potential buyers should add people with substantial prior experience in selling or buying businesses to their team of advisors. None of the principals or their advisors had this kind of experience in the early stages of this potential transaction.

3. *Determining the value of a privately held business can be a complex and confusing activity for owners.* There are multiple methodologies that can produce a wide range of possible answers. Brendan believed that $3.75 million was a reasonable asking price for his agency and the building. Jill and Tom initially were expecting to buy the agency for $1.5 million.

4. *Determining the value of a privately held business can be an expensive and time-consuming process.* Jill spent $14,000 for a "rush" 4-week valuation report.

5. *Valuation multiples are used widely in the determination of value, but the validity of these numbers is questionable.* There are no well-documented sources tracking the specifics of sales transactions for privately held businesses. Using public company multiples is problematic for reasons we will explain later. The details of privately held business transactions are rarely made public. It always makes sense to question someone offering a valuation multiple for your industry about the types of transactions used, the timeliness, and the method of calculation of the multiple.

6. *Valuation reports have short shelf lives.* The appraisal Brendan ordered in 1998 at a cost of $13,000 was not current, so it was essentially useless.

7. *Restating the expenses of a business to "disentangle" the current owner's preferences from ongoing business expenses is key to reaching a reasonable valuation of the business.* One of the biggest challenges to determining value of a privately held business is that the expenses and, therefore, the net income of a business represent to some extent the preferences of the individual who owns the business. Reasonable people can and do disagree over what constitutes a discretionary expense of an owner versus a necessary expense.

8. *The purpose of the valuation makes a difference as to how much time is spent on valuing each asset.* Neither the Continental nor the Simon appraisal spent much time in valuing the building. In the Continental appraisal, the purpose was to support a possible intrafamily sale, so a full "arm's-length" review was not necessary. In the Simon case, Jill was not interested in buying the building, so again little time was spent. Thus Brendan at this point has very little actionable information on the value of one of his two sizable business assets, the building.

OTHER IMPORTANT ISSUES TO CONSIDER

As noted earlier, the professional advisors in this example were not experienced in business sales transactions and thus could not offer Brendan or Jill much advice on how to bridge the valuation gap. There are two other possible problem areas that may emerge for Brendan over time from the inexperience of his current team of advisors in the area of selling a business—tax planning and portfolio diversification.

Tax Planning

While Brendan's lawyer, Ed, has offered to help with estate planning after the deal is done, the time to consider this is while the deal is being structured. Despite the phaseout of the death tax over the next several years, there is a reasonable chance, given Brendan's health situation, that his estate will be subject to estate taxes. An attorney experienced in business sales and their aftermath should be able to advise Brendan on ways to structure the sale that meet Brendan's objectives for the amount of money received, his control over that money, and the potential tax liabilities. *Business owners should know that incorporating estate and gift tax considerations into their exit strategy discussions rather than waiting until after the sale is transacted will save time, money, and potentially many headaches.*

Portfolio Diversification

Like most business owners, Brendan's current and future wealth are tightly linked to his business success. However, now that Brendan is planning his exit, he should be looking for advice on how to manage the money he will receive for his business. His initial offer to finance much of the deal for Jill keeps Brendan tied to Jill, the agency, and the building for *10 more years*, assuming that he does not sell the building right away. This should all be reviewed with a financial advisor experienced in working on business sales, so Brendan can look at the trade-offs of different deal structures on the overall price he gets and the financial risks. His goal should be to diversify his investments over time in order to minimize the risk that problems in the insurance brokerage sector or the Akron economy will wipe out some or most of his accumulated wealth.

Although business owners rarely want to ·face this, there inevitably comes a time when an owner is better off taking cash out of the business that has made him or her wealthy. They should either take the money out directly or borrow against the business, as long as the ongoing business operation can support this. They should invest this money into stocks, bonds, or other instruments that are unrelated to the owner's business. The best time to start this depends on the owner's financial objectives, current degree of asset diversification, his risk profile, and the ability of the business to handle this cash drain or interest payments. *Business owners should know that diversification of their financial resources is their second most important financial strategy behind managing a successful transition out of the business.*

SPECIAL FOCUS

DISCRETIONARY EXPENSES

Guidelines for Expenses in a Public Company

Business transactions carried out by publicly traded firms, such as IBM and General Motors, are assumed to be, and overwhelmingly are, "arm's-length" transactions; that is, the products and services purchased by the firm are authorized by competent managers operating under three basic criteria:

1. The managers are making spending decisions with the primary goal of increasing value for the shareholders of the company.
2. The managers receive no significant benefits individually from these purchases or from the suppliers of those products and services.
3. The owners of the company, generally through the board of directors, review whether the decisions of the company's managers are prudent and are adding value to the company.

The executives of a public company can make the decision to sponsor a golf tournament where they entertain clients. These executives and sales-people can enjoy playing golf in this setting, just as Brendan enjoys playing golf with his friends and clients at the country club. The big difference is that the owners of the public company, that is, the shareholders, can review whether these types of marketing decisions are producing a worthwhile return on their investment. If the board of directors finds that this spending is excessive relative to the sales results that follow, they have the choice of dismissing the executives that organized the golfing event.

Discretionary Expenses Can Equal Income in a Private Business

In privately held businesses, it is almost always true that there is no separa-tion of ownership and control. The owners of the business are frequently employee/managers of the business. The breakdown of the separation of ownership and control in privately held businesses can create serious prob-lems in valuing the business. This was a major problem in selling the O'Toole Insurance Agency. Brendan's salary, company car, country club membership and expenses, and salaries paid to his children were not "arm's-length" transactions. These expenses were at the discretion of the owner. From the perspective of valuing the O'Toole Insurance Agency, if one were to add back these discretionary expenses to taxable income, the value of the business certainly would increase.

Business owners should know that there are no completely objective standards for determining which expenses in a privately held business are "arm's length" and which are discretionary. There are generally accepted approaches used by valuation consultants that have been reviewed by the courts over time.

There is no need for business owners to become experts on the methods for separating discretionary from necessary expenses. *Business owners should know that the answers they and/or their accountants provide to valuation-related questions about whether certain expenses are discretionary or necessary may have an important impact on the valuation results.* Owners are more expert on running their types of businesses than any valuation consultant. They often know of better sources of information for their industry and location for making these kinds of discretionary versus necessary expense determinations than a valuation consultant (or the valuation consultant working for the owner's ex-spouse or the IRS; remember, owners are not always trying to make the value of their business larger). This does not make the owner the valuation expert; the owner is just helping the valuation consultant to find better information to make better estimates.

Business owners should know that the information they provide about discretionary versus necessary expenses should be reasonable and have solid backup. Owners cannot always anticipate whether the value of the business will be contested (e.g., by the IRS, a divorcing spouse, or a departing partner). Given the self-interest of a business owner in the valuation results, other participants in the valuation process are likely to look closely at the answers provided by the owner and accountant and the information that backs up these answers.

MORE ON VALUATION METHODS

THE ASSET APPROACH
The asset-based approach (ABA) assumes that a business is a collection of assets and that each asset should be valued separately by the most appropriate methods. In the O'Toole Insurance Agency example, Continental Appraisers, Inc., viewed the O'Toole Insurance Agency as having three major assets: a building, a generic insurance agency, and unique goodwill. There is a certain logic to this approach: Value the parts of a business, and then add them to get the value of the entire business. However, separating the business into its component assets presents challenges to the valuation process. In

addition, the quality of an asset-based valuation will depend on how robust the valuation methods are that are used to value the separate assets.

A number of issues arise in how Continental Appraisers used the ABA to value the O'Toole Insurance Agency.

1. *Separating the agency from the building.* Since the O'Toole Insurance Agency owns the building and the business, it does not pay rent on the part of the office space that the agency occupies. The Continental appraiser took an unfortunate shortcut and simply separated the two assets without making any adjustments to either side. A valuation consultant should construct separate sets of adjusted financial statements for the building as a stand-alone entity with revenue from its tenants, including an estimate of what the O'Toole Insurance Agency would pay based on market rents and for the O'Toole Insurance Agency as a rent-paying tenant.

2. *Valuing the building.* In the O'Toole example, the Continental appraiser used a simplistic value per square footage ratio for office buildings in Akron, Ohio. While this is one valid approach to valuation, it does not take into account how the agency building differs from others in the Akron business district in terms of the condition of the building. Lack of recent sales of comparable properties also was an issue that Continental never addressed adequately as part of the appraisal report. As we saw in this case, the earlier Continental valuation estimate of $1.4 million for the building became accepted as a reasonable standard by all parties involved in the O'Toole case despite the lack of specificity or timeliness of this estimate.

3. *Separating the business between generic and goodwill.* While it may make most business owners happy to hear how much unique goodwill they have in their businesses due to their excellent service and products, drawing this distinction simply shifts the challenge to figuring out how to value the generic from the unique. While a valuation consultant can try to examine whether the business is better or worse than the industry average in customer retention or profit per transaction or other measures, this type of analysis requires knowledge of and access to industry information that would not be readily available to the typical valuation consultant.

4. *Establishing an earnings base for valuing the generic ongoing insurance business.* As we saw in the O'Toole case, one of the most difficult issues is figuring out which expenses are necessary and which are discretionary, since there is no separation between ownership and control of the assets. This problem of establishing a reliable earnings

base exists also with all earnings-based valuation methods, including the ABA, and is complicated by the split between the generic value of the firm and the additional value associated with the firm's goodwill.

5. *Valuing the generic ongoing insurance business of the O'Toole Insurance Agency.* For this step, Continental relied on the earnings-multiple approach. As we have seen already and will demonstrate further, the valuation-multiple approach has important weaknesses. In the O'Toole case, the "eight times earnings" calculation got used both for valuing a generic ongoing insurance business and for the estimate prepared by Simon and Associates for valuing the O'Toole Insurance Agency without the office building.

6. *Valuing the unique goodwill.* In addition to our concerns about splitting the business into generic and unique goodwill, we are also skeptical of methods used for valuing goodwill. In this case, Continental did not document the $300,000 value estimate for O'Toole's goodwill. This lack of clarity only adds to the unnecessary mysteriousness of valuation.

In summary, valuation estimates constructed using ABA will only be as good as their underlying assumptions on how to split up the assets and the methods used to value the assets.

BACKGROUNDER

PUBLIC COMPANIES VERSUS PRIVATE COMPANIES
Brendan O'Toole was involved in two transactions related to the sale of a business. One transaction was his unsuccessful attempt to sell the O'Toole Insurance Agency. The other was his successful effort to sell 100 shares of General Electric stock to pay off the remaining college debts of his children.

In the United States, for-profit businesses can be separated into two categories: publicly traded businesses versus privately held businesses. Brendan's sale transaction for his privately held business was very difficult and costly (and unsuccessful); the other, a sale of publicly traded company shares, was very easy to complete. In this backgrounder, we examine the reasons why these transactions are so different.

Publicly Held Companies
Publicly traded businesses, which tend to be the larger businesses (e.g., General Electric), sell equity shares representing the ownership of the firm to the general public. These equity shares then trade in the so-called sec-

ondary (public) capital markets, for example, on the New York Stock Exchange (NYSE) or on the National Association of Security Dealers Automated Quote Market (Nasdaq). A large number of individuals and financial institutions own the shares. Every day that these markets are open, shares of virtually every public company are bought and sold. Anyone with the money to buy one share of stock is eligible to become an owner of any publicly held firm.

Privately Held Companies
In contrast, privately held businesses are owned by one person or by a small number of people. These tend to be smaller companies measured by revenue, employees, and assets, although there are exceptions. Mars, Inc., the candy company, and Koch Oil, Inc., are two multi-billion dollar firms that are privately held.

Stock in these companies is rarely exchanged. Most private businesses will sell stock to a person outside the company only once in the lifetime of the primary owner. Most minority owners, that is, people owning less than 50 percent of the stock of a private company, are restricted in selling their stock to anyone but the current owners (unless the current owners are also selling to a third party).

Key Differences between Public and Private Businesses
From the perspective of valuation and the buying and selling of businesses, there are three key differences between public and private businesses:

1. The legal form of ownership structure
2. The impact of ownership structure on taxation and value
3. Market liquidity (i.e., the number of potential buyers)

In this backgrounder we will address the first difference, the legal form of ownership structure. The others will be addressed in later chapters.

OWNERSHIP STRUCTURE
Ownership structure is the legal form in which the owners take title of the assets and liabilities of a business. There are seven primary types of ownership structure:

1. Sole proprietorship
2. General partnership
3. Limited partnership
4. Limited liability partnership

5. Standard corporation (C Corp)
6. Limited liability company
7. Corporation electing Subchapter S treatment (S Corp)

Almost all public companies are in number 5, the C Corp, form. Most private companies are set up as some form of a partnership or as a corporation electing Subchapter S treatment. Differences in ownership structure lead to ownership/control issues that make valuing a private business more difficult than valuing a public company. We will briefly review each form of ownership.

Legal Form 1: Sole Proprietorship

The sole proprietorship is the simplest way to own a business. One person, that is, the proprietor, owns the business. Proprietorships are usually small businesses, such as small retail stores (e.g., Mary's Dry Cleaners). Mary Johnson owns Mary's Dry Cleaners. There is no separation between Mary Johnson and her business. The assets used by Mary's Dry Cleaners belong to Mary, as do the liabilities of the business. The income earned by Mary's Dry Cleaners is the personal income of Mary Johnson and will be taxed accordingly. Mary will report the income and expenses of her business, along with her other income, on her personal income tax Form 1040.

The major advantage of forming a business as a sole proprietorship is the ease with which it can be set up. The major disadvantage is that there is no legal separation between the business and its owner. Assume that a customer of Mary's Dry Cleaners slips and falls on a wet floor in the store. The customer sues successfully for wrongful injury and is awarded $250,000 in damages. Mary has $100,000 in liability insurance, which is paid to the claimant. Mary, however, still owes the claimant $150,000. Mary's personal assets (e.g., her savings account, car, and home) may be seized for payment.

Legal Form 2: General Partnership

A partnership exists when a group of individuals join together to own and operate a business. In a general partnership, each partner has an ownership share in the business and receives income generated by the partnership in accordance with the partnership agreement. The advantage of a general partnership over a sole proprietorship is that the partnership can assemble the expertise and financial resources of a group of people. Partnerships are easy to form. Partnership income is not taxed on the partnership tax return. Instead, the income is "passed through" to each partner, who then reports her share of the partnership profits on her personal Form 1040 tax return, where the income is taxed at the individual level. Limited partnerships and limited liability partnerships, which are discussed in detail below, are pass-thru entities for tax purposes as well.

General partnerships also have significant disadvantages. As with sole proprietorships, there is no separation between the partners as individual persons and the business they own. The partners, like a sole proprietor, are personally responsible for all partnership liabilities. The partnership situation is more complex than a sole proprietorship because each partner in a general partnership is "jointly and severally liable" for all partnership liabilities, and each general partner may contract for the partnership.

Jointly and severally liable means that any one of the partners could be held responsible for the total liabilities of the partnership if the other partners for any reason could not come up with any resources to meet the partnership's liabilities. Because of the liability and contracting issues surrounding a general partnership, this form of business organization is not used widely.

Legal Form 3: Limited Partnership
In a limited partnership, one or more of the partners is a *general partner* and one or more is a *limited partner*. The general partner is in the same situation as a partner in a general partnership, as described earlier. Limited partners, on the other hand, do not take part in the decision making of the business (i.e., they cannot contract for the partnership), and their liability is limited to their investment in the business. The legal issues surrounding a limited partnership have been codified into the Uniform Limited Partnership Act adopted as law by all 50 states.

Limited partnerships offer some degree of protection to limited partners. They are used in professional practices such as medical practices. Another example of a limited partnership is the New York Yankee baseball team. George Steinbrenner is the general partner in the club, along with several limited partners.

Legal Form 4: Limited Liability Partnership
A limited liability partnership is a partnership in which the individual partners generally remain personally liable for their own acts but not for the acts of other partners. This form may be useful for partnerships that seek some limitation on the personal liability of their individual partners but that, for some reason, cannot operate as limited partnerships. This form is used most often for professional practices such as law firms.

Legal Form 5: Standard Corporation
In the United States, with some exceptions, publicly traded businesses take on this legal organizational form. Whether we are analyzing General

Electric, Boeing, Intel, or Disney, each is a standard incorporated business (i.e., a C Corp). Each of these firms is incorporated under the incorporation laws of one of the states, and the state incorporation laws have similar provisions on the basic issues of incorporation. Fundamentally, a corporation is considered to be a separate legal entity (sometimes referred to as a separate legal "person"), separate and distinct from its owners. Corporations have many legal rights that are normally associated with a human person. Corporations can enter into legally enforceable contracts to buy and sell goods and services, to hire employees, and to borrow money. Corporations can sue or be sued in courts just like persons.

The great advantage of doing business under the legal form of the standard business corporation is limited liability. Since the corporation is a separate legal person, separate and distinct from its owners, the stockholders of the corporation are risking only the money they invest in the stock of the corporation. Should the corporation fail, the stockholders would lose their investment in the corporation, but the stockholders would not be personally responsible for any unpaid debts or obligations of the corporation. The stockholders' liability in the corporation is limited to the amount of their equity investment. Since the corporation is a separate legal entity, separate and distinct from its owners, there is said to be a wall (sometimes referred to as the *corporate veil*) between the assets and liabilities of the corporation and the private assets of the stockholder owners.

The great disadvantage of doing business under the legal form of the standard corporation is that since, at law, the corporation is considered a separate legal entity (person), the corporation is subject to income and other forms of taxation. The problem for the stockholder of a standard corporation is that when the corporation makes a profit, that profit is subject to, and reduced by, the amount of the corporate income tax. When the corporation pays out some or all of its after-tax profits (net income) to its stockholders in the form of a dividend, the dividend is considered income to the stockholder and subject to personal income taxes. This is the so-called double taxation of corporate profits, once at the corporate level and again at the personal level, that is a disadvantage to doing business as a standard corporation.

This standardization of business form means that buyers or sellers of publicly traded equity shares know important aspects of the ground rules of the equity share they are considering buying or selling. Those who would seek to estimate the fair value of a publicly traded firm at a point in time know the legal form—and therefore important taxation and liability issues—of the business they are valuing. In contrast to the standardization of legal form in publicly traded firms, privately held businesses can be held in any one of at least seven legal forms.

Legal Form 6: Limited Liability Company

Limited liability companies (LLCs) are hybrid entities that combine certain attributes of the corporate form with certain attributes of the partnership form. For tax purposes, unless otherwise elected to be treated as a corporation, a limited liability company generally is treated as a partnership as long as it has one or more members, and therefore, the disadvantage of incorporating—double taxation—is eliminated. For liability purposes, a limited liability company is treated in most cases similar to a corporation by providing limited liability for all of its members, including those who are involved in management. LLCs can be more expensive and time-consuming to organize than corporations and typically require that the members enter into an operating agreement that contains specific information about the LLC, such as the management of the LLC, the capital contribution of the members, and the allocation of income and loss.

Legal Form 7: Corporation Electing to Be Treated as a
Subchapter S Corporation for Tax Purposes

Prior to 1958, the owner(s) of a small business had a difficult choice in selecting the legal form of ownership of the business. Owning a business as a C Corporation had the attraction of limited liability, but the C Corporation had the significant disadvantage of double taxation. The alternative was to own a business as a sole proprietorship or a partnership. These forms eliminated double taxation but made the owner(s) of the business personally liable for the business's debts.

In 1958, Congress amended the Internal Revenue Code to allow corporations with certain characteristics to make an election under Subchapter S that was designed to aid small businesses. In order to qualify for the election under Subchapter S, a corporation could only have 75 or fewer individual U.S. stockholders. Electing to be treated as a corporation under Subchapter S allows the corporation to be taxed as if it were a partnership; that is, it pays no income tax on the corporation profits. Each stockholder must report on her personal income tax return her proportionate share of the S Corporation's profit or loss. If there were two stockholders who owned an equal number of shares of an S Corporation that made $100,000 in profit, then each stockholder would have to report and pay personal income tax on $50,000 of income. This personal tax would have to be paid whether the S Corporation distributed the $100,000 to the stockholders or retained it in the business.

The S Corporation has become the most popular legal form for the ownership of Established Small businesses. It allows the owner of an Established Small business to have the advantage of limited liability without the cost of double taxation of income.

These distinctions between ownership structure types are summarized in Table 3-5.

TABLE 3-5   Summary of Ownership Structure Pros and Cons

Ownership Structure	Pros	Cons
Sole proprietor	Low cost to set up and maintain; no double taxation of income	Owner has unlimited liability for obligations of the business; cannot sell a part of the business without changing legal form
General partnership	Low cost to set up and maintain; no double taxation of income	Partners have unlimited liability for the obligations of the business
Limited partnership	Moderate cost to set up and maintain; no double taxation of income	General partners have unlimited liability
Limited liability partnership	Limited liability for partners; no double taxation of income	Could be slightly more complex/costly to form than basic partnership
C Corporation	Low cost to set up and maintain; limited liability of owners	Double taxation of income
Limited liability corporation	Limited liability similar to corporation; tax pass-thru entity like a partnership	Could be slightly more complex/costly to form than basic partnership
S Corporation	Low cost to set up and maintain; no double taxation of income; limited liability	Cannot have an owner that is a corporation; limited to 75 U.S. individuals

C H A P T E R

VALUATION FOR EXIT PLANS AND BUSINESS SUCCESSION

CASE BACKGROUND

BARTON AND SCHULER METAL FABRICATING, INC.

Barton and Schuler Metal Fabricating, Inc., was founded in 1958 in Lansing, Michigan, as a sole proprietorship by Fred Barton. Barton took plans from building contractors and fabricated metal parts to meet their construction needs. Most of the work involved fabricating the metal ductwork for heating, air-conditioning, and ventilation systems. Each job had to be customized to the design requirements of the building.

In 1972, Fred became acquainted with a young man named Larry Schuler who had graduated recently from Saginaw Technical College with a degree in construction design and management and a minor in accounting. Larry was working freelance for a number of contractors, drawing up the plans and blueprints that Fred used to fabricate his products. Fred and Larry collaborated on several projects and, in 1973, Fred suggested to Larry that they combine forces and develop a comprehensive metal-fabricating business that could handle all aspects of fabricating—design, manufacture, and installation. This was accomplished in August 1973 when the two men created Barton and Schuler Metal Fabricating, Inc., as a standard C Corporation under the laws of the State of Michigan. Fred's brother-in-law was an attorney who worked for an insurance company. As a favor, he did the legal work to set up the corporation.

Over the years, the business prospered, becoming one of the major metal-fabricating firms in central Michigan. The corporation owned a fabricating plant with associated offices in Lansing, Michigan. By 1999, the firm employed nine full-time employees, in addition to Fred and Larry, and generated in excess of $2 million in gross revenues. In a little under 30 years, Fred and Larry had built a business of which they were both proud.

Business Owner Segmentation for Fred and Larry

Despite their age difference, Fred and Larry appear to be similar in their attitudes and expectations concerning business life events (BLEs). They are conservative, prudent managers who spend very little time planning for the future. They have not relied on legal, financial, insurance, or accounting professionals for anything beyond the minimum level of support.

At this point, since neither has experienced any significant BLEs, we can only narrow down to two groups where they might be classified. They certainly cannot be considered in either of the advisor-led groups given their minimal use of advisors. Considering the size and structure of their business, they certainly could have needs for help in several areas, including business succession planning, retirement planning, estate planning, and executive disability insurance. They could become BLE Planners—Expert Independent. However, they also may end up in the Limited Needs group. Although Fred and Larry want their business to continue, if they do nothing to plan for this outcome, they are much less likely to see the anticipated result.

The Owner Officers

Fred is president of Barton and Schuler, and Larry is vice president. There are no other officers of the corporation. Fred owns 70 percent of the outstanding shares of the company, reflecting his contribution of the existing metal-fabrication business to the creation of Barton and Schuler, whereas Larry owns the remaining 30 percent. They are each paid $100,000 in salary and are covered by the company's benefits. Each year Fred and Larry review their after-tax profits and declare a per-share dividend. Over the last few years, they have paid out roughly $150,000 in dividends per year, split 70:30 based on their stock ownership. Between salary and dividends, their total officers' compensation reported on the corporate tax return was $350,000.

Larry has functioned as the de facto accountant for the company, drawing on what he learned in his undergraduate minor. Sandra Whitcomb is the bookkeeper/office manager who keeps the general ledger for the business, prepares monthly accounting reports with occasional help from Larry, and takes care of tax matters. This includes transmitting employee tax with-holdings to the Internal Revenue Service (IRS) in an appropriate manner, paying the corporation's quarterly tax payments, and preparing its tax return. She also serves as the secretary for the company's board of direc-tors, Fred and Larry, and makes sure that all the required state corporation filings are filed on time.

Discretionary Expenses

When the corporation was formed, Larry had suggested that the simplest way for the two owners to handle their car, entertainment, and family employee expenses was not to have any of these expenses. Each owner was reimbursed by the company for business use of his personal car based on logs each man kept. They had no entertainment-related marketing expens-es, and they had never hired any family members.

BUSINESS LIFE EVENTS

Exit Strategy

Fred and Larry have never talked seriously about how they might manage the departure of one or both from the company. Fred at age 64 jokes that he will never retire; his father and mother are still going strong at 90, and he expects to do better than that. Fred, like many owners of businesses that deliver customized products to their customers, lives for the crisis that aris-es in most customized jobs. Fred "rides to the rescue" and figures out a solution to the problem created by "some damn architect."

Larry at age 51, while not as passionate as Fred about working until he drops, is nonetheless unconcerned about the future. He too has to stay focused on the demands of each job. Part of his assignment is to make sure that Fred's solutions do not end up losing the company money on the job. They make an excellent team this way. Larry also half expects Fred to out-live him given his heredity.

Both Fred and Larry assume that their business will continue somehow after they are gone. They are well known and well respected in their market niche in central Michigan, and climate control of buildings in the area is now considered a necessity rather than a luxury.

The Precipitating Event

During the past year, Larry had some personal legal issues surrounding his decision to buy a parcel of land and to have a contractor build a new home for him and his family. The project involved several legal issues, such as applying for a zoning variance and a quality-of-work/payment dispute with a subcontractor. Larry retained Elmer Norton as his personal attorney in these matters. In a conversation with Larry, Elmer was surprised to learn that Larry's business did not have a law firm on retainer. When Larry told him that his partner Fred was over age 60, Elmer asked about plans for the business in the event of the death or retirement of one of the owners. Larry responded that they didn't have any such plans. Larry persuaded Fred that they should retain Elmer to perform a general legal review of the business. Fred went along but insisted that Elmer perform the review under a fixed price arrangement of $1000. Fred did not want the lawyer to start searching for all kinds of ways to spend their money. Elmer agreed to the arrangement and scheduled a meeting in 2 weeks with Fred and Larry to discuss his findings.

Elmer's Findings

It took two more tries to get the three of them together. Fred canceled the meeting twice due to customer crises. Finally, they met on a Monday morning in Elmer's office, away from the phones at Barton and Schuler.

Elmer pointed out that Fred and Larry had created a solid business that paid them well and should be worth quite a bit of money. Now they needed to take a few important steps to make sure that nothing would derail their success. The first step was business succession planning, and the second was estate planning.

First, Elmer reminded them of their ages: Fred 64 and Larry 51. Elmer emphasized that on the death of either man, his ownership share in the firm would go into his estate. As things currently stood, the new owner would be the inheritor of that estate, the wife of either Fred or Larry. Neither woman was interested in managing the firm. Elmer pointed out that the widow likely would have cash needs for estate taxes and living expenses. Instead of cash, her major asset would be an ownership share in a metal-fabricating firm. Elmer noted that very few private companies have cash, securities, or other liquid assets to finance a buyout of one of the owners.

Elmer also pointed out that given the differences in their ages, Fred would more likely wish to retire or become disabled earlier than Larry. Fred stopped him right there, saying that he would likely be working into his nineties. Elmer amended his suggestion that both men do some thinking and planning about possible ways in which they might exit the firm. Elmer asked if they could narrow down the possibilities, and then he could design a simple set of plans that would cover those eventualities. In this way, they could both reap the full benefits for themselves, their wives, and any other heirs they may wish to designate. He gave them a three-page briefing outlining the findings relevant to his review of the business, along with his bill for $1000.

Owner Reactions—Larry

Elmer's straightforward presentation made a strong impression on Larry. His training in both design and accounting gave him an appreciation of managing for contingencies. He realized how quickly the last 25 years had gone by, working in this exciting but somewhat chaotic business. If he and Fred did not spend time now to consider potential risks to themselves and their business, they could end up having to sell the business due to estate obligations of either man.

Owner Reactions—Fred

On the other side, Fred did not like hearing from Elmer, an overweight former smoker in his early fifties, about Fred's mortality prospects. Fred admitted to Larry that Elmer had logic and statistics on his side but noted that Fred had genetics on his side. Larry had seen this stubborn streak in Fred before and knew what would be necessary to move this forward.

Back at the office, Larry called his wife, Susan, and asked her to set up a lunch with Anne, Fred's wife. Larry went over Elmer's report with Susan that night. She saw immediately the risks that Fred and Larry were taking by not having a succession plan in place. While lunching with Anne that Friday, Susan asked what Anne thought of the lawyer's report. It turned out that Fred had not shown Anne the report. As Susan outlined the situation, Anne realized that Fred's previous assurances that he was adequately insured were not completely accurate.

In 1970, when Fred's business was just getting off the ground, Fred and Anne had purchased a $200,000 whole-life insurance policy on Fred to provide income for the family if Fred passed away. That had been an expensive decision; however, it was important to Anne that she and the children have protection against such a risk. She now realized that at this stage in their lives the value Fred and Larry had built in Barton and Schuler was the only sufficient source of funds for current income, for retirement funds, and for protection when Fred eventually dies and that Fred and Larry had not put in place any insurance to protect the business in case of the death of one of the owners.

That night, after Fred came home late from solving another last-minute proposal crisis, Anne asked to see the report. Fred and Larry often went into the office on Saturday mornings to clear their desks of the clutter emanating from the crises of the past week. When Larry saw Fred that morning, he knew instantly that Anne had weighed in on the business succession issue.

THE OWNERS TALK ABOUT EXIT STRATEGIES

For the first time in many years, Fred and Larry talked about their personal and company goals rather than cleaning up their desks. They talked about possible ways for the company to continue on with just one of them or at some point with a new ownership group. They talked about what retirement meant to each of them. They covered a lot of familiar ground but also learned important new things about each other.

Larry confessed that he was increasingly concerned about how they were managing the financials of the business. He knew that he was just an amateur accountant, not a real controller or even chief financial officer (CFO) of a $3 million company. They needed help here, especially since they were thinking about transition options. Fred admitted that while he still planned to work until he dropped, as he aged, he would need to take more time off from work. One of the many points that Anne had raised to him was that their three daughters were now married and talking about starting families. They all had moved away from Michigan. Anne knew that Fred would want to spend time with any grandchildren, which meant taking more personal time off. After several hours of discussion, Fred and Larry agreed on two concrete actions.

Business Succession

First, they agreed that Elmer should prepare a business succession agreement that would set the terms for one owner to buy out the other owner in the event of the death of one of them. The agreement would include a mechanism for setting a fair price for these shares. The firm would purchase a life insurance policy on each man, from which the proceeds would be sufficient to purchase his shares. In this way, the man surviving would own the entire firm, and the estate of the deceased would receive cash instead of illiquid stock, that is, stock that is not easily sold.

Ownership Transition

Second, Fred decided that whether his exit strategy was to "drop dead on the plant floor" or retire at age 70, he should start reducing his ownership share. This would facilitate several objectives, including

1. Changing the ownership to reflect current contributions.
2. Providing a pool of stock that could be sold to potential partners, perhaps a CFO or another fabricating expert, who would help build the company's ability to continue after Fred and Larry depart.
3. Helping Fred to diversify his investment portfolio. Like most owners, the bulk of his wealth is tied up in the company. He could take the

cash from selling a portion of his shares and invest in assets not tied to metal fabricating or the economy of Michigan.

As a first step, Fred proposed that he and Larry enter into a contract where Fred would sell Larry 4 percent of his ownership per year so that after 5 years Larry would own 50 percent (30 percent owned by Larry initially plus the additional 20 percent purchased from Fred). Larry would be an equal owner, and Fred would receive the cash needed to start diversifying his retirement assets. This process could be speeded up, and the percentage of stock sold by Fred could be increased or changed to include a new minority partner, if both parties agreed.

VALUING BARTON AND SCHULER
In both plans described above, the most important issue was determining the value of the firm. Neither Fred nor Larry had given any serious thought to the value of their business, although both knew it was substantial. Fred had heard that metal-fabricating businesses generally sell for 1.5 times revenues, but he was not sure from whom he had heard this number. Larry said that he would call some business acquaintances and the trade association to see if he could get some guidelines.

Elmer recommended that each owner use whatever valuation sources he felt comfortable with to come up with his own independent estimate of value. Elmer said that he would get an additional valuation estimate from bizownerHQ using the Internet-based Valuation GURU. Through this three-way process, they could have both Fred's and Larry's estimates of valuation and their rationales and an objective, third-party estimate. Hopefully, this process would lead to swift agreement for Fred and Larry. They all agreed to this process and went about their prescribed activities.

The reader can find the Barton and Schuler Metal Fabricating tax return used as the company financial inputs to the Valuation GURU and the "Valuation Snapshots report" from bizownerHQ in Appendix 4A.

Reviewing the Valuation Reports
Elmer met with Fred and Larry to go over the bizownerHQ reports. The key findings from the "Valuation Snapshots report" are shown in Table 4-1.

The Valuation GURU's estimate of the total fair market value of Barton and Schuler was $2,352,244. Fred thought that the valuation was low because the rule of thumb for valuation in the trade was 1.5 times revenues. This method places the value closer to $3 million. Larry, on the other hand, had gotten such a wide range of valuation rules of thumb from the people he spoke with that he was happy to accept these third-party valuation results.

TABLE 4-1 Value Concepts for Barton and Schuler

Value Concept	Value
Total fair market value	$2,352,244
Total fair market value (if valued as a tax pass-thru entity)	$3,206,207
Ownership equity for valuing a controlling interest	$2,051,505
Ownership equity for valuing a minority interest	$1,646,362

In response to Fred's concern, Elmer told Fred and Larry that the bizownerHQ report raised a serious issue concerning the legal form of ownership and the taxation of the business. Elmer explained the difference between C- and S-type corporations. Barton and Schuler is a C Corporation and, as such, pays corporate income taxes. Fred and Larry pay personal income taxes on any dividends received. The corporate income tax liability could be completely eliminated if the business were an S Corporation. Elmer asked Fred and Larry to pay particular attention to the section of the report that stated $3,206,207 is the Valuation GURU's estimate of what the firm would be worth if it could take advantage of the S Corporation tax provisions. Since formation of the company, Fred and Larry had been paying more taxes than necessary, and that reduced the value of the business by almost $900,000.

Elmer explained that any corporate income taxes paid in the past were history. He strongly recommended that the corporation become an S Corporation. He explained that this could be done for the upcoming tax year. Fred and Larry asked Elmer to proceed with the conversion to S Corp status, and they said that they wished to meet with Elmer in the near future to implement their plans for succession and estate planning.

Elmer then pointed out that for Larry's stock purchases from Fred, the value concept they needed was the minority equity value of the company, which is $1,646,362, rather than the ownership equity value of $2,051,505. Elmer explained that what Larry is buying is the equity value of the company, not the total value, which includes their debt. In addition, Larry would not be buying "control" of the company but rather buying enough shares to be an equal partner of Fred, so he should be paying only for the minority value, not for the control of the ownership equity.

However, for Fred's business succession insurance policy, they should base the coverage on Fred's 70 percent share using the ownership equity value, or $1,436,053. If Fred were to die before Larry, buying Fred's share of the business would give Larry control of the ownership equity. This control premium is discussed further in Chapter 5.

LESSONS LEARNED

This example demonstrates, in realistic terms, the major issues of valuing a privately held business for exit planning and business succession. The example business is relatively straightforward, with two owners in one line of a business.

As we see with many Established Small businesses, the valuation of the business is a necessary means to an important end. For Fred and Larry, they have not yet taken steps to protect their business from the substantial risk of one of the owners dying. Their business is now valuable enough to make it prudent to insure against this risk. In order to put in place a business succession plan (often called a *buy-sell agreement*), they will need to buy insurance policies with the value of their respective ownership shares of the business. The valuation is necessary to determine a fair value for the insurance policies. Along the way, they also learned that their corporate form, the C Corporation, was costing them money and value.

Business owners should know that

1. *Business succession means having a funded strategy in place for having sufficient cash for a business to continue operating after paying the estate of the deceased owner for his share of the value of the business.* For most situations, the funding likely will come from the proceeds of insurance policies on the lives of the owner or owners. In our research we have found that while most business owners recognize the need to have a business succession plan, few have implemented one.

2. *As the value of a business changes over time, the business succession insurance coverage should be updated to reflect the current value of the business.* Unlike homeowner insurance policies that can have automatic coverage increases, business succession insurance is sold at a fixed amount of coverage for the current value of the business and the current health of the owner. Business owners with a business succession insurance policy should review on a regular basis whether their coverage is adequate for the current value of the business.

3. *Business succession also means having a strategy in place for which person or persons will replace the current owner or owners.* Fred and Larry need to consider how to replace their complementary skill sets over time, since as a provider of custom services, the owners are involved in the day-to-day operations. They also should be considering whether they embed their knowledge of how to customize their projects into their design and bidding processes or, in other words, become a mass customization company.

4. *Business valuation for business succession and exit planning must take into account whether the purchase of a partial stake in the company will give an owner control of the company, that is, 50.1 percent or more of the shares.* Consider the situation where three equal owners decide to buy out one of the three. Before the purchase, none of the owners alone has control. It requires two owners to have majority control. This remains true after the buyout. The two 50 percent owners also must agree on an action to have majority control. Thus the purchase price for the third owner's stake does not have to include any control premium, according to generally accepted valuation principles. However, a minority partner sometimes can extract some of what the control premium would be through negotiation.

OTHER IMPORTANT ISSUES TO CONSIDER

As noted in the Barton and Schuler case, their original advice on establishing the corporate form came from Fred's brother-in-law, an attorney who worked for an insurance company and who was not experienced in small business accounting issues. Many small businesses take advantage of the various corporate or sole proprietor forms that avoid paying taxes at the corporate level. However, we continue to run across situations such as that of Barton and Schuler, where the company has been set up as a C Corporation, although the owners would be much better off from a tax standpoint and from a valuation perspective with a different corporate form.

Business owners should know that the corporate form of the business could have an important impact on the value of the business both for today and in the future when the owner is planning to exit. As with all valuation, legal, and accounting issues, owners should speak with their current professional advisors about whether the corporate form they currently have is most appropriate for their current strategies. They also should ask about the implications of the corporate form for their exit planning. For example, a sole proprietor who wants his two best salespeople to buy into the company will have to change the corporate form to allow for multiple owners. The EarthRight case used in Chapters 6 and 8 provides more information on the differences in value based on corporate form and how this can affect owner exit strategies.

Estate Tax Planning

While much has been written about the "death of the death tax" contained in the federal legislation approved by the Congress and signed by the President in 2001, what actually was approved was a phased-in reduction of estate tax rates and an increase in the size of estates exempted from the tax until 2010, when the tax rate becomes 0 percent. As currently implemented, the elimination of the estate tax in 2010 is temporary, and the current rates and exemptions return in 2011. *Business owners should know that estate tax planning is still a necessary activity if they want to ensure that a business does not have to be sold to meet estate taxes on the death of an owner.*

Portfolio Diversification

In this case, Fred (age 64), the majority owner of the business, will have the opportunity to diversify his net worth as Larry increases his ownership stake in the company. Larry (age 51) will become less diversified as more of his assets are tied up with Barton and Schuler. Given their different ages, these are sensible portfolio management strategies. Because of the importance of this issue, we repeat a maxim from Chapter 3:

> *Business owners should know that diversification of their financial resources is their second most important financial strategy behind managing a successful transition out of the businesses.*

MORE ON VALUATION METHODS

REVENUE AND EARNINGS MULTIPLES

The earnings- or revenue-multiples approach (ERMA) is based on the premise that a particular type of business is worth some multiple of its earnings or revenues based on an average or median of previous comparable transactions. Using ERMA requires information on the earnings and revenues and selling prices of comparable businesses that have changed ownership recently. The assumptions that are key to the reliability of ERMA are the degrees of

1. Comparability of businesses sold
2. Lack of deviation in the transaction multiples used to calculate the average or median
3. Timeliness of the sale transactions
4. Comparability of transaction circumstances

To illustrate these points, we have developed an example case where ERMA is used to value a service station business.

Valuing a Service Station Using ERMA

Tom Scott is a business appraiser based in Wichita who focuses on sales of service stations, convenience stores, fast-food restaurants, and other franchise operations in Kansas, Oklahoma, and Nebraska. Over the years, he has built a network of sources of information on transactions for these types of businesses, including attorneys, accountants, insurance agents, and other brokers. By sharing his transaction information, he has been able to get others to reciprocate. Also, he standardizes these transactions by setting an owner salary benchmark of $80,000. For any business in which the owner reports a higher salary, Tom takes the salary amount over $80,000 and adds it back to earnings.

Today, his assignment is to develop a valuation estimate for Barney's Sunoco on the west side of Wichita, Kansas. This business had revenues of $1,905,000 and net income of $105,500 for the year 2000. The owner's salary is $100,000, compared with Tom's benchmark of $80,000. Tom reduces the salary to $80,000 and adds $20,000 to net income to get an adjusted earnings figure of $125,500. He then searches his database of transactions for service stations and comes up with 16 transactions for the year 2000, as shown in Table 4-2. All these transactions involved a service station in a town or city of at least 25,000 people or more in Kansas and Oklahoma.

TABLE 4-2   Example Transactions for Service Stations

Sale	Date	Revenue	Adjusted Earnings	Sale Price	Revenue Multiple	Earnings Multiple
1	Jan 2000	$2,683,816	$ 24,880	$ 274,735	0.1	11.04
2	Mar 2000	$1,374,533	$ 64,835	$ 869,378	0.63	13.41
3	Apr 2000	$ 553,136	$ 23,075	$ 252,309	0.46	10.93
4	May 2000	$1,478,318	$ 52,399	$ 671,941	0.45	12.82
5	May 2000	$1,529,359	$ 65,050	$ 617,736	0.4	9.5
6	Jun 2000	$ 719,744	$ 30,025	$ 309,325	0.43	10.3
7	Jul 2000	$1,823,359	$111,360	$1,492,624	0.82	13.4
8	Jul 2000	$ 505,751	$ 17,926	$ 90,645	0.18	5.06
9	Sep 2000	$2,247,708	$ 82,734	$ 779,450	0.35	9.42
10	Sep 2000	$2,689,247	$123,623	$1,753,609	0.65	14.19
11	Oct 2000	$2,873,453	$119,869	$1,212,246	0.42	10.11
12	Oct 2000	$ 907,484	$ 42,805	$ 628,516	0.69	14.68
13	Nov 2000	$3,079,324	$128,457	$1,067,834	0.35	8.31
14	Dec 2000	$3,659,360	$194,559	$2,726,746	0.75	14.02

continued on next page

TABLE 4-2   Example Transactions for Service Stations *(continued)*

Sale	Date	Revenue	Adjusted Earnings	Sale Price	Revenue Multiple	Earnings Multiple
15	Dec 2000	$4,100,521	$195,877	$2,272,191	0.55	11.6
16	Dec 2000	$4,929,040	$205,620	$2,184,068	0.44	10.62
Average Jan-Jun 2000		$1,389,818	$ 43,377	$ 499,237	0.36	11.51
Jul-Dec 2000		$2,681,525	$122,283	$1,420,793	0.53	11.62
Jan-Dec 2000		$2,197,135	$ 92,693	$1,075,210	0.49	11.60

For these 16 transactions over the year 2000, the average valuation-to-revenue multiple is 0.49 and the average earnings multiple is 11.60. For Tom Scott, the valuation estimate for Barney's Sunoco takes only a minute. Using Barney's 2000 revenues of $1,905,000 and earnings of $125,500, he calculates that the current valuation based on revenue is $932,348 and the valuation based on earnings is $1,455,755. This information is presented in Table 4-3.

TABLE 4-3   Valuation of Barney's Sunoco Using ERMA

Barney's Sunoco	Revenue	Adjusted Earnings
Year 2000 financials	$1,905,000	$125,500
	Revenue Multiple	**Earnings Multiple**
Valuation multiple from Tom Scott's database	0.49	11.60
	Valuation Estimate	**Valuation Estimate**
Valuation of Barney's Sunoco	$932,348	$1,455,755

ERMA Advantages

The advantage of ERMA is its simplicity. A business is worth some multiple of the revenue or earnings it generates. As long as the transactions used to calculate ERMA are current, based on comparable businesses, adjusted if necessary for differences in the transaction arrangements, and closely clustered around the average, then ERMA should provide a highly reliable estimate. ERMA is used widely to value privately held businesses.

ERMA Disadvantages

The disadvantages of ERMA arise from deviations from the key ERMA requirements. First, the revenue or earnings approach to valuation assumes that businesses (service stations in our example) are comparable. Let us consider three factors that can make a significant difference in the financial performance of a service station:

1. *Mix of services.* Service stations can offer a variety of services; often they sell gasoline and have facilities to repair vehicles. The mix of revenue and profit from selling gasoline (a low-profit-margin business) and automobile repair (a high-profit-margin business) can differ dramatically from one station to another. Some service stations have replaced their repair business with a convenience store, which also provides a different revenue and profit picture. The value of a particular service station will be affected not only by the volume of its business (revenues) but also by the type. ERMA does not explicitly account for the difference.

2. *Who owns the real estate.* The real estate (land and building) of a service station is sometimes owned by the same person who operates the service station. Barney owns Barney's Sunoco, both the business and the real estate. Barney buys his gas exclusively from Sunoco, which allows him to use the Sunoco brand name. At other gas stations, the owner of the gas station leases the land and building usually from an oil company. Another service station owner, Steve, owns Steve's Sunoco. Sunoco owns the land and building and leases these to Steve—a franchisee. Steve pays rent to Sunoco for use of the land and building and agrees to buy gas exclusively from Sunoco. Sunoco allows Steve to use the Sunoco brand name. The relative valuations of Barney's and Steve's Sunoco service stations are different. Barney owns the real estate; Steve does not. The ERMA does not explicitly account for this difference.

3. *Size matters.* There are economies of scale in the retail sales of gasoline. The station has underground storage tanks and pumps. The station has a physical maximum capacity of gasoline it can sell at any time that is fixed. The costs associated with this capacity are fixed. Whether a station pumps 10 or 10,000 gallons of gas in a week, certain costs (e.g., maintenance, insurance, and inspection costs associated with the storage tanks) are fixed. The closer a service station owner can push

the gasoline sales of the station toward the maximum capacity of the station, the lower will be the per-gallon cost of the gasoline sold and the higher will be the profit. Volume sold relative to delivery capacity is a major determinant of service station profitability and value. The ERMA does not explicitly account for this difference.

Variability of Multiples within Comparables

The second assumption relates to how closely clustered around the average the actual multiples for individual transactions are. In looking at Tom Scott's database, we see a wide difference in the valuation multiples that service stations sell for within this area. For example, transaction 1 has the lowest revenue multiple of 0.1, whereas transaction 7 has the highest revenue multiple at 0.82. Six of the service stations sold near the average of 0.49 times revenue, whereas 10 were much higher or lower. What is the logic of applying the average multiple to a particular business such as Barney's Sunoco?

Timeliness of Multiples

Timeliness also can be a significant concern for using transactions. Tom Scott's database covers all of the year 2000. Over the year, the economic and financial situation changed considerably as the economy weakened; gasoline prices increased, and the Federal Reserve began to cut interest rates. These changes have an impact on the valuation of service stations and most other businesses. As we can see from the valuation multiples for both revenue and earnings in Table 4-2, the multiples are somewhat higher for the second half of the year than for the first half. This is a likely reflection that interest rates declined, which lowered the cost of capital required to buy a business, and that demand for gasoline and other services was still relatively strong despite the weakening economy. Both these factors would tend to push valuations of service stations higher. In addition, the transactions in the second half of the year were mostly service stations with higher revenues that tended to have higher multiples on both revenue and earnings.

Comparability of Transactions

The final key assumption in ERMA is the comparability of transaction arrangements. This is typically the hardest information to obtain, since the details of most private sales are never publicized. Tom Scott's database does not include information on whether owner financing is involved in the sales transaction or whether the owner was paid a portion of the purchase price over time based on meeting revenue and/or earnings objectives established when the transactions were finalized. While Tom generally knows this information about his own deals, there is no comprehensive structure for listing this information about a private company sales transaction.

VALUATION USING ERMA

What is the right valuation multiple to use for Barney's Sunoco? Table 4-4 shows the high, average, and low revenue and earnings multiples. These are used to produce a range of values for Barney's Sunoco based on Barney's year 2000 revenue and earnings results. The highest estimate of value is $1,842,340, which is station-adjusted earnings times the highest earnings multiplier of 14.68. The lowest estimate of value is $190,500, which is station revenue times the lowest revenue multiplier of 0.10. This is a wide range of valuations for an industry that many people would consider relatively homogeneous. With ERMA, there is no objective way to determine which estimate is superior. The act of averaging or taking the median is considered to be the end of the analysis.

TABLE 4-4   Valuation Ranges for Barney's Sunoco Using ERMA Approach

Barney's Sunoco	Revenue	Adjusted Earnings
Year 2000 financials	$1,905,000	$125,500
Multiples from Service Station Transactions	**Revenue Multiples**	**Earnings Multiples**
High multiple	.82	14.68
Average multiple	.49	11.60
Low multiple	.10	5.06
Valuation Results	**Valuation Estimates**	**Valuation Estimates**
High	$1,562,100	$1,842,340
Average	$ 932,348	$1,455,755
Low	$ 190,500	$ 635,030

Revenue versus Earnings Multiples

Another concern about the use of multiples is that ERMA provides two possible answers for a valuation, one based on the revenue multiple and the other based on the earnings multiple. As we see with Barney's Sunoco, even using the average for the revenue and earnings concepts generates estimates that are over 10 percent apart.

There is a logical case for using earnings, since earnings are the economic measure of the return to a business. However, we have already seen that the measurement of earnings in a private business is complicated by the lack of separation between ownership and control. In situations where reliable measurement of earnings can be established, earnings multiples should provide superior measures of value compared with revenue multiples.

Business owners should know that the reliability of valuation multiples depends on the degree of business comparability, time period of the transactions, similarity of transaction financing arrangements, and the tightness of the transaction values around the median or average. We strongly encourage business owners to find out as much as possible about the transactions underlying valuation multiples for their industry offered by business brokers, investment intermediaries, and valuation consultants to determine whether to use this information as an input in valuing their business.

BACKGROUNDER

LEGAL FORM AFFECTS TAXATION AND VALUE

The legal form in which a business is held can affect the taxation and relative owner liability of the business, as discussed in the Chapter 3 "Backgrounder." These differences in legal form can affect value in two ways.

First, a corporate structure that causes higher tax payments makes a business less valuable than a structure that causes lower tax payments. Indeed, any particular privately held business could have a higher value if it is or could be held in a lower-tax business form. All else equal, an S Corporation will have a higher value than a C Corporation. In a later section of this book, we refer to this difference as the *tax pass-thru value*—the additional value that arises because S Corporations, partnerships, and sole proprietorships are not taxed at the business level. Consequently, owners of these business forms are allowed to keep a greater percentage of their before-tax income than owners of C Corporations. Table 4-5 shows the relationship between tax pass-thru value and business legal form.

The tax pass-thru legal form can have substantial advantages over a C Corporation primarily where the business being sold and the business buying are already tax pass-thru type businesses. However, the tax pass-thru corporate forms have one major drawback, a limit on the number of owners, which restricts their use to firms under a certain size. For example, S Corporations are limited to 75 owners. This generally means that the amount of capital a tax pass-thru business can raise is also limited. It is possible for an S Corporation to become a C Corporation, and visa versa. However, such a change could be complicated and expensive. As always, when contemplating a change in ownership structure, an owner always should get the advice of a well-informed tax attorney.

TABLE 4-5   Tax Pass-Thru Value Depends on the Legal Form of the Business

	Seller: C Corporation	Seller: Pass-Thru Type of Entity
Buyer: C Corporation	No tax pass-thru advantage	No tax pass-thru advantage
Buyer: Pass-thru	Potential tax pass-thru advantage if buyer can convert C business to pass through at a reasonable cost	Tax pass-thru advantage

Appendix 4A
BARTON AND SCHULER: VALUATION INPUTS AND OUTPUTS

Partial 2000 Tax Return
Valuation Snapshots Report

Barton & Schuler tax return, page 1.

Form 1120
Department of the Treasury
Internal Revenue Service

U.S. Corporation Income Tax Return

For calendar year 2000 or tax year beginning .... , 2000, ending .... , 20 ....
▶ Instructions are separate. See page 1 for Paperwork Reduction Act Notice.

OMB No. 1545-0123

2000

A Check if a:	Use IRS label. Other- wise, print or type.	**Name** Barton and Schuler
1 Consolidated return (attach Form 851) ☐		**Number, street, and room or suite no.** (If a P.O. box, see page 7 of instructions.)
2 Personal holding co. (attach Sch. PH) ☐		**City or town, state, and ZIP code** Lansing, MI
3 Personal service corp. (as defined in Temporary Regs. sec. 1.441-4T— see instructions) ☐		

B Employer identification number

C Date incorporated 1973

D Total assets (see page 8 of instructions) 921,639 | 00

E Check applicable boxes: (1) ☐ Initial return (2) ☐ Final return (3) ☐ Change of address $

Income

1a	Gross receipts or sales 2,054,723 | 00 **b** Less returns and allowances 32,000 | 00 **c** Bal ▶	1c	2,022,723 | 00
2	Cost of goods sold (Schedule A, line 8)	2	1,272,000 | 00
3	Gross profit. Subtract line 2 from line 1c	3	600,723 | 00
4	Dividends (Schedule C, line 19)	4	10,050 | 00
5	Interest	5	5,650 | 00
6	Gross rents	6	
7	Gross royalties	7	
8	Capital gain net income (attach Schedule D (Form 1120))	8	
9	Net gain or (loss) from Form 4797, Part II, line 18 (attach Form 4797)	9	
10	Other income (see page 8 of instructions—attach schedule)	10	
11	**Total income.** Add lines 3 through 10 ▶	11	616,423 | 00

Deductions (See instructions for limitations on deductions.)

12	Compensation of officers (Schedule E, line 4)	12	350,000 | 00
13	Salaries and wages (less employment credits)	13	89,125 | 00
14	Repairs and maintenance	14	980 | 00
15	Bad debts	15	1,800 | 00
16	Rents	16	32,900 | 00
17	Taxes and licenses	17	16,750 | 00
18	Interest	18	25,985 | 00
19	Charitable contributions (see page 11 of instructions for 10% limitation)	19	
20	Depreciation (attach Form 4562) 20 | 18,150 | 00		
21	Less depreciation claimed on Schedule A and elsewhere on return 21a | 12,150 | 00	21b	6,000 | 00
22	Depletion	22	
23	Advertising	23	
24	Pension, profit-sharing, etc., plans	24	9,100 | 00
25	Employee benefit programs	25	50,500 | 00
26	Other deductions (attach schedule)	26	12,000 | 00
27	**Total deductions.** Add lines 12 through 26 ▶	27	445,140 | 00
28	Taxable income before net operating loss deduction and special deductions. Subtract line 27 from line 11	28	171,283 | 00
29	**Less:** a Net operating loss (NOL) deduction (see page 13 of instructions) 29a		
	b Special deductions (Schedule C, line 20) 29b | 9,800 | 00	29c	9,800 | 00

Tax and Payments

30	Taxable income. Subtract line 29c from line 28	30	445,140 | 00
31	Total tax (Schedule J, line 11)	31	44,050 | 00
32	Payments: a 1999 overpayment credited to 2000 32a		
	b 2000 estimated tax payments 32b | 72,129 | 00		
	c Less 2000 refund applied for on Form 4466 32c ( ) **d** Bal ▶ 32d | 72,129 | 00		
	e Tax deposited with Form 7004 32e		
	f Credit for tax paid on undistributed capital gains (attach Form 2439) 32f		
	g Credit for Federal tax on fuels (attach Form 4136). See instructions 32g	32h	72,129 | 00
33	Estimated tax penalty (see page 14 of instructions). Check if Form 2220 is attached ▶ ☐	33	
34	**Tax due.** If line 32h is smaller than the total of lines 31 and 33, enter amount owed	34	
35	**Overpayment.** If line 32h is larger than the total of lines 31 and 33, enter amount overpaid	35	28,079 | 00
36	Enter amount of line 35 you want: **Credited to 2001 estimated tax** ▶ Refunded ▶	36	

Sign Here

Under penalties of perjury, I declare that I have examined this return, including accompanying schedules and statements, and to the best of my knowledge and belief, it is true, correct, and complete. Declaration of preparer (other than taxpayer) is based on all information of which preparer has any knowledge.

▶ Signature of officer　　　　　Date　　　　　▶ Title

Paid Preparer's Use Only

Preparer's signature ▶	Date	Check if self-employed ☐	Preparer's SSN or PTIN
Firm's name (or yours if self-employed), address, and ZIP code ▶		EIN	
		Phone no. ( )	

Cat. No. 11450Q　　　　　　　　　　　　　　　　　　Form **1120** (2000)

Barton & Schuler tax return, page 4.

Form 1120 (2000)   Page **4**

Schedule L — Balance Sheets per Books

	Assets	Beginning of tax year (a)	Beginning of tax year (b)	End of tax year (c)	End of tax year (d)
1	Cash		15,100		31,336
2a	Trade notes and accounts receivable	100,100		105,700	
b	Less allowance for bad debts	( )	100,100	( )	105,700
3	Inventories		141,000		301,520
4	U.S. government obligations				
5	Tax-exempt securities (see instructions)		112,000		124,150
6	Other current assets (attach schedule)		27,200		17,243
7	Loans to shareholders				
8	Mortgage and real estate loans				
9	Other investments (attach schedule)		135,000		95,000
10a	Buildings and other depreciable assets	265,405		315,650	
b	Less accumulated depreciation	89,285)	176,120	110,475)	205,175
11a	Depletable assets				
b	Less accumulated depletion	( )		( )	
12	Land (net of any amortization)		21,000		21,000
13a	Intangible assets (amortizable only)				
b	Less accumulated amortization	( )		( )	
14	Other assets (attach schedule)		17,530		20,515
15	Total assets		745,050		921,639
	Liabilities and Shareholders' Equity				
16	Accounts payable		31,225		36,856
17	Mortgages, notes, bonds payable in less than 1 year		4,105		4,105
18	Other current liabilities (attach schedule)		7,160		7,150
19	Loans from shareholders				
20	Mortgages, notes, bonds payable in 1 year or more		206,540		296,634
21	Other liabilities (attach schedule)				
22	Capital stock: a Preferred stock				
	b Common stock	210,000	210,000	210,000	210,000
23	Additional paid-in capital				
24	Retained earnings—Appropriated (attach schedule)		32,000		42,000
25	Retained earnings—Unappropriated		254,020		322,894
26	Adjustments to shareholders' equity (attach schedule)				
27	Less cost of treasury stock		( )		( )
28	Total liabilities and shareholders' equity		745,050		921,639

Note: *The corporation is not required to complete Schedules M-1 and M-2 if the total assets on line 15, col. (d) of Schedule L are less than $25,000.*

Schedule M-1 — Reconciliation of Income (Loss) per Books With Income per Return (See page 20 of instructions.)

1	Net income (loss) per books		7	Income recorded on books this year not included on this return (itemize):	
2	Federal income tax	44,022		Tax-exempt interest $	
3	Excess of capital losses over capital gains			....	
4	Income subject to tax not recorded on books this year (itemize):		8	Deductions on this return not charged against book income this year (itemize):	
	....		a	Depreciation . . . . $............	
5	Expenses recorded on books this year not deducted on this return (itemize):		b	Contributions carryover $..........	
a	Depreciation . . . . $............			....	
b	Contributions carryover $..........			....	
c	Travel and entertainment $		9	Add lines 7 and 8	
	....		10	Income (line 28, page 1)—line 6 less line 9	
6	Add lines 1 through 5				

Schedule M-2 — Analysis of Unappropriated Retained Earnings per Books (Line 25, Schedule L)

1	Balance at beginning of year		5	Distributions: a Cash	
2	Net income (loss) per books			b Stock	
3	Other increases (itemize):			c Property	
	....		6	Other decreases (itemize):	
	....		7	Add lines 5 and 6	
4	Add lines 1, 2, and 3		8	Balance at end of year (line 4 less line 7)	

✪   Form **1120** (2000)

VALUATION SNAPSHOTS REPORT

WHAT IS BARTON AND SCHULER WORTH?

The Valuation GURU estimates that the fair market total value of Barton and Schuler is $2,352,244 as of January 1, 2001, based on the business tax return information entered. Please review the bizownerHQ key assumptions to make sure that they apply to this business.

The Valuation GURU builds up the fair market total value of a business by estimating values separately by source, as shown in Figure 4A-1:

FIGURE 4A-1   Barton and Schuler—Total value estimate.

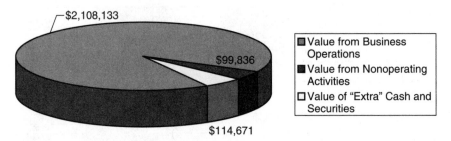

1. *Value from business operations.* Generally, the primary source of value in a business is based on the cash flows from the earnings of the business operations, that is, the products or services the company sells less the cash needed for investments in operations. The Valuation GURU uses a sophisticated proprietary approach to forecasting the revenues and adjusted earnings of the business operations and then calculates the present value of those future anticipated earnings to determine the value shown in the graph.

2. *Value from nonoperating activities.* Many businesses have other sources of income, such as rental income from buildings or licensing income, that are generated outside the normal business operations. While these cash flows have value, they are not given the same valuation treatment as income from business operations, reflecting that buyers often will not value these nonoperating cash flows as highly as those from operating activities. The Valuation GURU, following standard practices, calculates the present value of the current income flow to the business owner(s).

3. *Value of extra cash and securities.* The final source of value that the Valuation GURU analyzes is whether the company has on its balance

sheet a level of cash and marketable securities above what is considered necessary to fund working capital. The Valuation GURU draws on financial analysis research across thousands of companies for a revenue-based factor to estimate the working capital needs of a company. If the cash and securities on the balance sheet are greater than this estimate, the Valuation GURU makes an adjustment to the fair market total valuation to reflect this extra difference.

4. *Valuation of Barton and Schuler as an S Corporation.* The Valuation GURU's estimate of what the firm would be worth if it could take advantage of the tax pass-thru provisions of the S Corp election is $3,206,207. You should review with your accountant whether switching to S Corp status is possible and whether you would gain from such a switch.

DEFINITIONS

1. *Fair market value.* The price at which the property would change hands between a willing buyer and a willing seller when the former is not under any compulsion to buy and the latter is not under any compulsion to sell, both parties having reasonable knowledge of relevant facts (Internal Revenue Service Revenue Rule 59-60, 1959-1, C.B. 237).

2. *Fair market total value.* The sum of the fair market values of the cash flows from business operations, nonoperating activities, and the tax pass-thru *plus* the value of the current dollar amount of the extra company cash and marketable securities, if any.

bizownerHQ KEY ASSUMPTIONS

1. *Company growth rate forecasts.* Revenue and cash flows for Barton and Schuler are projected to grow at rates consistent with the baseline or average performing growth segment of companies in this industry.

2. *No greater use of assets.* The assets of Barton and Schuler, including production equipment, technology, patents, intangible assets, and real estate used by the company, have no greater value as stand-alone assets than they have as profit-generating assets for this business.

GURU Alert

Please review with your accountant or other business professional whether these assumptions are correct for your business before using this valuation as input to decision making.

WHAT IS THE OWNERSHIP EQUITY IN
BARTON AND SCHULER WORTH?

The estimated value of the ownership equity in Barton and Schuler is
$2,051,505. This is the amount the owner would receive if the company
were sold today for the fair market total value of $2,352,244 minus an esti-
mate of the amount necessary to pay off company debts and long-term liabilities, as shown in Figure 4A-2. Ownership equity is equal to the firm's
minority interest value (i.e., $1,646,362) plus a control premium of
$405,143, the amount necessary to obtain full control of the firm.

FIGURE 4A-2   Barton and Schuler—Total ownership value.

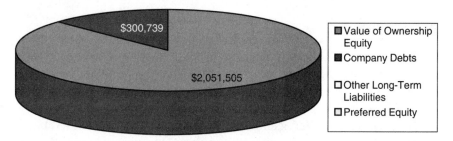

The Valuation GURU separates the business value into its ownership
components, as shown in Figure 4A-2:

1. *Value of ownership equity.* This is the estimate of the market value of
   owner equity in the business.
   - *Minority value of equity.* Minority owners own less than 51 per-
     cent of the equity of a firm and do not have the right to direct
     how the firm's assets are used. Minority owners have claims on a
     firm's earnings after taxes and interest and a right to vote on firm
     agenda items.
   - *Control premium.* When a business is sold, the buyer or buyers
     typically purchase full control of the firm. This gives the new buy-
     ers the right to change the way the firm is managed, the types of
     products and services the firm desires to produce, and the number
     of employees that are required. In return for the right to make
     these and other decisions, a buyer will pay a premium above the
     minority equity value of the firm. This premium is not a constant
     percentage. It varies with the level of interest rates, the riskiness of
     the firm, and the long-term growth of the firm's earnings.

2. *Company debts (book value)*. This book-value concept from the tax return balance sheet is the closest estimate of the market value of the company's debt given the information provided.

Caution: The terms and conditions of any business loans should be reviewed by the company's accountant or by the owner(s) to determine whether there are any prepayment penalties or other charges that would make the market value of the company's debts different from the book value. Any differences found should be included in the preceding estimate to refine the valuation of the company.

WHAT ARE THE VALUATION MULTIPLES FOR BARTON AND SCHULER?

The Valuation GURU estimates that the value-to-revenue multiple for Barton and Schuler is 1.16 and the value-to-earnings multiple is 6.49 as of January 1, 2001, as shown in Figure 4A-3.

FIGURE 4A-3   Barton and Schuler—Valuation multiples.

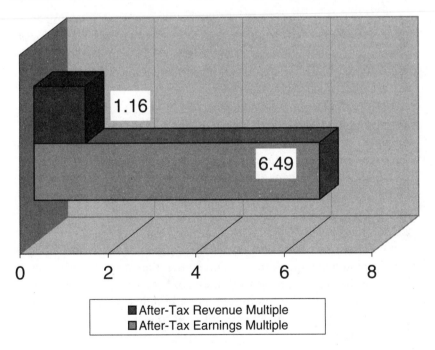

What Business Owners Need to Know about Industry Valuation Multiples

1. *Beware of the industry valuation multiples.* These industry valuation multiples are used by business brokers and investment bankers to provide owners with a quick and supposedly costless way to find out the value of their companies. For example, a broker might tell a landscaping business owner that landscaping businesses typically sell for 1 times revenue.

2. *Typical concerns with industry valuation multiples.* Industry valuation estimates generally are based on the company sales experiences of, at worst, a single broker and, at best, a number of brokers. For most industries, there are no consistently reliable data sources where transaction data on the prices and terms of privately held businesses can be found. There are many factors in these sales, such as how quickly the owner needs to sell and the financing of the business before and after the sale, that have a significant impact on the actual price and hence the valuation multiple. Decisions owners make based on the valuation, such as selling a business, should be made on more solid evidence.

3. *Is this an average business for this industry?* An owner applying an industry multiple to his business should wonder whether his business is likely to have a value right at the average or median level. If a business is more productive and efficient than most, then that business should be worth a higher multiple.

4. *Problems with earnings-based multiples.* Valuation multiples based on earnings are particularly troublesome because how privately held companies report earnings varies significantly. Industry valuation estimates tend to be based on transactions over a long period of time, yet business valuations change frequently as interest rates change and as perceptions about industry growth opportunities and industry risk change.

5. *Valuation multiples are rarely used for the benefit of the current owner.* Business brokers and investment bankers have a natural incentive to encourage a quick transaction so that they maximize their compensation for the amount of work they do. By encouraging business owners and business buyers to rely on these industry valuation multiples, brokers reinforce the "value" of their role and justify their sizable commission.

HOW CAN bizownerHQ VALUATION MULTIPLES BE USED?

1. *Valuation multiples can be useful shorthand tools.* The bizownerHQ company-specific valuation multiples are useful shorthand tools for understanding the current valuation of a company and how that valuation may vary in the short run from changes in revenue or earnings. For example, a business with a company-specific valuation-to-revenue multiple of six can estimate that if the company can increase revenues by $50,000, the company should be worth approximately $300,000 more. (This assumes that the company is able to generate higher earnings and cash flow after investments at the same rate as before.)

   - **Business owners should know that company-specific valuation multiples will change as interest rates and economic conditions change.** For example, as a general rule, when the Federal Reserve increases interest rates in the U.S. economy by pushing up the federal funds rate, the valuation of all U.S. companies will decline somewhat.

2. *Valuation multiples vary within industry and over time.* There is generally a wide difference in the revenue and earnings growths of companies in the same industry. Companies with higher growth in revenue and earnings typically will have a higher multiple than companies in their industry with lower revenue and earnings.

   - *Owners need to be aware of this potential valuation range within their industry.* They should evaluate potential risks and rewards that go along with a more aggressive growth strategy. They also should review whether a more aggressive growth strategy might lead to less control for the owner. For example, borrowing money for expansion from a bank increases the influence of the bank on the company's decisions.

C H A P T E R

VALUATION FOR OWNER BUY-INS AND BUYOUTS

CASE BACKGROUND

HACHEY AND NELSON, ATTORNEYS

Nancy Hachey and David Nelson were classmates at the University of Florida Law School. Both graduated in 1978, and both joined the Florida bar soon after. Nancy and David had become friends during law school, and they had discussed the type of law and setting in which each would like to practice. Neither wanted to work for a large law firm. Both initially considered setting up a solo practice, but after discussion, they decided to start a new law firm as partners.

The Orlando, Florida, metropolitan area was experiencing enormous growth during 1978. The opening of Disney World sparked a great economic expansion with associated restaurants and hotels. Nancy and David created Hachey and Nelson, Attorneys at Law, as a Subchapter S Corporation on January 3, 1979, and started their practice in leased office space. The initial years were a struggle. The two young attorneys took whatever work they were offered as a general law practice—wills and estates, some real estate work, and divorces.

In 1982, a construction worker who had been injured on the job retained Hachey and Nelson. The worker had several grievances, which related to inadequate and unfair treatment from the worker's compensation system of the state of Florida. Nancy and David took on the worker's case and in 1984 won a significant legal suit against the state of Florida. The decision was appealed, and in every instance, the appellate court agreed with the original decision. The worker's compensation system eventually appealed the ruling to the Florida Supreme Court, where it lost. The ruling quickly became a definitive part of Florida case law on the disability rights of workers and the responsibilities of the state's worker's compensation system. From the work on this case, Nancy and David acquired a great deal of knowledge about the law surrounding work-related injuries, and their reputations in the legal community grew as knowledgeable attorneys and successful litigators. Soon the law firm of Hachey and Nelson prospered as it specialized in employment-related injury cases.

Business Owner Segmentation for Nancy and David
These two attorneys, with Nancy taking the lead, are in the needs being met—expert dependent grouping of business owners. They have taken several important steps in the management of their business life events (BLEs), and they have put significant faith in the advice and recommendations of their accountant, attorney, and insurance agent.

Coverage and Advisors
Nancy and David are very careful in their management of BLE risks. They have put in place a business succession plan funded by insurance policies on both of them, similar to the one that Fred Barton and Larry Schuler planned to buy in Chapter 4. Nancy also insisted that they purchase executive disability insurance as soon as they could afford it. They also had a 401(k) plan, their wills are up to date, and they have started exploring their estate-planning options.

Nancy scheduled an annual review meeting for herself and David with the firm's accountant, estate-planning lawyer, and insurance advisor. She considered this the financial equivalent of her annual medical checkup. She encouraged these advisors to keep her and David informed about the latest and greatest advances in managing BLEs.

Owner Compensation
Nancy and David each pay themselves $150,000 per year, which includes the value of the company-paid portion of the costs of nonmandatory benefits, such as health insurance. In addition, any ordinary income reported at the Subchapter S Corp level is allocated between the two owners on their Schedule K tax forms. The firm has no significant discretionary expenditures.

BUSINESS LIFE EVENTS

Exit Strategy

Nancy and David were both comfortable with their business lives. They had reached a similar trade-off point between income and stress. They knew that they could earn more either by hiring more attorneys or by being absorbed into a larger firm, but these were not attractive options to either of them.

Their preferred exit strategy was to sell the business in installments over several years to two or three of their best and most ambitious associates. In this way, Nancy and David could

1. Continue their desired balance of income and stress for now
2. Stay involved with the firm as long as either desired
3. Earn a return on the capital they have built

This exit strategy does entail some risks; most notably, if one or more of the associates were not up to the task of keeping the practice growing and profitable, then Nancy and David might not earn the amounts they expected.

Adding a New Partner

During the fall of 2000, Nancy and David had several conversations about an attorney, Donna Young, they had hired as a legal associate 8 years earlier. Donna had developed as an attorney during her time with Hachey and Nelson. She had contributed positively to the firm. Donna had told both Nancy and David that she believed that her contributions to the firm and her current level of experience supported her promotion to partner (actually a part owner) in the firm. Nancy and David agreed that Donna was ready to become a partner, but the details of how to accomplish this in a manner that was financially reasonable to them and Donna was not clear. After considerable discussion, they made the following proposal to Donna that she found acceptable:

On January 1, 2001, Donna would become a partner (really a one-third owner of the stock of Hachey and Nelson). Donna would accomplish this by buying one-third of the shares owned by Nancy and David. Nancy and David would lend Donna the money to buy the shares. Starting on January 1, 2001, Donna would receive a significant raise in salary, reflecting her status as a partner of the firm, and would receive one-third of any profits earned by the firm. With these extra resources, she would pay off her debts to Nancy and David. Donna would become a member of the board of directors of Hachey and Nelson.

Valuing Hachey and Nelson, Attorneys at Law

The practical problem now was to value Hachey and Nelson, Attorneys at Law. Being attorneys, Nancy, David, and Donna were familiar with valuation issues and were well aware of the difficulties of accomplishing this for a privately held firm. They did not want their agreement to fall apart because they could not come up with a mutually satisfactory estimate of the firm's value.

In their worker's compensation practice, Nancy, David, and Donna were all familiar with the measurement of the economic loss when a worker is injured or permanently disabled. They also understood the concept of discounting future lost earnings to determine a value of those losses. This is how the courts can issue a judgment for a payment to be made in today's dollars to compensate for future losses. They liked the "scientific" nature of this type of measurement because one can examine the impacts of different assumptions on the final answer. Consequently, they were interested in using a similar type of scientific approach to the related issue of determining the value of their business. Instead of a future stream of wage payments, the buyer of a business is anticipating a future stream of profits. These must be similarly discounted back to the value they represent today.

Nancy, David, and Donna decided to get an estimate of the value of their business from bizownerHQ using the Internet-based Valuation GURU. This expert system uses the discounted free cash flow method of valuation, which was acceptable to all three attorneys. The three agreed that the valuation from the site would not be binding but would serve as the basis for further discussions. The reader can find the Hachey and Nelson tax return used as the company financial inputs to the Valuation GURU and the "Valuation Snapshots report" from bizownerHQ in Appendix 5A.

Reaching Agreement on the Value of Hachey and Nelson

The total fair market value of Hachey and Nelson, Attorneys at Law, as shown in Table 5-1 was $739,070. The valuation multiples showed that the firm was worth 0.94 times revenue and 6.08 times earnings.

Just to be sure, David pulled out his calculator and quickly confirmed that the revenue-multiple math was correct. However, even without his calculator, he saw that the earnings multiple must be wrong. Their year 2000 ordinary income was $73,046, and six times that was well short of $739,070. He then saw that the earnings multiple was based on adjusted earnings. The primary adjustment to earnings is for owner compensation.

TABLE 5-1 Value Concepts for Hachey and Nelson

Value Concept	Value
Total fair market value	$739,070
Ownership equity for valuing a controlling interest	$733,888
Ownership equity for valuing a minority interest	$591,290
Revenue multiple	0.94
Earnings multiple	6.08

OWNERS' COMPENSATION ISSUES

As described in the O'Toole case (see Chapter 3), the owners of privately held companies basically can set their own salaries. They can choose to pay themselves a low salary and then pay themselves dividends from the firm's profits or pay themselves a high salary, perhaps high enough to "wipe out" any reported profit for tax purposes. This potential variability in earnings creates a significant challenge for all earnings-based methods of valuation.

The approach that valuation experts use to standardize the earnings across companies for differences in owners' compensation is to develop an estimate of the market salary paid to people in similar senior management positions, including public companies, adjusted for the industry and the size of the company. This information can come from several different sources. This market-salary benchmark provides the "reasonable person" standard for determining what an owner would pay himself or herself, separate from the ownership dividends, which are considered a return to capital.

bizownerHQ has constructed a detailed owners' compensation database by industry, by size of company (as measured by total assets), and by location, either state or metropolitan area. The salary estimate for owners of small legal practices in Florida is used for dividing up the as-reported salaries for Nancy and David into a return for their labor and a return on their capital. The net effect of these adjustments is shown in Table 5-2.

After reviewing these compensation adjustments, Nancy, David, and Donna agreed that the valuation estimate was reasonable and within the various estimates each had generated from various rules of thumb and discussions of valuations of legal practices they had with other attorneys.

TABLE 5-2   Adjustments to Compensation

Partner Salaries*	As Reported on Tax Return	After Adjustment by the Valuation GURU
Nancy's salary	$150,000	$125,790
David's salary	$150,000	$125,790
Total expenses	$683,577	$635,157
Taxable income	$ 73,046	$121,466

*Including nonmandatory benefits.

VALUING A MINORITY INTEREST

The next step was to look at the value of the ownership equity, that is, the total value of the firm minus debts and other liabilities. The ownership equity is similar to the equity in a house, which is determined by the value of the house minus the payoff of the mortgage. As shown in Table 5-1, the ownership equity value of Hachey and Nelson is $733,888. However, since Donna is buying only a minority (noncontrolling) interest in the firm, Nancy and David have to make an adjustment for the difference between a controlling and a noncontrolling purchase. The minority value of the firm is $591,290.

In the Hachey and Nelson situation, neither of the two 50 percent owners has complete control individually; that is, all key decisions require their joint agreement. Nancy and David's current ownership positions are minority positions. By adding a third owner and dividing the shares equally among the three, all three ownership positions will be valued as minority stakes.

Ownership of less than 50 percent of a firm, whether publicly or privately held, is generally considered a minority position. Without a majority (i.e., one share more than 50 percent), an owner cannot by himself make fundamental decisions about running the business. Gaining a majority of shares and hence control of a firm typically requires paying more than the current stock price. Examples can be seen in public company acquisitions, where the purchasing company offers a "premium" over the current stock price. The current stock price, or the price to buy one or more shares—but fewer than 50 percent—is the minority price for a public company stock.

In a valuation in which the valuation expert starts by determining what a willing buyer would pay a willing seller as of a specific date, this *control premium* must be estimated as part of the valuation process and then subtracted from the total ownership equity value to get the minority value.

There is a further complication that private company shares are generally sold at a discount to comparable public company shares due to a lack of liquidity—a *liquidity discount*. This simply means with no public market for the stock, there are fewer likely buyers, and the cost of getting information on the company is higher. Fewer buyers and higher costs translate into lower prices for private companies. This is described in more detail in Chapter 6.

These two valuation adjustments, the control premium and the liquidity discount, were initially confusing to Nancy, David, and Donna, so they turned to the bizownerHQ "Valuation Report." This excerpt is included in Appendix 5A for readers looking for more background on these issues.

Removing the Control Premium

Valuation experts make two important adjustments to the discounted-cash-flow estimate for a firm, the control premium and the liquidity discount. Chuckling over the use of this impressive-sounding jargon, Donna described the control premium to David and Nancy as the extra amount she would have to pay to be their boss. David and Nancy realized that if Donna had not developed as strongly, then they would have considered selling out to a larger firm over the next few years. Another firm clearly would have to pay them more to get control of their clients and their time. Reducing the value of the company by subtracting out this control premium to determine the price for Donna's shares made sense to David and Nancy.

Applying the Liquidity Discount

Donna went on to describe the liquidity discount as the amount the business loses in value because it is not available for sale on a public stock exchange. For example, Donna cannot become a part owner of Hachey and Nelson by buying shares of Hachey and Nelson on the Nasdaq. Hachey and Nelson is a privately held, not a publicly held, company. In order to be a part owner of Hachey and Nelson, Donna has to be a lawyer, she has to be willing to buy a sizable amount of stock, and she has to participate in the growth of the company. There are very few people who would offer to buy into this private firm and few whom the existing owners would accept as part owners. Thus it makes sense that there are fewer people available to buy into a private business. Fewer potential buyers translates into a lower value. Nancy and David agreed with this as well.

FINALIZING THE MINORITY VALUE

Using the information from the "Valuation Report" and "Valuation Snapshots," Nancy, David, and Donna came to an agreement on the price that Donna should pay to buy into the ownership of the firm, as shown in Table 5-3. They rounded the resulting number to come up with $600,000 as the minority value of the company. The price Donna would pay for one-third of Hachey and Nelson would be based on this amount, or $200,000.

TABLE 5-3   Ownership with Liquidity Discount and without Control Premium

Lack of Liquidity Reduces Minority Ownership	Value
Minority ownership value before discount	$739,112
Loss of minority ownership value due to liquidity discount	$147,822
Minority ownership value after discount	$591,290

The Arrangement

As outlined in their previous discussions, Nancy and David each loaned Donna $100,000, which she used to buy $200,000 of the stock of Hachey and Nelson. Donna thus became a partner (really a one-third owner) of the law firm. Nancy and David continue to receive their respective salaries and profits from the firm, as well as loan repayments from Donna. Donna now has a significantly increased salary, a share of the profits of the firm, and a vote on the major policies of the firm. She realistically expects to repay her loans to Nancy and David in 7 years. At that time, she fully expects that her one-third ownership in a growing firm will be worth considerably more than her $200,000 investment.

LESSONS LEARNED

As in purchasing other businesses, purchasing an interest in a professional practice has its complications. In this case, Donna was familiar with the firm's clients and how Nancy and David ran the firm. Disclosure inaccuracy, always an issue when a private firm is sold, was less of an issue for Donna because of her working relationship with Nancy and David. Nevertheless, for Donna, valuing the practice had a bit of the proverbial "black box" associated with it. Nevertheless, all three lawyers came to appreciate the importance of the various adjustments that needed to be made to develop an accurate estimate of the business's value, especially the review of owners' compensation, the control premium, and the liquidity discount.

Business owners should know that

1. *For valuation purposes, owners' compensation needs to be reviewed against an owner's salary benchmark for the industry, size of firm,*

and location. If the owners' compensation in the firm being valued is greater than the average CEO's salary benchmark for peer-group companies, then this difference may be added back into the company's earnings to use as the base from which the valuation calculations are made. This is the approach valuation consultants typically use to make the split between what an owner is paid for her labor and what the owner receives as dividends representing a return on her capital.

2. *The value of a portion of any business depends on whether a majority or minority interest is being sold.* The value of a partial stake in a business is larger, all else being equal, if the buyer of that stake gains majority control of the business than if the buyer only gets a minority position. For example, consider a company with three owners, Alex with 50 percent, Joe with 30 percent, and Jeff with 20 percent. Alex would pay more for Jeff's 20 percent stake than Joe would because Alex would get majority control of the company. If Joe buys Jeff's 20 percent, then Joe and Alex are equal minority partners. The reason a controlling owner will pay more is that he is buying not only the right to the firm's cash flows but also the right to change the way the firm conducts its business. This last right has a great deal of value, although it varies depending on the nature of the business being valued.

3. *A privately held firm is not worth as much as a publicly held firm that has the same level of current and projected cash flows.* A private firm, by not being part of a public market with easily accessible information on the company's operations, is, in essence, penalized for this lack of information and transparency. In a discounted cash flow valuation, the cash flows of a firm are valued as if they were for a public company. Then this value is reduced by the factor called a liquidity discount.

MORE ON VALUATION METHODS

DISCOUNTED CASH FLOW
The discounted cash flow approach (DCFA) is based on the premise that a person buying a business is buying the opportunity to earn the future cash flows of the business. There are three central elements to determining valuation by DCFA:

1. An estimate of current free cash flows of the business
2. A forecast of the most likely growth for the company's free cash flows
3. A discount rate that reflects the relative riskiness of the company and industry

Key Assumptions

As with each of the valuation approaches, key assumptions are made by a valuation expert in conducting a valuation using DCFA. These include

- The estimate of current free cash flows represents a reasonable basis for forecasting these cash flows into the future.
- There are business forecasting methods that provide reasonable estimates of future free cash flows for all ongoing businesses.

To illustrate the DCFA, we have developed an example case in which DCFA is used to value a construction company.

VALUING A CONSTRUCTION COMPANY USING DCFA

Len Rosenthal is the owner of Middlesex Construction Company that builds commercial office buildings in Massachusetts and surrounding states. Len wishes to retire in early 2002 and would like to sell his business. He is not clear about the business's estimated value and, more important, how he could justify the asking price to a potential buyer. Len is by trade an electrician who started his own electrical contracting firm 30 years ago. That firm grew into the general construction firm Len owns today. Len met with his CPA, Jim Diulio, and asked for advice about valuing his business. Jim suggested that they look at the business from the point of view of a logical potential buyer and come up with a valuation and supporting rationale that could be explained clearly. Jim went over Middlesex's books in detail and looked at the contracts it had for future work. He then prepared a projected free cash flow statement for the year 2003, as shown in Table 5-4.

TABLE 5-4   Free Cash Flow Statement for Middlesex Construction (Values in Dollars, Projected for 2003)

Financial Concept	Year 2003
Gross revenue	$950,000
Less returns and allowances	$ 12,000
Net revenue	$938,000
Cost of goods sold	$401,000
Gross profit	$537,000
Total income	$537,000
Compensation of officers	$100,000
Salaries and wages	$145,000
Repairs and maintenance	$ 20,000

continued on next page

TABLE 5-4 Free Cash Flow Statement for Middlesex Construction (Values in Dollars, Projected for 2003) (continued)

Financial Concept	Year 2003
Bad debts	$ 10,000
Rents	$ 19,000
Taxes and licenses	$ 40,000
Interest	$ 5,000
Depreciation	$ 22,000
Advertising	$ 1,500
Pension	$ 27,000
Employee benefits	$ 26,500
Other deductions	$ 8,000
Total expenses	$424,000
Net income	$113,000
Depreciation	$ 22,000
Retained earnings needed for growth	$ 35,000
Free cash flow	$100,000

Free Cash Flows: Now and in the Future

Free cash flow is the amount of money, in addition to salary and benefits, that an owner of a business could remove from a business in a year and still have the business operate and grow. Free cash flow is related to net income, but it is not the same thing. Jim believed that if the future buyer ran the business in a reasonable manner and paid himself a reasonable salary ($100,000), he could remove an additional $100,000 from the business in 2003. This extra $100,000 is referred to as *free cash flow*.

Jim estimated that Middlesex would have revenues of $950,000 in 2003, with gross profit of $537,000 and total expenses of $424,000, producing a net income of $113,000. Could the owner remove the $113,000 from the business and still have it operate and grow in a reasonable manner? The answer is no. The reasons are twofold. First, not all expenses in an accrual accounting system are necessarily paid in cash in the year the expense is recognized. In 2003, Middlesex is expected to report a depreciation expense of $22,000. Depreciation is a legitimate expense that recognizes the decline in value during the year of the assets (e.g., backhoes, power tools) used by the business. Although a depreciation expense of $22,000 is recognized in 2003, it is a noncash expense in that Middlesex does not write a check for $22,000 and send it to some external party. Middlesex paid for the assets in the year(s) in which it purchased them.

Therefore, to arrive at a net cash flow figure, the $22,000 in depreciation expense is added to net income.

Second, if Middlesex is going to remain in business and grow, then additional new equipment will have to be purchased in 2003 to replace old existing equipment that is being retired and to purchase additional equipment needed to support a growing business. Jim said he thought that the business would grow close to its recent history, or 5 percent per year, and that $35,000 of new equipment would need to be purchased in 2003. This $35,000 expenditure could then not be removed by the future owner and therefore is subtracted to estimate free cash flow. The result is an estimate of free cash flow for Middlesex Construction of $100,000 in 2003.

Len studied Jim's data and assumptions carefully and agreed with his analysis. A future owner of Middlesex Construction, in addition to being fairly compensated for her labor, could remove $100,000 from the business in 2003. The free cash flow an owner could take from the business also would grow at 5 percent, so in year 2006 the owner could take $121,551. Len found this reasonable.

In financial terms, a person who purchases Middlesex Construction Company is purchasing a series of future cash flows. These cash flows would have a value of $100,000 in 2003 and grow 5 percent per year into the future. The value of Middlesex Construction is the present value of these future cash flows. All that is needed to value the business now that cash flows have been estimated is a discount rate.

Discount Rate

Len and Jim had a conversation about what discount rate would be appropriate to use for a construction company. Jim noted that the construction business is an above-average-risk business that is very sensitive to the level of general business activity. A reasonable buyer would expect to earn a return that would be greater than those available on government or corporate bonds or those to be earned by investing in the stock of large Fortune 500 companies. Jim thought that a 15 percent discount rate was reasonable, and after some discussion, Len agreed.

DCFA VALUATION RESULTS

Jim plugged the numbers into his computer's spreadsheet software and produced a report of the estimated value of Middlesex, as shown in Table 5-5.

In 2003, a future owner could expect to remove $100,000 in free cash flow from Middlesex Construction. At a 15 percent discount rate, each of those future dollars would be worth about $0.87 in 2002, so the present value of $100,000 in 2003 is $86,957. Similarly, in 2006, a future owner

TABLE 5-5   Middlesex Construction Company Valuation as of January 1, 2002. Key Assumptions: Growth Rate 5 percent; Discount Rate 15 percent

Year	2003	2004	2005	2006	2007
Cash flow	$100,000	$105,000	$110,250	$115,762	$121,550
Discount factor	0.87	0.76	0.66	0.57	0.50
Present value	$86,956	$79,395	$72,491	$66,187	$60,432

Year	2008	2009	2010	2011	2012
Cash flow	$127,628	$134,009	$140,710	$147,745	$155,132
Discount factor	0.38	0.25	0.14	0.07	0.03
Present value	$47,980	$33,125	$19,886	$10,381	$4,097

could expect to remove $115,956 in free cash flow from Middlesex Construction. At a 15 percent discount rate, those future dollars would be worth about $0.57 in 2002, so the present value in 2006 is $66,188. In 2012, a future owner could expect to remove $155,132 in free cash flow from Middlesex Construction. At a 15 percent discount rate, those future dollars would only be worth about $0.025 in 2002, so the present value in 2012 is $4097. Cash flows beyond 2012 would not increase present value in any significant amount. The estimated value of Middlesex Construction Company in 2002 is the sum of the present values of the future free cash flows generated by the business, or $480,933, as shown in Table 5-6.

TABLE 5-6   Projected Present Values of Future Free Cash Flows for Middlesex Construction

Year	Present Value
2003	$ 86,956.52
2004	$ 79,395.09
2005	$ 72,491.16
2006	$ 66,187.59
2007	$ 60,432.14
2008	$ 47,980.15
2009	$ 33,125.11

continued on next page

TABLE 5-6   Projected Present Values of Future Free Cash Flows for Middlesex Construction (continued)

Year	Present Value
2010	$ 19,886.36
2011	$ 10,381.39
2012	$ 4,097.89
Total value	$480,933.40

SELLING THE BUSINESS

Len took the report and listed the business for sale for $500,000. Several people responded to his ad, and he explained in detail how a buyer could purchase the firm for $500,000 and have good reason to expect to receive future cash flows from the business starting in 2003 at $100,000 and growing at a rate of 5 percent per year. He entered into a purchase and sale agreement with an electrician like himself for $500,000 contingent on the buyer being able to borrow $400,000 from a commercial bank at a reasonable rate of interest to finance the transaction. The prospective owner used Jim Diulio's spreadsheet valuation model to support a bank loan application for $400,000 to finance part of the purchase. The bank approved the loan application, and the loan officer complimented the new owner on his presentation. The new owner made it very easy for the loan officer to understand the nature of the business he was buying and how he was going to have the resources to repay the loan in a timely manner.

SPECIAL FOCUS

CALCULATING PRESENT VALUE

The DCFA is used widely in the investment community and is based on the simple idea that the value of an asset is the value today (i.e., the present value) of benefits to be received in the future.

Time Value of Money

One of the basic principles of finance is that money has a time value. This principle is frequently stated as: "a dollar to be received today is worth more than a dollar to be received at some future time (e.g., 1 year from today)." The primary reason for this truism is that the U.S. economy (and for that matter, the world economy) tends to grow over time, and people have the opportunity to save money and invest in and benefit from that growth. If, for example, a bank is paying 10 percent interest per year on deposits, one could take a dollar today, and it would be worth $1.10 (not $1.00) in a year.

Future Value
The formula for this relationship is

$$PV*(1 + i) = FV$$

That is, the future value FV equals the present value PV times 1 plus the interest rate. In the preceding example,

$$\$1.00*(1.10) = \$1.10$$

That is, $1.00 invested today at 10 percent interest will be worth $1.10 in 1 year. A dollar invested today is definitely worth more in the future in a growing economy with positive interest rates.

Present Value
Conversely, the $1.10 received 1 year from now is worth $1.00 today. We can use the preceding formula to determine this result. The formula can be rearranged to

$$PV = FV/(1 + i) \text{ or } \$1.00 = \$1.10/1.10$$

where $1.10 to be received 1 year from now is worth $1.00 today if the relevant interest rate is 10 percent.

This present-value equation can be rewritten as

$$PV = FV*[1/(1 + i)] \text{ or } \$1.00 = \$1.10*(1/1.10)$$

where the $1.10 to be received in 1 year is worth $1.00 today if the relevant interest rate is 10 percent. We can present the preceding as $1.00 = $1.10(0.90909) because 1/1.10 equals 0.90909.

In this example, 0.90909 is called the *discount factor*. It tells an analyst that $1.10 to be received in 1 year is worth a little less than $0.91 cents today if the relevant interest rate is 10 percent.

TIME VALUE OF MONEY AND VALUATION
This basic time value of money principle underlies a great deal of financial analysis. An understanding of the time value of money, and of interest rates, is central to understanding a range of tools that have been developed to support financial analyses, especially valuation. Interest rates play an important role in time value of money calculations. As demonstrated in the pre-

ceding bank deposit example, the interest rate is the "bridge" that connects the present value of a sum to its future value. It is important to understand and be comfortable with the various ways interest rates are calculated and the related terminology that is used. Interest rates can, like many things, be calculated and expressed in a number of ways.

For example, interest can be computed on a simple or compound basis. A $1.00 deposited in a bank for 2 years at 10 percent simple interest will grow to $1.20. One will earn 10 percent of $1.00 for 2 years. However, if the 10 percent interest is compounded annually (which is the normal situation), a $1.00 deposit will grow to $1.21 in 2 years. The extra $0.01 one receives comes from the fact that during the second year, one earns 10 percent interest not on a deposit of $1.00 but on a deposit of $1.00 plus the $0.10 interest earned during the first year. Under compound interest, during the second year, one earns interest on the interest previously earned. Clearly, interest computed on a simple versus compound basis will produce different values over time. This can be restated in the following formula:

$$PV*(1 + i)*(1 + i) = FV \quad \text{or} \quad \$1.00*(1.10)*(1.10) = \$1.21$$

where $1.00 invested today at 10 percent interest compounded annually will be worth $1.21 in 2 years.

The same relationship can be stated as

$$PV*(1 + i)^2 = FV \quad \text{or} \quad \$1.00*(1.10)^2 = \$1.21$$

where $1.00 invested today at 10 percent interest compounded annually will be worth $1.21 in 2 years. Conversely, $1.21 to be received in 2 years time is worth only $1.00 today. We can use the preceding formula to determine this. The formula can be rearranged to

$$PV = FV/(1 + i)^2 \quad \text{or} \quad \$1.00 = \$1.21/(1.10)^2$$

where $1.21 to be received in 2 years is worth $1.00 today at a 10 percent rate of interest. This present-value equation can be rewritten as

$$PV = FV*[1/(1 + i)^2] \quad \text{or} \quad \$1.00 = \$1.21*[1/(1.10)^2]$$

where $1.21 to be received in 2 years is worth $1.00 today at a 10 percent rate of interest. Alternatively, since $(1/1.10)^2$ equals 0.82644, we can present the preceding as

$$\$1.00 = \$1.21*(0.82644)$$

In this example, 0.82644 is called the *discount factor*. It tells an analyst that $1.21 to be received at the end of 2 years is worth a bit less than $0.83 today if the relevant interest rate is 10 percent.

In the preceding bank deposit example, we call the $1.00 today a *present value* and the $1.10 in 1 year from now a *future value*. At a 10 percent interest rate, $1.00 today is worth $1.10 in a year. Also, $1.10 a year from now (future value) at a 10 percent interest rate is worth $1.00 today (present value). This basic analysis can be extended to different amounts of money over different periods of time with different interest rates. For example, at 10 percent interest, what would $1.00 today be worth in 12 years? The general time value of money equation is

$$PV = FV*[1/(1 + i)^N]$$

This formula tells us that present value PV of a sum of money to be received at some number of years in the future is equal to that future sum FV multiplied by the discount factor. If, for example, $1.00 (FV) to be received in 12 years (N) at a discount rate of 10 percent is only worth a little less than $0.32 today:

$$PV = \$1.00*[1/(1.10)^{12}]$$

$$\$0.3186 = \$1.00*(0.3186)$$

Computing Present Values

Since the time value of money comes up so frequently in finance, a range of tools (i.e., formulas, tables and specialized financial calculators) have been developed to assist in this analysis. For example, time value of money functions are preprogrammed into spreadsheet software such as EXCEL.

The DCFA thus gives an analyst a powerful valuation tool. Its greatest advantage is that it is a logical construct based on the simple idea that the value of money to be received in the future is worth less today. The amount that it is worth less (i.e., discounted) is a function of how far into the future it is and what an acceptable discount rate (i.e., interest rate) is for the particular cash flow. To perform a DCFA and value an asset, an analyst must estimate two types of variables:

1. The future cash flows that an asset likely will generate
2. The appropriate discount rate to use for those cash flows

This discount rate is a function of how risky the cash flows are.

BACKGROUNDER

FOCUS ON OWNERS' COMPENSATION

In Established Small businesses, there is typically no division between owners and managers. Among other things, this means that owners are free to establish their own compensation levels based on both their personal needs and the cash flow–generating capacity of their businesses. The distinction between wage or salary income and return on investment is generally not considered. There is no reason to make this distinction because the manager is also the owner. In contrast, this distinction is made all the time when one considers the compensation of CEOs of public firms. There is an ongoing debate about the size of public company CEOs' compensation packages and the appropriate split between stock options and cash bonuses received and salary paid. Any stock options awarded and any cash paid as part of a bonus are analogous to what an owner/manager pays herself above and beyond salary.

While the total compensation of officers of public and private firms reflects both wage and return-on-capital components, the return on capital paid to the owners of private firms often represents all of or a significant part of the total cash flow generated by the firm. The need to distinguish these two components is far more critical to determining the value of a private firm than it is for a public firm counterpart. This means that to value a private firm properly, one needs to establish the salary level of the owner. bizownerHQ has developed an extensive officer wage and salary database. Analysis indicates that officer wages and salaries vary by industry, size of firm, and location. An example of this variation is given in Chapter 6.

Appendix 5A
HACHEY AND NELSON, ATTORNEYS: VALUATION INPUTS AND OUTPUTS

Partial 2000 Tax Return

Valuation Snapshots Report

Section 5 Excerpt on Liquidity Discount and Control Premium
    Adjustments from the bizownerHQ Business Valuation Report

Hachey and Nelson Tax Return, page 1.

Form **1120S**		**U.S. Income Tax Return for an S Corporation**		OMB No. 1545-0130
Department of the Treasury Internal Revenue Service		▶ Do not file this form unless the corporation has timely filed Form 2553 to elect to be an S corporation. ▶ See separate instructions.		**2000**

For calendar year 2000, or tax year beginning , 2000, and ending 20

A Effective date of election as an S corporation	Use IRS label. Other- wise, print or type.	**Name** The Law Office of Hachey and Nelson		**C** Employer identification number
B Business code no. (see pages 29–31) 541110		Number, street, and room or suite no. (If a P.O. box, see page 11 of the instructions.)		**D** Date incorporated
		City or town, state, and ZIP code Orlando, FL		**E** Total assets (see page 11) $

F Check applicable boxes: (1) ☐ Initial return   (2) ☐ Final return   (3) ☐ Change in address   (4) ☐ Amended return
G Enter number of shareholders in the corporation at end of the tax year . . . . ▶

Caution: *Include only trade or business income and expenses on lines 1a through 21. See page 11 of the instructions for more information.*

Income	1a	Gross receipts or sales	782,452 00	**b** Less returns and allowances		**c** Bal ▶	**1c**	782,452 00
	2	Cost of goods sold (Schedule A, line 8)					**2**	25,829 00
	3	Gross profit. Subtract line 2 from line 1c					**3**	756,623 00
	4	Net gain (loss) from Form 4797, Part II, line 18 *(attach Form 4797)* . . .					**4**	
	5	Other income (loss) *(attach schedule)*					**5**	
	6	**Total income (loss).** Combine lines 3 through 5 . . . . ▶					**6**	756,623 00
Deductions (see page 12 of the instructions for limitations)	7	Compensation of officers					**7**	300,000 00
	8	Salaries and wages (less employment credits)					**8**	82,421 00
	9	Repairs and maintenance					**9**	1,845 00
	10	Bad debts					**10**	42,841 00
	11	Rents					**11**	89,721 00
	12	Taxes and licenses					**12**	8,114 00
	13	Interest					**13**	2,481 00
	14a	Depreciation *(if required, attach Form 4562)* . . .	**14a**					
	b	Depreciation claimed on Schedule A and elsewhere on return . .	**14b**					
	c	Subtract line 14b from line 14a					**14c**	
	15	Depletion **(Do not deduct oil and gas depletion.)**					**15**	
	16	Advertising					**16**	3,815 00
	17	Pension, profit-sharing, etc., plans					**17**	52,471 00
	18	Employee benefit programs					**18**	28,187 00
	19	Other deductions *(attach schedule)*					**19**	71,681 00
	20	**Total deductions.** Add the amounts shown in the far right column for lines 7 through 19 . ▶					**20**	683,577 00
	21	Ordinary income (loss) from trade or business activities. Subtract line 20 from line 6. . . .					**21**	73,046 00
Tax and Payments	22	**Tax: a** Excess net passive income tax *(attach schedule)* . . .	**22a**					
	b	Tax from Schedule D (Form 1120S)	**22b**					
	c	Add lines 22a and 22b (see page 15 of the instructions for additional taxes)					**22c**	
	23	**Payments: a** 2000 estimated tax payments and amount applied from 1999 return	**23a**					
	b	Tax deposited with Form 7004	**23b**					
	c	Credit for Federal tax paid on fuels *(attach Form 4136)*	**23c**					
	d	Add lines 23a through 23c . . . . ▶					**23d**	
	24	Estimated tax penalty. Check if Form 2220 is attached . . . . ▶ ☐					**24**	
	25	**Tax due.** If the total of lines 22c and 24 is larger than line 23d, enter amount owed. See page 4 of the instructions for depository method of payment . . . . ▶					**25**	
	26	**Overpayment.** If line 23d is larger than the total of lines 22c and 24, enter amount overpaid ▶					**26**	
	27	Enter amount of line 26 you want: **Credited to 2001 estimated tax** ▶ **Refunded** ▶					**27**	

Sign Here
Under penalties of perjury, I declare that I have examined this return, including accompanying schedules and statements, and to the best of my knowledge and belief, it is true, correct, and complete. Declaration of preparer (other than taxpayer) is based on all information of which preparer has any knowledge.

▶ _____   _____   ▶ _____
Signature of officer   Date   Title

Paid Preparer's Use Only	Preparer's signature ▶		Date	Check if self-employed ☐	Preparer's SSN or PTIN
	Firm's name (or yours if self-employed), address, and ZIP code ▶			EIN	
				Phone no. ( )	

For Paperwork Reduction Act Notice, see the separate instructions.   Cat. No. 11510H   Form **1120S** (2000)

Hachey and Nelson Tax Return, page 4.

Form 1120S (2000)   Page **4**

Schedule L — Balance Sheets per Books

Assets	Beginning of tax year (a)	(b)	End of tax year (c)	(d)
1 Cash		21,604		28,425
2a Trade notes and accounts receivable	32,060		36,149	
b Less allowance for bad debts	3,000	29,060	3,000	33,145
3 Inventories		456		503
4 U.S. Government obligations				
5 Tax-exempt securities				
6 Other current assets (attach schedule)		1,846		1,954
7 Loans to shareholders				
8 Mortgage and real estate loans				
9 Other investments (attach schedule)				
10a Buildings and other depreciable assets	26,751		28,756	
b Less accumulated depreciation	3,245	23,506	3,376	25,308
11a Depletable assets				
b Less accumulated depletion				
12 Land (net of any amortization)				
13a Intangible assets (amortizable only)				
b Less accumulated amortization				
14 Other assets (attach schedule)		84,781		87,952
15 Total assets		161,253		177,363
Liabilities and Shareholders' Equity				
16 Accounts payable		2,376		2,618
17 Mortgages, notes, bonds payable in less than 1 year		4,672		5,182
18 Other current liabilities (attach schedule)				
19 Loans from shareholders				
20 Mortgages, notes, bonds payable in 1 year or more				
21 Other liabilities (attach schedule)				
22 Capital stock		30,000		30,000
23 Additional paid-in capital				
24 Retained earnings		124,205		139,563
25 Adjustments to shareholders' equity (attach schedule)				
26 Less cost of treasury stock		( )		( )
27 Total liabilities and shareholders' equity		161,253		177,363

Schedule M-1 — Reconciliation of Income (Loss) per Books With Income (Loss) per Return (You are not required to complete this schedule if the total assets on line 15, column (d), of Schedule L are less than $25,000.)

1 Net income (loss) per books	5 Income recorded on books this year not included on Schedule K, lines 1 through 6 (itemize):
2 Income included on Schedule K, lines 1 through 6, not recorded on books this year (itemize):	a Tax-exempt interest $ ....
3 Expenses recorded on books this year not included on Schedule K, lines 1 through 11a, 15f, and 16b (itemize):	6 Deductions included on Schedule K, lines 1 through 11a, 15f, and 16b, not charged against book income this year (itemize):
a Depreciation $	a Depreciation $ ....
b Travel and entertainment $	
4 Add lines 1 through 3	7 Add lines 5 and 6
	8 Income (loss) (Schedule K, line 23). Line 4 less line 7

Schedule M-2 — Analysis of Accumulated Adjustments Account, Other Adjustments Account, and Shareholders' Undistributed Taxable Income Previously Taxed (see page 27 of the instructions)

	(a) Accumulated adjustments account	(b) Other adjustments account	(c) Shareholders' undistributed taxable income previously taxed
1 Balance at beginning of tax year			
2 Ordinary income from page 1, line 21			
3 Other additions			
4 Loss from page 1, line 21	( )		
5 Other reductions	( )	( )	
6 Combine lines 1 through 5			
7 Distributions other than dividend distributions			
8 Balance at end of tax year. Subtract line 7 from line 6			

Form **1120S** (2000)

VALUE SNAPSHOTS REPORT

WHAT IS HACHEY AND NELSON WORTH?

The Valuation GURU estimates that the fair market total value of Hachey and Nelson is $739,070 as of January 1, 2001, based on the business tax return information entered. Please review the bizownerHQ key assumptions to make sure that they apply to this business.

The Valuation GURU builds up the fair market total value of a business by estimating separately value by source, as shown in Figure 5A-1.

FIGURE 5A-1   Hachey and Nelson—Total value estimate.

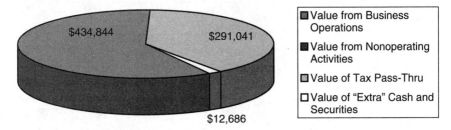

1. *Value from business operations.* Generally, the primary source of value in a business is based on the cash flows from the earnings of the business operations, that is, the products or services the company sells, less the cash needed for investments in operations. The Valuation GURU uses a sophisticated proprietary approach to fore-casting the revenues and adjusted earnings of the business operations and then calculates the present value of those future anticipated earnings to determine the value shown in the graph.

2. *Value from nonoperating activities.* Many businesses have other sources of income, such as rental income from buildings or licensing income, that are generated outside the normal business operations. While these cash flows have value, they are not given the same valuation treatment as income from business operations, reflecting that buyers often will not value these nonoperating cash flows as highly as those from operating activities. The Valuation GURU, following standard practices, calculates the present value of the current income flow to the business owner(s).

3. *Value of tax pass-thru.* Companies that are not C Corporations filing Tax Form 1120 have a tax advantage; any earnings that the company reports are not taxed at the corporate level but are "passed through" to the owner's individual tax return. The Valuation GURU shows this value separately so that an owner can determine the likely reduction in value that would occur if the business were sold to a C Corporation rather than to a corporation that can take advantage of the tax pass-thru, such as an S Corporation, partnership, or sole proprietorship (all other elements of the deal being equal).

4. *Value of extra cash and securities.* The final source of value that the Valuation GURU analyzes is whether the company has on its balance sheet a level of cash and marketable securities above what is considered necessary to fund working capital. The Valuation GURU draws on financial analysis research across thousands of companies for a revenue-based factor to estimate the working-capital needs of a company. If the cash and securities on the balance sheet are greater than this estimate, the Valuation GURU makes an adjustment to the fair market total valuation to reflect this extra difference.

DEFINITIONS

1. *Fair market value.* The price at which the property would change hands between a willing buyer and a willing seller when the former is not under any compulsion to buy and the latter is not under any compulsion to sell, both parties having reasonable knowledge of relevant facts (Internal Revenue Service Revenue Rule 59-60, 1959-1, C.B. 237).

2. *Fair market total value.* The sum of the fair market values of the cash flows from business operations, nonoperating activities, and the tax pass-thru *plus* the value of the current dollar amount of the extra company cash and marketable securities, if any.

bizownerHQ KEY ASSUMPTIONS

1. *Company growth rate forecasts.* Revenue and cash flows for Hachey and Nelson are projected to grow at rates consistent with the baseline or average-performing growth segment of companies in this industry.

2. *No greater use of assets.* The assets of Hachey and Nelson, including production equipment, technology, patents, intangible assets, or real estate, used by the company have no greater value as stand-alone assets than they have as profit-generating assets for this business.

GURU Alert

Please review with your accountant or other business professional whether these assumptions are correct for your business before using this valuation as input to decision making.

WHAT IS THE OWNERSHIP EQUITY IN HACHEY AND NELSON WORTH?

The estimated value of the ownership equity in Hachey and Nelson is $733,888. This is the amount the owners would receive if the company were sold today for the fair market total value of $739,070 minus an estimate of the amount necessary to pay off company debts and long-term liabilities, as shown in Figure 5A-2. Ownership equity is equal to the firm's minority interest value, $591,290, plus a control premium of $142,598, the amount necessary to obtain full control of the firm.

FIGURE 5A-2   Hachey and Nelson—Total ownership value.

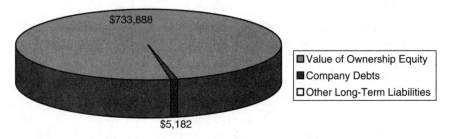

The Valuation GURU separates the business value into its ownership components, as shown in Figure 5A-2.

1. *Value of ownership equity.* This is the estimate of the market value of owner equity in the business.
   - *Minority value of equity.* Minority owners own less than 51 percent of the equity of a firm and do not have the right to direct how the firm's assets are used. Minority owners have claims on a firm's earnings after taxes and interest and a right to vote on firm agenda items.
   - *Control premium.* When a business is sold, the buyer or buyers typically purchase full control of the firm. This gives the new buy-

ers the right to change the way the firm is managed, the types of products and services the firm desires to produce, and the number of employees that are required. In return for the right to make these and other decisions, a buyer will pay a premium above the minority equity value of the firm. This premium is not a constant percentage. It varies with the level of interest rates, the riskiness of the firm, and the long-term growth of the firm's earnings.

2. *Company debts (book value).* This book-value concept from the tax return balance sheet is the closest estimate of the market value of the company's debt that the Valuation GURU can make with the information provided.

Caution: The terms and conditions of any business loans should be reviewed by the company's accountant or by the owner(s) to determine whether there are any prepayment penalties or other charges that would make the market value of the company's debts different from the book value. Any differences found should be included in the preceding estimate to refine the valuation of the company.

WHAT ARE THE VALUATION MULTIPLES FOR HACHEY AND NELSON?
The Valuation GURU estimates that the value-to-revenue multiple for Hachey and Nelson is 0.94 and the value-to-earnings multiple is 6.08 as of January 1, 2001, as shown in Figure 5A-3.

FIGURE 5A-3   Hachey and Nelson—Valuation multiples.

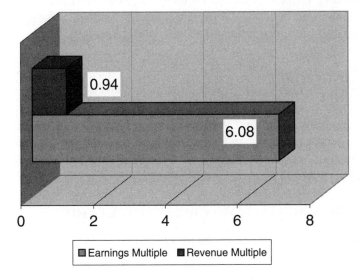

What Business Owners Need to Know about Industry Valuation Multiples

1. *Beware of the industry valuation multiples.* These industry valuation multiples are used by business brokers and investment bankers to provide owners with a quick and supposedly costless way to find out the value of their companies. For example, a broker might tell a landscaping business owner that landscaping businesses typically sell for one times revenue.

2. *Typical concerns with industry valuation multiples.* Industry valuation estimates generally are based on the company sales experiences of, at worst, a single broker and, at best, a number of brokers. For most industries, there are no consistently reliable data sources where transaction data on the prices and terms of privately held businesses can be found. There are many factors in these sales, such as how quickly the owner needs to sell and the financing of the business before and after the sale, that have significant impact on the actual price and hence the valuation multiple. Decisions owners make based on the valuation, such as selling a business, should be made on more solid evidence.

    *   *Is this an average business for this industry?* An owner applying an industry multiple to his business should wonder whether his business is likely to have a value right at the average or median level. If a business is more productive and efficient than most, then that business should be worth a higher multiple.

    *   *Problems with earnings-based multiples.* Valuation multiples based on earnings are particularly troublesome because the ways privately held companies report earnings vary significantly. Industry valuation estimates tend to be based on transactions over a long period of time, yet business valuations change frequently as interest rates change and as perceptions about industry growth opportunities and industry risk change.

    *   *Valuation multiples are rarely used for the benefit of the current owner.* Business brokers and investment bankers have a natural incentive to encourage a quick transaction so that they maximize their compensation for the amount of work they do. By encouraging business owners and business buyers to rely on these industry valuation multiples, brokers reinforce the "value" of their role and justify their sizable commissions.

HOW CAN bizownerHQ VALUATION MULTIPLES BE USED?

1. *Valuation multiples can be useful shorthand tools.* The bizownerHQ company-specific valuation multiples are useful short-hand tools for

understanding the current valuation of a company and how that valuation may vary in the short run from changes in revenue or earnings. For example, a business with a company-specific valuation to revenue multiple of six can estimate that if the company can increase revenues by $50,000, the company should be worth approximately $300,000 more. (This assumes that the company is able to generate higher earnings and cash flow after investments at the same rate as before.)

- *Business owners should know that company-specific valuation multiples will change as interest rates and economic conditions change.* For example, as a general rule, when the Federal Reserve increases interest rates in the U.S. economy by pushing up the federal funds rate, the valuation of all U.S. companies will decline somewhat.

2. *Valuation multiples vary within industries and over time.* There are generally wide differences in the revenue and earnings growth paths of companies in the same industry. Companies with higher growth in revenue and earnings typically will have a higher multiple than companies in their industry with lower revenue and earnings.

- *Owners need to be aware of this potential valuation range within their industry.* They should evaluate potential risks and rewards that go along with a more aggressive growth strategy. They also should review whether a more aggressive growth strategy may lead to less control for the owner. For example, borrowing money for expansion from a bank increases the influence of the bank on the company's decisions.

LIQUIDITY DISCOUNT AND CONTROL PREMIUM ADJUSTMENTS[1]

TWO KEY VALUATION ADJUSTMENTS FOR HACHEY AND NELSON
There are two important adjustments that should be made in the valuation of a privately held firm when the valuation is centered on the total business entity. These are the liquidity discount and the control premium. In any valuation where these adjustments are made, it is important to understand the rationale for making these adjustments and the basis on which a valuation expert selected the values to use in making these adjustments. These adjustment factors can be large, often ranging from 20 to 45 percent of the total

[1]Excerpt from bizownerHQ Business Valuation Report Section 5 for Hachey and Nelson.

business value before adjustment; and yet the general explanations in the valuation literature of how to choose a value for either the liquidity discount or control premium appear to be based on weak analyses or questionable data. The topic of how to select these values likely would be more controversial, if they did not have the effect often of largely canceling each other out. For example, a valuation expert may choose a liquidity discount of 30 percent to apply but then also choose a control premium of 30 percent. Since they are applied at the same time, the net effect of the two adjustments is 0.

The Liquidity Discount

The liquidity discount reduces the ownership value to reflect the fact that the ownership interest cannot be sold easily. Any potential buyer of the ownership value faces the risk that he cannot sell the ownership interest in a timely way because there are a limited number of potential buyers. This is to be contrasted with shares of stock that trade on the New York Stock Exchange. These shares can be readily purchased and sold, and except for rare cases, the price received will reflect the fair market value of these shares. Thus the liquidity discount reflects the additional risk that a buyer faces because he may not be able to receive a price that would be obtained if ownership interest in the firm were sold in a highly liquid market.

Although much has been written on the liquidity discount, and several organizations have routinely attempted to measure it, the values traditionally reported are far too high. The reason is that what is reported as a marketability or liquidity discount is really a private company discount. This private company discount reflects a number of factors that are not related to lack of liquidity. The differences between private firm valuations and those of public firms can occur because of differing cash flow growth prospects, timing of cash flows, and differing ratios of debt to equity. The result is that reported discounts for marketability are too high, and private company valuations that use them are too low. Table 5A-1 offers evidence of this variation.

The Willamette results are the best known and, as can be seen, are generally consistent with those reported by other researchers. The problem with Willamette's results is that their data are proprietary, and Willamette has not disclosed this information for peer review and analysis by academic researchers. This is an important qualification. This creates the potential that the empirical work presented simply may be fraught with errors. The peer-review process, while it does not remove this possibility completely, nevertheless minimizes the potential for drawing incorrect conclusions due to errors related to measurement, research design, and statistical method. It is particularly important to use peer-reviewed research when one is valuing a private asset because many of the issues that arise have been addressed by finance scholars and there is a well-developed academic literature.

TABLE 5A-1   Representative Studies That Attempt to Measure the Liquidity Discount

Author(s)	Peer Review	Discount	Reported Dispersion	Type of Study
William Silber	Yes	35%	14% for large creditworthy companies; 50% for small firms with negative earnings	Restricted stock study
M. Hertzel and R. Smith	Yes	Not reported	0.2–43.7 %	Private equity study
John Emory	Yes	47%	Not reported	Pre-IPO study
John Koeplin et al.	Yes	20.39%	Depending on the multiple used, discount varied from 0% based on sales revenue to 28.26% using the ratio of enterprise value to Earnings Before Interest and Taxes	Identified all acquisitions of private firms from 1984 to 1998
Willamette Associates	No	40.1%	Wide dispersion from a premium to a maximum discount of 99%	Pre-IPO study

Source: bizownerHQ.

This peer-review issue aside, Willamette's numbers appear far too high to only account for a private firm's lack of liquidity. Based on bizownerHQ's review of this research, we believe that the most appropriate value to use is the average private company discount published in the Koeplin study. This conclusion is based on two factors. First, their research controls for capital structure differences. Second, selection of the private company's public company peer was dictated by whether they were in the same four-digit Standard Industrial Classification (SIC) industry. Based on this, bizownerHQ uses 20 percent as the liquidity discount adjustment factor. Table 5A-2 indicates how the minority ownership value of Hachey and Nelson is affected by applying bizownerHQ's liquidity discount.

TABLE 5A-2   The Impact of the Liquidity Discount on the Minority
             Ownership Value for this Firm

Lack of Liquidity Reduces Minority Ownership	Value
Minority ownership value before discount	$739,112
Loss of minority ownership value due to liquidity discount	$147,822
Minority ownership value after discount	$591,290

Source: bizownerHQ.

The Control Premium

The control premium is an additional sum that an investor would pay above the fair market value of a minority interest in the firm in question. This means that if a share of common stock of a public company is selling for $100 and an investor is willing to purchase all shares for $140 per share, the control premium is 40 percent. bizownerHQ first calculates the minority interest ownership value of Hachey and Nelson. We then factor up this value to reflect a control premium. Multiple factors give rise to a control premium, including

1. The ability of the owner to manage the cash flow of the firm in a way that is consistent with lifestyle and family responsibilities
2. The nature and magnitude of business nonoperating assets
3. The quality of management
4. Synergies between the buying and target firm, such as removal of overlapping functions and the consequent reduction of expenses per dollar of revenue
5. Taking advantage of growth opportunities that either would not be possible or would be highly expensive to take advantage of without purchasing the assets of the target firm

The approach used by bizownerHQ to estimate the control premium for this firm reflects several factors. They include the firm's business risk, which is directly related to its industry, as well as the firm's size and capital structure. As a general rule, most business appraisers apply a median markup value to the minority equity value to obtain the majority equity value. The source of this median value and related control premium statistics is the annual *Mergerstat Review*, which is published by Houlihan, Lokey, Howard, and Zukin of Los Angeles. *Mergerstat* compiles data on publicly announced mergers, acquisitions, and divestitures involving operating entities, where the transfer involves at least 10 percent of the subject company's equity, the purchase price is at least $1 million, and at least one of the parties to the transaction is a U.S. entity. *Mergerstat* sells data on control premiums by industry, but only at a very aggregate level, and data for individual firm transactions. Table 5A-3 indicates the extent to which median control values change over time.

TABLE 5A-3 *Mergerstat* **Aggregate Control Premiums over Time**

Control Premiums Change Over Time

Year	No. of Transactions	Historical Control Premiums: Median Values
1998	512	30.1%
1997	487	27.5%
1996	381	27.3%
1995	324	29.2%
1994	260	35%
1993	173	33%
1992	142	34.7%
1991	137	29.4%
1990	175	32%
1989	303	29%

Source: Mergerstat.

As can be seen, median control values indeed vary, reaching a low of 27.3 percent in 1996 and a high of 35.0 percent in 1994. There has been a good deal of academic research that has addressed the issue of the factors that determine the size of control premiums. These studies have analyzed the following variables:

1. Method of payment: cash versus stock
2. Purpose of acquisition:
   - Purchase new product line

- Enter new domestic or foreign market
- Purchase patents and other intangible assets
- Leverage financial synergy based on a mismatch between growth opportunities between the target and acquiring firm

3. Size of acquirer

Published research in refereed journals has not shown any of the preceding variables to consistently or powerfully contribute to the size of the control premium. For this and other reasons, business appraisers often default to using the median control value. This is generally the wrong value to use based on both theoretical considerations and the large variability in reported control premiums.

1. *Public company comparison.* When adjusting a private asset value for control, one should ask what the premium would be if the firm in question were a public firm that is being purchased. The answer, as it turns out, is related to the purchased firm's cost of equity capital. The reason is that the greater the risk, the less a rational buyer would be willing to pay for the cash flows despite whatever strategic value the firm's assets may have. Thus, by applying the median control premium to a firm that is of below-average risk, one would be underestimating the value of control. Similarly, one would be overestimating the value for control if the firm is of above-average risk.

2. *Lack of industry specificity.* The median control premium is not industry-specific, and thus, using it in a year when there were few transactions in the firm's industry may provide a biased benchmark, the preceding comments notwithstanding.

3. *Significant variation in values.* One should be very cautious about applying a median value as a markup factor because there is wide variation around these values. For example, in 1998, of the 560 transactions reported by *Mergerstat*, the maximum control premium value was 423.5 percent, the minimum was 0 percent, the average was 40.4 percent, and the standard deviation was 43.4 percent. This means that the chances are high that simply applying the median control premium will result in considerable error.

The Control Premium for This Firm

For these reasons, bizownerHQ estimates the control premium directly. This premium varies by our industry detail and is further customized to the size and capital structure of Hachey and Nelson. The control premium applied to this firm is 24.1 percent. Table 5A-4 shows bizownerHQ.com's final estimate of this firm's ownership value.

TABLE 5A-4   The Impact of Control Premium and Liquidity Discount on Ownership Value

Adjusting Ownership Value for Control and Liquidity	$ Value
1. Minority ownership value before adjustment for liquidity discount and control premium	$739,112
2. Loss of ownership value due to liquidity discount	$147,822
3. Minority ownership value after discount	$591,290
4. Gain in ownership value due to applying control premium	$142,598
5. Final estimated ownership value (row 3 + row 4)	$733,888

Source: bizownerHQ.

C H A P T E R

6

VALUATION FOR DIVORCE
AND OTHER LIFE EVENTS

CASE BACKGROUND

THE EARTHRIGHT GROUP

The EarthRight Group is an environmental consulting firm located in
Natick, Massachusetts. The firm was founded in 1989 by Robin Leggett,
Randy Milton, and Laura Simon and is organized as a general partnership.
Each of the three partners has a degree in environmental science.

Within the Commonwealth of Massachusetts, there is a body of state
environmental laws and regulations. In addition, each city and town in the
state has a conservation commission, which has specified authority to
ensure the maintenance of a safe environment within the community.
Moreover, Massachusetts' residents and businesses must comply with federal environmental laws and regulations. EarthRight advises clients about
specific environmental laws and regulations and provides guidance on efficient ways to comply. The firm works with clients to prepare documents
and plans to be submitted to government agencies, prepare testimony for
hearings, and help in securing needed permits, variances, and so on.

The firm primarily helps clients who have water or septic system issues
before the conservation commission of a city or town. EarthRight has considerable expertise in determining suitable uses for a specific parcel of

land. For example, it renders opinions on what is a wetland. It also renders opinions on the geologic and soil composition of a specific parcel.

Outside the Boston area, most Massachusetts' cities and towns rely on groundwater wells for public drinking water supplies. Development has threatened the quality of these public water supplies. Significant new regulations and aggressive regulatory oversight control the waste discharges that residences and businesses can release into the ground and the amount of water that businesses and new housing developments may withdraw from the ground. The siting of new facilities near sensitive groundwater areas has become more difficult, and as a result, EarthRight has witnessed an increase in consulting contracts related to groundwater issues. This segment of the business should see substantial growth in the future.

The partnership operates out of leased space in Natick. Gross revenues for 2000 were in excess of $600,000. Besides the three partners, the firm employs two people in clerical positions. The partners enjoy their work and each other's company.

Ownership
The EarthRight Group is organized as a general partnership. Each partner owns an equal share in the business. Each partner receives the same salary and benefits and shares of any distributed profits. All major decisions are made after discussion among the three partners, with the majority opinion prevailing. The partners have never disagreed about a major business decision.

Business Owner Segmentation for Robin, Randy, and Laura
These three partners are best classified as business life event (BLE) planners. They recognize the need to get prepared, but as yet, they have done little to manage their BLEs. Thus far they have been expert independent, that is, skeptical of working with advisors in this area, because they are well-educated professionals. However, they may shift to the expert-dependent BLE planner segment if they find that managing these issues takes too much time away from running their own business.

Discretionary Expenses
The partners agreed at the outset that EarthRight would be run in a reasonable but modest manner. For example, each partner owns his or her own vehicle and is reimbursed for business mileage. Customers are taken to lunch or dinner when appropriate, but the expenses are reasonable. Each partner attends scientific meetings and purchases professional materials at firm expense, but the annual spending by the three partners is comparable. EarthRight does not have significant discretionary expenses.

Exit Strategy

From time to time, the partners of EarthRight had discussed their individual futures and the future of the firm. Randy had been pushing to incorporate the business and seeking to expand the business more rapidly in terms of both additional services offered and additional geographic markets and locations. Robin and Laura were not very interestesd in Randy's plan. Both found their lives hectic enough with existing business and family commitments.

Two issues did, however, concern the partners. The first had to do with the growth in environmental knowledge, equipment, and regulation. Knowledge about the environment in general and specific issues such as soil, water, and air contamination was growing rapidly. Each partner found it difficult just to keep up with the flood of new information. Larger firms had the luxury of allowing partners to specialize and to have support staff so that the burden of "keeping up" was not so overwhelming. The partners also worried about how their small firm was going to acquire the increasingly sophisticated and expensive equipment that was needed to do serious environmental testing and analysis. Laura noted that when she graduated from college, a young environmental scientist needed about $1000 worth of equipment to do the normally expected work. Today that number could easily reach $40,000. Finally, although each partner was physically robust with many years before retirement, each worried about the eventual time when one or more of them might wish to retire or might become disabled or die. As things now stood, they did not have any business succession plan and no disability or life insurance program in place. These were the things that these three busy professionals just never seemed to have the time to get done.

THE PRECIPITATING EVENT

In early 2001, Randy Milton's wife, Catherine, filed for divorce. The Miltons had been experiencing marital differences for some time. Randy's partners were aware of his personal situation and had hoped that it would work out for the best. Unfortunately, the Miltons were going to divorce. As part of the divorce settlement, the marital assets would have to be divided equally between Randy and Catherine. The assets they own, with one exception, are tangible and relatively easy to value, for example, a home, two cars, and some mutual funds.

The one exception is Randy's ownership interest in EarthRight. Randy's wife, Catherine, through her attorney, is claiming that EarthRight is a profitable business, with excellent prospects, that is worth in excess of $1.8 million. Since three partners own EarthRight equally, Randy's ownership share is worth in excess of $600,000. Catherine Milton wants $300,000 from Randy's ownership in EarthRight plus 50 percent of the value of the couple's other assets.

Division of Assets

Randy Milton reacted angrily when he received the letter outlining the proposed division of martial assets from his wife's lawyer. He did not have any good idea what EarthRight was worth, and he didn't think his wife or her lawyer did either. To him, the $1.8 million figure had been pulled out of thin air. What especially upset Randy was his fear that determining the value of EarthRight would become a football between him and his estranged wife as their personal relationship became more and more strained. Randy feared that the divorce would become a protracted, nasty affair with large amounts of money being paid to his lawyer, his wife's lawyer, and various accountants and business appraisers who would render opinions on the value of his partnership share in EarthRight.

Randy's partners, Robin and Laura, also were concerned about Randy and his divorce. Besides the personal anguish of seeing two people they both liked and respected involved in a serious dispute, Robin and Laura had concerns about the effect of the divorce on EarthRight. They had worked hard, along with Randy, to build a successful business. The value of EarthRight, however, was illiquid. If Randy was ordered as part of a divorce decree to pay Catherine $300,000, where would he get the cash to do so? Could the divorce somehow force the breakup of EarthRight?

Laura Simon's husband, Andrew, is a CPA, and his advice to everyone was to take a deep breath. The first issue to be resolved, or at least clarified, was the value of EarthRight. If EarthRight, by some reasonable method of valuation, were worth approximately $1.8 million, then some settlement along the lines suggested by Randy's wife would seem justified. How such a settlement would be funded with cash was another matter. If, however, EarthRight were worth considerably less than $1.8 million, which he suspected, then the divorce settlement should be contested vigorously. In any event, getting an objective estimate of the valuation of EarthRight would base the analysis and discussion more on fact and less on emotion. In his professional experience, this is always a step in the right direction in conflicted situations. Andrew suggested that EarthRight get a valuation as of January 1, 2001, from the bizownerHQ.com Web site.

The reader can find the EarthRight Group tax return used as the company financial inputs to the Valuation GURU and the "Valuation Snapshots report" from bizownerHQ in Appendix 6A.

Valuing EarthRight

Randy was somewhat relieved when he read the valuation reports for the EarthRight Group. The key findings are shown in Table 6-1. First, he learned that the estimated fair market value of the firm was $722,027, which is a lot less than the $1.8 million valuation asserted by his wife. As he read on, he happily found that his one-third share of EarthRight was worth even less than that. ***Business owners should know that the intended use of a valuation will make a critical difference in how they respond to the results.*** When an owner wants to sell a business, she will be looking for the highest number. When a higher value for a business means either having to pay more to the IRS or to an ex-spouse or ex-partner, then an owner will want the lowest reasonable number.

Valuing a Minority Interest

As noted in Chapter 2, a valuation depends on exactly what is being valued. In this case, the "what" is a minority interest because none of the three owners has control of the firm; nor will anyone have control of the firm after buying Catherine Milton's ownership stake.

A key assumption of the fair market value concept is that the "willing buyer" would be getting control of the firm. As one sees in the business press for public companies, an acquirer typically pays a premium above the current market value of a company's stock to attract enough of the current shareholders to gain at least 51 percent control. Similarly, in a valuation analysis for a privately held company, the valuation expert should make an estimate of what the control premium would be to attract enough of these owners to sell 51 percent or more.

TABLE 6-1 Owner Equity and Minority Interest for The EarthRight Group

Valuation Concept	Value
Fair market value of business	$722,027
Minus debts and other long-term liabilities	$ 5,600
Equals fair market value of ownership equity	$716,427
Minus control premium	$130,350
Equals value of ownership equity—minority interests (MI)	$586,077
Divided by 3: Milton's share of ownership equity—MI	$195,359
Divided by 2: Catherine's share of Milton's ownership equity—MI	$ 97,670
Compared with Catherine's estimate of Milton's ownership equity—MI	$300,000

Randy ran through the calculations to make sure that he followed the logic. First, he subtracted EarthRight's debts of $5600 from the fair market value to get the fair market value of ownership equity of $716,427. This is what the three owners would divide after selling the company for $722,027 and paying off their loan, as would be required by the bank.

The fair market value of ownership equity includes an estimate of the control premium that a buyer would have to pay to attain at least a controlling interest in the company of 51 percent or more. The Valuation GURU estimates that the control premium would be $130,350, or roughly 18 percent of the ownership equity. To get a value for EarthRight's equity for minority interest purposes, Randy subtracted the control premium from the fair market value of ownership equity to get $586,077. Since EarthRight was not changing control, this minority interest amount for ownership equity was what he needed to then do the specific calculations for his ownership share information.

Randy divided the minority interest value of $586,077 by 3 to get the value of the one-third share, $195,359, owned jointly by him and his wife, Catherine. Then he divided the value of their share by 2 to get the amount that he would have to pay Catherine to buy her ownership rights in the company, which came to $97,670, over $200,000 less than Catherine's estimate of $300,000.

The Alternative Proposal Using the New Valuation Results

Randy met with his attorney and shared this valuation information. They proposed to Randy's wife that she is entitled to $97,670, representing 50 percent of the value of Randy's ownership of EarthRight. They proposed that Randy would pay the sum, with interest, over a 5-year period. They also forwarded to Randy's wife and her attorney a copy of the bizownerHQ valuation report that included all the detail necessary to evaluate the reliability of the valuation result.

Randy left his attorney's office feeling better than he had for some time. He certainly believed that a $97,670 payment for his wife's share of EarthRight was more reasonable than a $300,000 payment. More important, he knew that he provided a rationale for his offer and that if it were to be rejected, he would be a strong position to contest the matter in court.

Business owners should know that in valuations of firms with multiple owners, determining when an owner's interest should be valued as a majority or controlling interest or as a minority interest can become quite complex. Owners should always seek professional legal assistance to review any proposed changes in ownership and to provide guidance to the valuation process.

THE SECOND PRECIPITATING EVENT

Randy Milton had recently run into Jawarhal "JW" Shah, a friend from college, who now was a senior executive for New England Environmental

Services, Inc. (NEESI), based in Hartford, Connecticut. NEESI does the same kind of environmental engineering work as EarthRight but primarily for industrial, commercial, and government customers. Randy told JW of his recent troubles and his concerns over how EarthRight could make it through this difficulty. JW lent a sympathetic ear and told Randy that he would give this situation some thought.

NEESI is a larger firm with annual revenues around $25 million. NEESI is a publicly traded C Corporation. JW and others in NEESI's management were concerned about the slowdown in their primary markets, industrial and government capital spending. While they had solid billability for their staff over the next 6 months, the number of projects being put up for bid had slowed over the last year. At the same time, demand for environmental engineering services for new home building and septic system repair projects was stronger than ever in the New England area. JW had already begun looking into how NEESI could penetrate the residential market directly. Now, with Randy's problem in mind, he began looking at whether a targeted acquisition program might work, starting with EarthRight as the entrée to the residential and small business Boston metropolitan area market.

After talking this idea over with the NEESI senior management team, JW got the go-ahead to put together a prototype acquisition deal with EarthRight as the first candidate. JW called Randy with this news. For Randy, this was the first good news he had heard in a while. His wife's attorney had called earlier that day to say that she and Catherine wanted more time to review the detailed bizownerHQ report. The attorney implied that this was not going to be a short or easy process.

Randy told his two partners that NEESI would be interested in EarthRight if they were interested in joining NEESI. While this had not been part of their initial exit strategy, they felt that the NEESI overture definitely was worth a serious look. They agreed to let Randy share the bizownerHQ results with JW and NEESI.

The Initial Valuation
JW quickly got up to speed on the EarthRight business from the "Valuation Snapshots" (shown in Appendix 6A). At first glance, an acquisition of EarthRight by NEESI did not seem to make sense. EarthRight was a partnership not subject to corporate income taxation. EarthRight's value was $722,027, of which $245,799 (or 34 percent) of value represented the tax pass-thru. Since NEESI is a taxable C Corporation, it would have to pay corporate income tax on EarthRight's profits and therefore would lose the value of the tax pass-thru. Under this logic, EarthRight would be worth $476,228 to NEESI.

JW also set up an alternative scenario, with the assumption that the EarthRight partners list their business for sale with a broker and sell it to another environmental consulting partnership that could continue to take advantage of the tax pass-thru of company earnings. His findings are shown in Table 6-2.

TABLE 6-2   EarthRight's Alternative Selling Strategies

Potential Selling Alternatives	Selling to NEESI	Selling to Another Partnership
Fair market value for EarthRight as a stand-alone business	$722,027	$722,027
Minus adjustment for tax pass-thru status	$245,799	$0
Equals sale price	$476,228	$722,027
Minus business broker fee of 10 percent	Not applicable	$ 72,203
Minus legal fees and other transaction costs	$ 25,000	$ 25,000
Net proceeds to owners	$451,228	$624,824

In short, based on the fair market value minus the tax pass-thru, NEESI could offer EarthRight $476,228 for the business. However, if it could be sold through a broker to another firm that could take advantage of the tax pass-thru, then a $722,027 sale price seemed indicated. After paying the broker's fee, EarthRight's owners still would be better off with the sale to a tax pass-thru type of firm—by over $170,000. The incompatible tax status of the two firms seemed to doom an NEESI acquisition.

However, it was the "Value Maximizer" report that gave JW the best perspective on how the EarthRight team and his colleagues at NEESI would look at any NEESI offer. The reader can find EarthRight's "Value Maximizer" report in Appendix 6A.

STRATEGIC USE OF VALUATION

At this point, JW shifted from fair market valuation, that is, what a willing buyer would pay a willing seller, to valuation from an acquisition perspective. For him, the question is: What is the value of the additional earnings that could be gained from the strategic integration of EarthRight as a new market distribution channel for NEESI? We call this kind of valuation analysis, *finding the strategic buyer premium*. This addresses the questions of which companies would gain the most from buying a company and estimating the value of higher earnings gained from greater revenue or expense productivity. *Business owners should know that most valuation experts are only trained in conducting fair market valuations.*

Owners who want assistance in finding a buyer willing to pay a significant buyer premium can pay a business broker or a regional investment banking firm to conduct a valuation that includes calculating the potential strategic buyer premium. Owners with their management and advisory teams also can do much of the analysis themselves because they know their industries and competition well. In this example, a senior manager from the potential acquirer does the analysis, and then he shares the findings with the owners of the potential acquisition.

Increasing Value: Higher Earnings Growth

JW saw on the first page of the "Value Maximizer" report how the value of EarthRight could increase under a higher growth scenario for earnings. Based on an assumption of earnings increasing by 8.6 percent per year compared with a 7 percent per year growth rate in the baseline growth case, the value of EarthRight rises by 9 percent to $779,394. JW believed that if NEESI acquired EarthRight, it could move EarthRight to a higher growth path. EarthRight's expertise in residential environmental issues and its expertise in groundwater quality issues could be leveraged across New England through NEESI's existing network.

Increasing Value: Lower Expense Base

JW also was certain that there were significant expense savings that EarthRight could achieve, net of integration costs. Once the companies were combined, they could get rid of duplicate association memberships, get more favorable rates on health insurance, and eliminate their annual audit. JW put together a list of net expense savings that came to $50,000. He then reran the Valuation GURU combining the two strategic changes, using the high-growth path for earnings and making a $50,000 addition to earnings. The reader can find the "Valuation Snapshots report" for EarthRight as part of NEESI in Appendix 6A.

JW took the results from this revised run and quickly updated his analysis of EarthRight's alternative selling strategies, as shown in Table 6-3.

The results now made the decision for EarthRight's management easy because there was over $200,000 more on the table for the NEESI offer compared with the potential option of selling at fair market value to another environmental consulting partnership.

TABLE 6-3   JW's Revised Version of EarthRight's Alternative Selling Strategies

Potential Selling Alternatives	Selling to NEESI	Selling to Another Partnership
Fair market value for EarthRight as a stand-alone business	$722,027	$722,027
Incremental value from NEESI acquisition (high-growth earnings + $50,000 in expense savings)	$496,478	Not applicable
Value of EarthRight to potential acquirer	$1,218,505	$722,027
Minus adjustment for tax pass-thru status	$359,672	$0
Equals sale price (rounded to nearest $10,000)	$860,000	$720,000
Minus business broker fee of 10 percent	Not applicable	$ 72,000
Minus legal fees and other transaction costs	$ 25,000	$ 25,000
Net proceeds to owners	$835,000	$623,000

NEESI's Maximum Incremental Gain from EarthRight

For NEESI's internal acquisition analysis shown in Table 6-4, JW had estimated that there was an additional $25,000 in annual expense savings from this acquisition. When he put this additional amount into the Valuation GURU valuation of EarthRight, the incremental value of EarthRight to NEESI increased from $860,000 to $1,024,216 (total value of $1,438,060 minus the tax pass-thru value of $413,844). This makes for a total incremental value of $302,189 (the maximum value of $1,024,216 minus the original stand-alone value of $722,027) from EarthRight joining with NEESI compared with continuing as a stand-alone business.

    This case highlights the importance of identifying potential strategic buyers for a business when the owner gets ready to sell the business. There can be a substantial value increment over the business value as a stand-alone business. The challenge for the owner is to make her own estimate of the incremental value to the potential acquirer and to negotiate for a higher percentage of this value. Based on JW's second analysis just described, EarthRight's owners would get 46 percent of the total incremental value ($137,973 divided by $302,189), and NEESI would retain 54 percent, or $164,216.

TABLE 6-4   JW's Internal Analysis of EarthRight's Potential

Potential Selling Alternatives	Selling to NEESI
Fair market value for EarthRight as a stand-alone business	$ 722,027
Incremental value from NEESI acquisition (high-growth earnings + $50,000 in expense savings)	$ 496,478
Value of EarthRight to NEESI	$1,218,505
Additional incremental value from NEESI acquisition ($25,000 additional expense savings)	$ 219,555
Maximum value of EarthRight to NEESI	$1,438,060
Minus adjustment for tax pass-thru status	$ 413,844
Equals maximum sale price	$1,024,216
Maximum gain from EarthRight acquisition by NEESI	$ 302,189
NEESI acquisition price for EarthRight	$ 860,000
EarthRight owners' share of maximum gain (acquisition price minus fair market value as stand-alone business)	$ 137,973
NEESI's share of maximum gain (maximum sale price minus NEESI's acquisition price)	$ 164,216

Business owners should know that an existing competitive or complementary business should be able to identify clear cost savings or revenue enhancements that would justify paying a strategic buyer premium above the stand-alone value of their businesses. Business owners can make their own estimates of the revenue gains and/or expense savings that the acquirer will gain from taking over their business and then use those estimates to find out the total incremental value. They can then negotiate with the potential acquirer to receive a larger share of this incremental value being created.

The Resolution
JW met with the NEESI management team and presented his results. He recommended that NEESI make an offer to buy EarthRight for $860,000 in NEESI common stock. The price was based on the assumption that NEESI could turn EarthRight from an average-growth to a high-growth environmental business and make at least $50,000 in ongoing expense savings, net of integration costs. The NEESI board of directors approved the offer.

JW then met with the three partners of EarthRight and explained the $860,000 offer in detail. He emphasized that this price was much better than what the partners could expect if they sold the business, through a broker, to another partnership or S Corporation. JW also explained that each EarthRight partner would receive $286,667 ($860,000 divided by 3) of NEESI common stock. Since NEESI common stock trades on the Nasdaq market, the transaction would take each partner's share from being an illiquid asset to being a liquid asset. In addition, JW prepared NEESI employment agreements for the three EarthRight owners and showed them the salary, benefits, and profit sharing they would receive as the ongoing managers of their new division of NEESI. He emphasized that NEESI was looking to acquire EarthRight as an ongoing business, which included its most important assets—its current partners.

After some discussion, the EarthRight partners agreed to accept the NEESI offer. Although the NEESI acquisition will mean big changes for EarthRight's current owners, they have decided to sell the business. The pluses outweigh the potential negatives for all three owners, but especially for Randy. Randy informed his wife's attorney that he no longer owned one-third of EarthRight that would be valued as a minority interest but approximately $287,000 worth of stock in NEESI. Since the value of the NEESI stock was not in dispute, he believed that his wife was entitled to $143,500 in stock rather than his previous offer of $97,670 for the half share of his ownership in EarthRight. The NEESI outcome provides Randy's wife with a higher number than before, since it now includes the control premium and a strategic buyer premium. Most important, it takes the question of the value of EarthRight out of the realm of costly litigation. There can no longer be any doubt as to the value of EarthRight because the company has just been sold. There is now a current market price for the EarthRight portion of the Milton's assets.

LESSONS LEARNED
As we have noted previously, a professional valuation of a business looks at the value of the business from the fair market value standpoint. This standard is based on the assumption of what any reasonable buyer would pay to own the right to earn the future cash flows to be produced by the business. However, *business owners should know that when one turns from fair market valuation to what is the price that a specific buyer might pay, there are several other factors that emerge, including*

1. *Compatible tax status.* Does the buying firm have the same tax status as the business being sold; that is, is the business taxed at the corpo-

rate level, or is the income passed through to the tax return of the individual owner(s)? NEESI is a fully taxable C Corporation; EarthRight is a partnership. The value of the same business (EarthRight) to owners and potential buyers with different tax statuses can influence the price at which they are willing to buy or sell the business.

2. **The strategic buyer.** Does the potential buyer have a complementary business to the business being sold? If so, is the combination of the businesses likely to produce higher cash flows than the sum of the individual businesses? EarthRight is a small partnership whose expertise and marketing reach are limited. NEESI is a larger firm that could use its existing customer base, scientific expertise, and marketing to leverage EarthRight into a more rapidly growing, higher cash flow, more valuable business. NEESI is willing to pay a strategic buyer premium to acquire EarthRight.

3. **The transaction costs.** Will a business broker be involved? What will be the due diligence and document preparation expenses for accountants and attorneys? The acquisition of EarthRight by NEESI can be accomplished with no brokerage fees and a minimum of attorney and other fees.

Being Prepared

As the former owners of EarthRight now know, an owner cannot always predict accurately when he should sell the business. Precipitating events such as a divorce of one of the owners, a falling out between partners, or an unexpected buyout offer can occur and reshape the landscape overnight. However, unless Robin, Randy, and Laura go back to owning their own business, this learning comes too late.

Business owners should know what the value of their business is and update the valuation annually. This information provides a fundamental context for owners to evaluate the full range of strategic decisions that may arise. Knowing for certain that EarthRight was not worth $3 million would have saved Randy a great deal of unnecessary stress.

Business owners should know what the businesses in their industry are selling for and what kinds of strategic buyers exist in their industry. Owners always should keep on top of transactions taking place in their industry even if they are not prepared to sell at the moment. They can either request that the valuation include private company market multiples or get this information through their industry contacts. While knowledge of transaction prices and associated multiples is important, the far more important piece of information is why the purchases are made. Knowing if buyers have tended to be strategic buyers or not may suggest the timing of an exit strategy. For example, if other niche environmental consulting firms have been purchased by much larger firms in the hope of entering new markets, one can reasonably conclude that a strategic buyer trend is developing. If EarthRight partners were on top of transaction developments in their industry, they might have been able to get competing bids from other, larger firms that compete with NEESI. Since timing is critical to the success of every decision, owners always must be prepared when that once-in-a-lifetime buyer comes calling.

MORE ON VALUATION METHODS

bizownerHQ APPROACH

As noted several times, the most widely accepted standard for valuing a closely held business is fair market value. This is the standard used in all matters related to state and federal tax matters, including estate taxes, gift taxes, and so on. The American Society of Appraisers and the IRS have defined *fair market value* as "the amount at which property would change hands between a willing seller and a willing buyer when neither is acting under compulsion and when both have reasonable knowledge of the relevant facts."

This being said, the question remains how one calculates fair market value prior to the sale of a business. Common sense would dictate that the best way to do this is to find a business that was just sold that is identical to the one being valued. This certainly would meet the IRS definition of fair market value. Calculating fair market value in this way would be easy, except for two crucial facts:

1. There is no business quite like the one under consideration.
2. Finding a transaction that occurred recently for a business exactly like the one under consideration is even less likely.

The preceding chapters discussed several notable problems with both the multiple- and asset-based approaches as well as the difficulty for a non-expert to use the discounted cash flow approach (DCFA).

So what is one left with? One might ask the following question: What would a savvy investor look at, and how would she assess the information collected to come up with a logically determined value that would be equivalent to the value that a market populated by a large number of informed buyers and sellers would produce? bizownerHQ has developed an expert valuation system, the Valuation GURU, that does exactly this.

The Valuation GURU

The Valuation GURU incorporates the uniqueness of a firm being valued by

1. Accurately predicting the firm's revenue and future cash flows using a statistical method that reflects the growth of the unique detailed industry segment the firm is in.
2. Incorporating the sensitivity of the business to economy- and industry-wide risks.
3. Assessing the firm's unique cost of short- and long-term debt using bizownerHQ's credit-risk model.
4. Considering the firm's unique capital mix between debt and equity and the impact of this on the firm's cost of financial capital.
5. Making adjustments to the firm's officers' compensation based on the industry and firm asset size.
6. Allowing for legitimate discretionary expense and revenue adjustments that better reflect the firm's current cash flow.
7. Explicitly considering capital expenditures necessary to support the expected growth of the business.

We have already noted that DCFA business valuation is complex. Remember, however, that the valuation of the Middlesex Construction Company (see Chapter 5) was driven by only three inputs:

1. Initial estimate of free cash flow—$100,000
2. Growth rate—5 percent
3. Discount rate—15 percent

All the rest of the numbers simply were calculated from these inputs.

The critical point here is that the major drivers of the DCFA are easy to calculate when one has the right tools but difficult and expensive to obtain and virtually not accessible or understandable to anyone but an expert in business valuation. The advantage of the DCFA is that it forces one to be as explicit as possible about the determinants of a firm's expected cash flow growth and as accurate as possible in estimating the firm's cost of capital. From a business buyer's point of view, understanding the realistic cash flow growth potential of the business is certainly critical to understanding what the business is worth. In the process of doing this, one must come to terms with the underlying competitive forces that will shape the business's success. Typically, both the owner and the business buyer are uninformed about the determinants of business value and are at a loss when discussing these issues with their financial advisors. This no longer has to be the case. By using the information in this book, owners can translate their knowledge of the earnings potential of their businesses into realistic estimates of the value of the business. Potential buyers also can examine the impact on the firm's value of their plans to improve earnings through cost reductions and/or new revenue sources.

The Expert System

The bizownerHQ method of valuing a business is encoded in the Valuation GURU, a web-based expert system. bizownerHQ uses this system to quickly and cost-effectively estimate the fair market value of a privately held business for owners and advisors. bizownerHQ also incorporates the Valuation GURU results in their signed valuation analyses that meet the IRS and legal requirements for tax filings and litigation settings. The Valuation GURU uses a sophisticated version of the DCFA that was used to value Middlesex Construction Company in Chapter 5. The most important determinants of a firm's value are its financial performance and the industry (business activity) that it engages in. Essentially, a highly profitable business in a rapidly growing industry is going to be worth more than a firm with the same sales volume that is a low-profit business in a slowly growing or declining industry.

Firm-Specific Inputs

As in the Middlesex Construction Company example in Chapter 5, three inputs (initial cash flow, growth rate, and discount rate) are needed for a discounted free cash flow valuation. The owner of the business to be valued provides data about the business from the business's most recent tax return. The most important pieces of information are the business activity code (which is a government code that specifies the specific industry the business operates in) and information about revenues, expenses, profits, officer compensation, income from nonoperating assets such as real estate, royalties, both taxable and nontaxable interest, and several items from the firm's balance sheet, including net working and plant and equipment capital.

Next, the user responds to a series of questions that enable the Valuation GURU to incorporate adjustments to the tax return data entered. These questions relate to categories of discretionary expenses, expenses that are not necessary for the ongoing viability of the business, and various revenue adjustments. The answers to the second set of questions allow the Valuation GURU to determine which growth segment of the industry the firm is in. Determining whether the firm is in the high-, middle-, or low-growth segment allows the Valuation GURU to identify how the firm is likely to perform relative to its industry and to the overall economy, a decision that all valuation experts have to make when they value a firm. All of these inputs to the expert system are reviewed by bizownerHQ staff with the user by phone to make sure that the inputs and assumptions are consistent with DCFA.

VALUATION FACTORS BY INDUSTRY

bizownerHQ maintains several detailed databases that contain information about the financial performance of 981 distinct industries. These databases are used to transform the information from the tax return provided by the owner into an estimate of the free cash flow that could be taken from the business by a new owner.

Owner Compensation

One database contains information on officer compensation by industry, size of firm, and location. The officer compensation actually paid by a firm will be compared with that paid by other firms of the same size, in the same industry, and in the same geographical area, either a state or metropolitan statistical area. If actual officer compensation differs from the norm, then the officer compensation number used is the norm not the actual. In this way, the model adjusts for the well-known problem of owners setting their own "salaries" in privately held firms.

Industry Growth Projections

bizownerHQ evaluates and forecasts the rates of revenue and cash flow growth by industry using a unique combination of proprietary databases, statistical models, and experienced analyst input. This provides the second input needed for the discounted free cash flow valuation—the growth rate in operating profits. The user will be prompted to provide information about whether the particular company to be valued is expected to grow at the industry average or slower or faster. The user has the option of letting the expert system choose the appropriate growth path based on the user's responses to a brief business performance survey. The expert system then transforms the tax return data into free cash flow data by adjusting for new investment needed to support growth.

Discount Rate

The third input needed for a discounted free cash flow valuation is the appropriate discount rate to use for a particular firm. bizownerHQ maintains two databases that produce estimates of the appropriate discount rate, frequently called the *cost of capital*, for a specific company in a specific industry. One is a credit-rating (scoring) model that calculates the risk and therefore the cost of investment debt capital for a specific business. Commercial banks and other business lenders frequently use these types of models to estimate the appropriate interest rate to require on a loan to a particular business. The other database contains equity risk estimates by industry calculated by sophisticated statistical techniques. With the assistance of these databases, an appropriate risk-adjusted discount rate can be used to value the free cash flows of a particular firm.

This combination of resources, along with bizownerHQ's valuation model, and input by bizownerHQ's valuation staff provides the basis for developing a customized valuation of a particular business.

ADJUSTMENTS TO VALUE
From the preceding information, the Valuation GURU determines the discounted free cash flow value of the business. However, there are two adjustments that must be made to make the valuation more accurate. The discounted free cash flow valuation methodology was developed for and is used widely to value the stock of publicly traded companies. However, two adjustments must be made when a private firm is being valued under the assumption that the total firm is being sold. The first adjustment is for lack of liquidity, the liquidity discount, and the second, the control premium, reflects an additional sum the new owner would be willing to pay to have control over the firm's assets. These adjustments are made only to the ownership equity in the firm, not to any portion of total value that is attributable to debt or other liabilities.

The Liquidity Discount
The liquidity discount reduces the ownership value to reflect the fact that the ownership interest cannot be sold easily. Put differently, any potential buyer of the ownership value faces the risk that he cannot sell his ownership interest in a timely way because there are a limited number of potential buyers. As Donna Young noted in the Hachey and Nelson case in Chapter 5, only a Florida lawyer experienced in worker's compensation law and willing to work with the existing partners would want to buy into or be considered by the owners as a buyer. This is a small set of potential buyers.

This is to be contrasted with shares of stock that trade on the New York Stock Exchange, for example. These shares can be purchased and sold readily, and except for rare cases, the price received will reflect the fair market value of these shares. Thus the liquidity discount reflects the additional risk that a buyer faces because she may not be able to receive the price that would be obtained if ownership interest in the business were sold in a highly liquid market.

Much has been written on the liquidity discount, and several organizations have routinely attempted to measure it. Based on our review of this research, we believe that the most appropriate value to use is the average private company discount published in an academic peer-reviewed study by John Koeplin and colleagues.[1] This conclusion is based on two factors: The Koeplin study controls for capital structure differences, and selection of the private company's public company peer was dictated by whether they were in the same four-digit Standard Industrial Classification (SIC) industry. Based on this, the Valuation GURU uses 20 percent as the liquidity discount.

The Control Premium

The second adjustment is the control premium. It is an additional sum that an investor would pay above the fair market value of a minority interest in the firm in question. This markup reflects that the buyer is an owner that not only has a claim on the firm's cash flow but also has an additional right to "control" the firm's assets and has the power to redirect their use. Minority interest owners do not have the "right" to deploy the assets. This means that if a share of common stock of a public company is selling for $100 and an investor is willing to purchase all shares for $140 per share, the control premium is 40 percent. The Valuation GURU first calculates the minority interest ownership value of the company. It then factors up this value to reflect a control premium.

As a general rule, most business appraisers apply a median markup value to the minority equity value to obtain the majority equity value. The source of this median value and related control premium statistics is the annual *Mergerstat Review* that is published by Houlihan, Lokey, Howard, and Zukin of Los Angeles. *Mergerstat* compiles data on publicly announced mergers, acquisitions, and divestitures involving operating entities, where the transfer involves at least 10 percent of the subject company's equity, the purchase price is at least $1 million, and at least one of the parties to the transaction is a U.S. entity. *Mergerstat* sells data on control premiums by industry, but only at a very aggregate level, and data for individual firm transactions. Median control values indeed vary over time, having reached a low of 27.3 percent in 1996 and a high of 35.0 percent in 1994.

One should be very cautious about applying a median value as a markup control factor because there is wide variation around these values. For example, in 1998, of the 560 transactions reported by *Mergerstat*, the

---

[1]J. Koeplin, A. Sarin, and A. Shapiro, "The Private Company Discount," *Journal of Applied Corporate Finance* 12(4):94–101, Winter 2000.

maximum was 423.5 percent, the minimum was 0 percent, the average was 40.4 percent, and the standard deviation was 43.4 percent. This means that the chances are quite high that simply applying the median control premium will result in considerable error. For these reasons, the Valuation GURU estimates the control premium directly. The methodology used is based on academic research that has been published in refereed journals. The bizownerHQ control premium varies by detailed industry and is customized to the size of the company being valued. The control premium applied to a company is stated explicitly in the valuation report.

BACKGROUNDER

MORE ON LIQUIDITY DIFFERENCES

A great advantage that the owners of equity shares in publicly traded businesses have is that at any time the market is open the stockholder can quickly know the price (value) of the shares he owns or might wish to buy or sell. Also, the buyer or seller of publicly traded shares can execute orders at or near the last transactions price for low transactions costs (i.e., brokerage commissions). The buyer or seller of 100 shares of a publicly traded business rarely would have to retain specialized advisors (e.g., an attorney) to complete a transaction successfully. As this is being written, online brokerage firms are offering to buy or sell 100 shares of publicly traded common stock for a commission of $10 or less.

In the terminology of modern finance, the owner of a publicly traded share of stock owns a liquid asset that trades in a highly efficient market. This ability of the owners of publicly traded shares to buy and sell quickly at or near a known price (value) for nominal transactions costs is called *liquidity*. Holding a liquid asset is thus an enormous advantage over holding an asset that can only be sold after a long period of time, for a value that is difficult to determine, at large transactions costs (i.e., an illiquid asset). To underscore the importance of liquidity, recall when Brendan O'Toole easily sold 100 shares of General Electric stock (a liquid asset) to pay off college loans for his children, and compare this transaction with the time and effort Brendan put in to sell his insurance agency (an illiquid asset) (see Chapter 3).

What Makes Publicly Traded Shares Liquid?

There are several factors that need to be present if we are to have a liquid market and thus allow ownership shares in a firm's equity to be bought and sold cost-effectively. These factors are

1. Standardization
2. Quality low-cost information
3. Knowledgeable financial analysts
4. Low-cost sales transactions

Standardization

As noted earlier, the potential buyer of a publicly traded share knows that the business is a C Corporation and therefore knows the general liability and tax status of the firm. The potential buyer of a privately held business must discover the ownership structure of the business and therefore important liability and taxation issues.

The buyer of a publicly traded share normally will buy that share on a regulated public market. The NYSE and Nasdaq are organized markets with established listing and trading rules and regulations. Businesses must meet and agree to certain standards to be listed and traded. For example, in order to be listed and traded on a stock exchange, a business must show that it is legally incorporated and that the directors have been elected in compliance with its articles of incorporation and the law. Brokers agree to a series of rules about how prices will be quoted and how long the parties have after the transaction to come up with the money and deliver the shares. Each transaction, to the extent practical, is not customized but rather standardized.

Standardization means that buyers and sellers and their brokers know the agreed-upon rules that govern a transaction in general and do not have to spend time and money discovering the unique or unusual rules of this particular transaction. Privately traded businesses have no comparable standardization.

Quality Low-Cost Information

Publicly traded businesses are required by law to make available financial and other information so that investors can value the businesses and decide whether to buy or sell securities. The Securities Acts of 1933 and 1934 established a federal agency, the Securities and Exchange Commission (SEC), to establish rules and regulate the public capital markets in the United States. Publicly traded firms must issue financial statements that are prepared in accordance with generally accepted accounting principles and are audited by an independent CPA firm. Publicly traded firms also must supply detailed financial data on a so-called 10K report to the SEC, which makes this information available to the public. Intentional misrepresentation of financial information in either the audited financial statements or the 10K is a serious crime. Investors, whether potential buyers or sellers, have easy, low-cost access to information about the business especially through audited financial statements and 10K reports. Investors, through brokerage houses and investment advisory services, also have access to forecasts of a firm's future revenues and earnings and forecasts concerning the larger economy, such as growth in economic output, employment, and inflation.

Information discovery for a public company has been driven lower by Internet technology. News stories, especially in the financial press, about the operations of publicly traded firms are easy and inexpensive to acquire. There is a high degree of transparency about the operations of a public company. This is not the case for a private firm like the O'Toole Insurance Agency (see Chapter 3).

While Brendan was honest and ethical, information discovery was expensive. Brendan did not have to produce an annual report, for example, that met predefined disclosure standards. Jill, the potential buyer of the O'Toole Agency, had to have her financial representatives do an extensive due diligence of the financial records and other related private information. These efforts were both qualitatively and quantitatively different from analyzing the disclosure information from a public company, where the data are standardized to a significant degree. In this case, for example, Jill's CPA had to differentiate the types of expenses and the amounts that were necessary for the running of the business from those expenses which were truly discretionary. These efforts cost a great deal of time and money, costs that are far less for the public company counterpart.

Knowledgeable Financial Analysts

The ability of the markets to value shares, in turn, is based on the availability of reliable financial and other information and the existence of professional financial analysts to evaluate the information and produce estimates of the value of the shares or give buy or sell recommendations. Brokerage houses, mutual funds, and other financial institutions hire people whose job is to evaluate information and convert that information into estimates of the value of shares. Although these financial analysts may use different valuation methodologies (i.e., valuation models) and give more or less weight to a particular piece of information, there are standardized models of valuation that lay out what information is important and how it should be weighed in valuing a publicly traded business. Analysts armed with accepted valuation models produce the estimates of firm earnings, value, and the buy, hold, and sell recommendations of the brokerage houses and investment advisory services. The potential buyer or seller of a publicly traded share can quickly and inexpensively get access to the valuation estimates of the shares made by professionals and the rationale for this valuation estimate and its buy, hold, or sell recommendation. Note that all financial analysts are not going to agree on the same value of a particular stock at a particular point in time. However, the potential buyer or seller can quickly and at low cost get the opinion, the valuation methodology, and the rationale of an expert. If the potential buyer or seller finds the valuation and its supporting documents persuasive, then confidence rises and transactions occur quickly.

Low-Cost Sales Transactions

At any time the market is open, the value (i.e., the last transaction price) of the shares of a publicly traded business is known. Indeed, it is the bidding of knowledgeable buyers and sellers that establishes the price of a share. The fact that the price of share at a point in time is known makes trading shares quick and inexpensive; that is, it makes it liquid.

Since sellers and buyers set the price through supply and demand and know the price through information technology, transactions occur quickly and at low cost. Sellers and buyers do not have to go through long face-to-face negotiations to determine the price of a share, and the standardized trading rules of the NYSE and the Nasdaq make trades easy and therefore inexpensive to execute. The fact that high-quality estimates of value can be transmitted to a large number of potential buyers and sellers means that transactions occur quickly and at low cost. Indeed, the buyer of publicly traded shares does not even know, or care, who the seller of the shares is. Contrast this situation with the sale of the O'Toole Insurance Agency.

THE O'TOOLE INSURANCE AGENCY FROM A LIQUIDITY PERSPECTIVE

The defining characteristic of a privately held business is exactly what the name implies: The business is owned by one or more individuals. Brendan owns the O'Toole Insurance Agency. He is owner and manager and has a number of his family members as employees. Brendan, like other owners of privately held businesses, not only views his business as the tangible result of years of hard work and the primary source of his income but also as the major financial asset he owns. The O'Toole Insurance Agency is also the major component of his net worth.

In contrast, an equivalent public firm has numerous shareholders. Family members may be employees, but the rules that guide their business positions are, at least on paper, no different from those of other employees. While Brendan's counterpart in the public company manages the business and makes all the critical business decisions, in the end, he must report to the shareholders and the board of directors. In contrast, Brendan is only accountable to himself and perhaps the bank with which he maintains a line of credit.

A major problem for the owner of a privately held business is precisely that the business is privately held. In the terminology of modern finance, the owner of a privately held business is holding an illiquid asset that trades in an inefficient market—unlike the owners of publicly traded businesses. On each of the four characteristics of an efficient, liquid market for publicly traded businesses, privately traded businesses are poorer.

Lack of Standardization

Brendan cannot easily and cost-effectively sell his business, unlike a public firm. The reason is that there is no well-organized market to buy and sell the assets that represent the ownership of a privately held business such as the O'Toole Insurance Agency. There is much less standardization in these transactions, and each transaction needs, at cost and time, to be customized to discover exactly what is being offered for sale, by whom, how the title to the asset will be transferred, and how the payment will be received.

High-Cost Information

Information about the privately held business is of lower quality than that about publicly traded businesses. Financial statements of a privately held firm, for example, may not have been audited by an independent CPA firm. Getting reliable, low-cost information about the larger economy and the industry in which the business operates may be difficult or impossible. Getting reliable, low-cost expert estimates of value also may be impossible. During the negotiations, there may be only one buyer or, at best, a small number of buyers. Both buyer and seller have limited access to what other similar businesses may be for sale or recently sold, and they do not have the benefit of competing, real-time bids for the asset.

Lack of Knowledgeable Analysts

Without the sales volume of the public markets, there is no way to support the numbers of analysts necessary to track and analyze the available private businesses.

High-Cost Sales Transactions

For these reasons, if the owner(s) of a small business decided to sell the business, the process would likely take a long time (e.g., 6 months) and would have significant transactions costs such as commissions to a broker, legal fees, accounting fees, and appraisal fees.

IMPROVING THE MARKET FOR
PRIVATE BUSINESS SALES

We expect that the coming business transition tidal wave described in Chapter 1 will greatly exacerbate the myriad difficulties facing sellers and buyers of private businesses unless new approaches and advances in how these businesses transact emerge soon. While helping owners make their way through this business transition tidal wave is one of the largest business and financial services opportunities of the next decade, few services have yet to emerge in the private business transition/transaction market offering both customization and cost-effectiveness, attributes necessary to serve this market.

Online Services for Posting/Finding a Business for Sale

One way to make information more readily available about businesses for sale is to have online business-for-sale listing services. Over the last few years, a number of Internet-based businesses have begun offering relatively low-cost business-for-sale posting services for owners and free viewing for potential buyers. Two of the largest examples are bizbuysell.com, with 16,000 businesses for sale, and USBX.com, with 14,000 businesses for sale as of May 2002. Neither service provides information on how many businesses actually have sold through their listing services.

While these services have the potential to improve efficiency in the private business-for-sale market, it is important to put these numbers in perspective. Their current combined listings, approximately 30,000, represent only 3 percent of the total number of private businesses for sale at any given time, which is estimated at 1.2 million, according to Tom West.[2]

The business brokerage community also has become Web-enabled. The International Business Brokerage Association Web site, *www.ibba.com*, has over 4000 business-for-sale listings and also offers a search engine to find brokers by location. This is also a positive step, but it is only a small improvement, given the current volume and the expected growth in businesses to transact over the next several years.

Business Valuation

We are contributing to making the private business sales and transition marketplace more efficient by writing this book and by developing a cost-effective valuation capability. We have designed our approach specifically to bring down the cost of valuing firms and analyzing alternative valuation

---

[2]Tom West, 2002 *Business Reference Guide*, 12th ed. Concord, MA: Business Brokerage Press, 2002.

scenarios and to make valuation assumptions and inputs transparent to owners and buyers. All of this should make the process of completing a sale of
a privately held business quicker and less expensive to buyers and sellers in
terms of transactions costs.

Appendix 6A

THE EARTHRIGHT GROUP: VALUATION INPUTS AND OUTPUTS

Partial 2000 Tax Return

Valuation Snapshots Report: EarthRight as a Stand-alone Business

EarthRight's Value Maximizer Report for JW Shah

Valuation Snapshots Report: EarthRight as a NEESI Acquisition

The EarthRight Group Tax Return, page 1.

Form **1065**			**U.S. Return of Partnership Income**		OMB No. 1545-0099
Department of the Treasury Internal Revenue Service			For calendar year 2000, or tax year beginning .... , 2000, and ending .... , 20.... . ▶ See separate instructions.		**2000**

A Principal business activity	Use the IRS label. Other- wise, print or type.	Name of partnership **The EarthRight Group**	D Employer identification number
B Principal product or service		Number, street, and room or suite no. If a P.O. box, see page 13 of the instructions. **274 Northern Ave**	E Date business started **10-1-1989**
C Business code number **541360**		City or town, state, and ZIP code **Natick, MA 01760**	F Total assets (see page 13 of the instructions) $

G   Check applicable boxes: **(1)** ☐ Initial return   **(2)** ☐ Final return   **(3)** ☐ Change in address   **(4)** ☐ Amended return
H   Check accounting method: **(1)** ☐ Cash   **(2)** ☑ Accrual   **(3)** ☐ Other (specify) ▶ ....
I   Number of Schedules K-1. Attach one for each person who was a partner at any time during the tax year ▶ ....

Caution: Include only trade or business income and expenses on lines 1a through 22 below. See the instructions for more information.

Income

1a Gross receipts or sales	1a	503,638	00	
b Less returns and allowances	1b	5,420	00	1c	498,218	00
2 Cost of goods sold (Schedule A, line 8)				2	237,482	00
3 Gross profit. Subtract line 2 from line 1c				3	260,736	00
4 Ordinary income (loss) from other partnerships, estates, and trusts *(attach schedule)*				4		
5 Net farm profit (loss) *(attach Schedule F (Form 1040))*				5		
6 Net gain (loss) from Form 4797, Part II, line 18				6		
7 Other income (loss) *(attach schedule)*				7	795	00
8 Total income (loss). Combine lines 3 through 7				8	261,531	00

Deductions (see page 14 of the instructions for limitations)

9 Salaries and wages (other than to partners) (less employment credits)			9	42,475	00
10 Guaranteed payments to partners			10	220,000	00
11 Repairs and maintenance			11	2,456	00
12 Bad debts			12	354	00
13 Rent			13	25,000	00
14 Taxes and licenses			14	16,280	00
15 Interest			15	2,050	00
16a Depreciation (if required, attach Form 4562)	16a	1,291	00	
b Less depreciation reported on Schedule A and elsewhere on return	16b			16c	1,291	00
17 Depletion **(Do not deduct oil and gas depletion.)**			17		
18 Retirement plans, etc.			18		
19 Employee benefit programs			19		
20 Other deductions *(attach schedule)*			20	9,872	00
21 Total deductions. Add the amounts shown in the far right column for lines 9 through 20			21	319,778	00
22 Ordinary income (loss) from trade or business activities. Subtract line 21 from line 8			22	58,247	00

Sign Here

Under penalties of perjury, I declare that I have examined this return, including accompanying schedules and statements, and to the best of my knowledge and belief, it is true, correct, and complete. Declaration of preparer (other than general partner or limited liability company member) is based on all information of which preparer has any knowledge.

▶ Signature of general partner or limited liability company member	▶ Date

Paid Preparer's Use Only	Preparer's signature ▶		Date	Check if self-employed ▶ ☐	Preparer's SSN or PTIN
	Firm's name (or yours if self-employed), address, and ZIP code ▶			EIN ▶	
				Phone no. ( )	

For Paperwork Reduction Act Notice, see separate instructions.   Cat. No. 11390Z   Form **1065** (2000)

The EarthRight Group Tax Return, page 4.

Form 1065 (2000)						Page 4

Analysis of Net Income (Loss)

1 Net income (loss). Combine Schedule K, lines 1 through 7 in column (b). From the result, subtract the sum of Schedule K, lines 8 through 11, 14a, 17f, and 18b **1**

2 Analysis by partner type:	(i) Corporate	(ii) Individual (active)	(iii) Individual (passive)	(iv) Partnership	(v) Exempt organization	(vi) Nominee/Other
a General partners						
b Limited partners						

Schedule L — Balance Sheets per Books (Not required if Question 5 on Schedule B is answered "Yes.")

Assets	Beginning of tax year (a)	(b)	End of tax year (c)	(d)
1 Cash		4,585		6,458
2a Trade notes and accounts receivable	8,255		12,456	
b Less allowance for bad debts		8,255		12,542
3 Inventories		24,897		28,542
4 U.S. government obligations				
5 Tax-exempt securities		2,000		2,500
6 Other current assets *(attach schedule)* . . .				
7 Mortgage and real estate loans				
8 Other investments *(attach schedule)*		2,000		1,850
9a Buildings and other depreciable assets . .	16,000		18,750	
b Less accumulated depreciation	4,550	11,450	5,841	18,750
10a Depletable assets				
b Less accumulated depletion				
11 Land (net of any amortization)				
12a Intangible assets (amortizable only)				
b Less accumulated amortization				
13 Other assets *(attach schedule)*				
14 **Total assets**		33,400		53,187
Liabilities and Capital				
15 Accounts payable		12,250		18,195
16 Mortgages, notes, bonds payable in less than 1 year .		5,600		9,046
17 Other current liabilities *(attach schedule)* . . .				
18 All nonrecourse loans				
19 Mortgages, notes, bonds payable in 1 year or more .				
20 Other liabilities *(attach schedule)*				
21 Partners' capital accounts		35,550		43,315
22 **Total liabilities and capital**		53,400		70,556

Schedule M-1 — Reconciliation of Income (Loss) per Books With Income (Loss) per Return
(Not required if Question 5 on Schedule B is answered "Yes." See page 30 of the instructions.)

1 Net income (loss) per books		6 Income recorded on books this year not included on Schedule K, lines 1 through 7 (itemize):	
2 Income included on Schedule K, lines 1 through 4, 6, and 7, not recorded on books this year (itemize):		a Tax-exempt interest $	
3 Guaranteed payments (other than health insurance)		7 Deductions included on Schedule K, lines 1 through 11, 14a, 17f, and 18b, not charged against book income this year (itemize):	
4 Expenses recorded on books this year not included on Schedule K, lines 1 through 11, 14a, 17f, and 18b (itemize):		a Depreciation $	
a Depreciation $		8 Add lines 6 and 7	
b Travel and entertainment $		9 Income (loss) (Analysis of Net Income (Loss), line 1). Subtract line 8 from line 5	
5 Add lines 1 through 4			

Schedule M-2 — Analysis of Partners' Capital Accounts (Not required if Question 5 on Schedule B is answered "Yes.")

1 Balance at beginning of year		6 Distributions: a Cash	
2 Capital contributed during year		b Property	
3 Net income (loss) per books		7 Other decreases (itemize):	
4 Other increases (itemize):		....	
		8 Add lines 6 and 7	
5 Add lines 1 through 4		9 Balance at end of year. Subtract line 8 from line 5	

Form **1065** (2000)

VALUATION SNAPSHOTS REPORT: VALUE OF EARTHRIGHT AS A STAND-ALONE BUSINESS

WHAT IS THE EARTHRIGHT GROUP WORTH?

The Valuation GURU estimates that the fair market total value of The EarthRight Group is $722,027 as of January 1, 2001, based on the business tax return information entered. Please review the bizownerHQ key assumptions to make sure that they apply to this business.

The Valuation GURU builds up the fair market total value of a business by estimating value separately by source, as shown in Figure 6A-1.

FIGURE 6A-1   The EarthRight Group—Total value estimate.

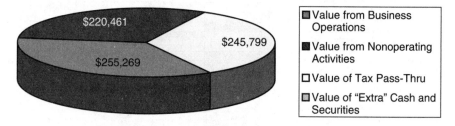

1. *Value from business operations.* Generally, the primary source of value in a business is based on the cash flows from the earnings of the business operations, that is, the products or services the company sells, less the cash needed for investments in operations. The Valuation GURU uses a sophisticated proprietary approach to forecasting the revenues and adjusted earnings of the business operations and then calculates the present value of those future anticipated earnings to determine the value shown in the figure.

2. *Value from nonoperating activities.* Many businesses have other sources of income, such as rental income from buildings or licensing income, that are generated outside the normal business operations. While these cash flows have value, they are not given the same valuation treatment as income from business operations, reflecting that buyers often will not value these nonoperating cash flows as highly as those from operating activities. The Valuation GURU, following standard practices, calculates the present value of the current income flow to the business owner(s).

3. *Value of tax pass-thru.* Companies that are not C Corporations filing an 1120 Tax Form have a tax advantage: Any earnings that the company reports are not taxed at the corporate level and are "passed through" to the owner's individual tax return. The Valuation GURU shows this value separately so that an owner can determine the likely reduction in value that would occur if the business were sold to a C Corporation rather than to a corporation that can take advantage of the tax pass-thru, such as an S Corporation, partnership, or sole proprietorship (all other elements of the deal being equal).

4. *Value of extra cash and securities.* The final source of value that the Valuation GURU analyzes is whether the company has on its balance sheet a level of cash and marketable securities above what is considered necessary to fund working capital. The Valuation GURU draws on financial analysis research across thousands of companies for a revenue-based factor to estimate the working capital needs of a company. If the cash and securities on the balance sheet are greater than this estimate, the Valuation GURU makes an adjustment to the fair market total valuation to reflect this extra difference.

DEFINITIONS

1. *Fair market value.* The price at which the property would change hands between a willing buyer and a willing seller when the former is not under any compulsion to buy and the latter is not under any compulsion to sell, both parties having reasonable knowledge of relevant facts (Internal Revenue Service Revenue Rule 59-60, 1959-1, C.B. 237).

2. *Fair market total value.* The sum of the fair market values of the cash flows from business operations, nonoperating activities, and the tax pass-thru plus the value of the current dollar amount of the extra company cash and marketable securities, if any.

bizownerHQ KEY ASSUMPTIONS

1. *Company growth rate forecasts.* Revenue and cash flows for The EarthRight Group are projected to grow at rates consistent with the baseline or average-performing growth segment of companies in this industry.

2. *No greater use of assets.* The assets of The EarthRight Group, including production equipment, technology, patents, intangible assets, or real estate, used by the company have no greater value as stand-alone assets than they have as profit-generating assets for this business.

GURU Alert

Please review with your accountant or other business professional whether these assumptions are correct for your business before using this valuation as input to decision making.

WHAT IS THE OWNERSHIP EQUITY IN EARTHRIGHT WORTH?

The estimated value of the ownership equity in The EarthRight Group is $716,427. This is the amount the owners would receive if the company were sold today for the fair market total value of $722,027, minus an estimate of the amount necessary to pay off company debts and long-term liabilities, as shown in Figure 6A-2. Ownership equity is equal to the firm's minority interest value, $586,077, plus a control premium of $130,350, the amount necessary to obtain full control of the firm.

FIGURE 6A-2   The EarthRight Group—Total ownership value.

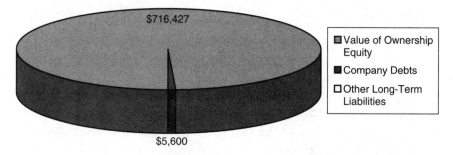

The Valuation GURU separates business value into its ownership components, as shown in Figure 6A-2.

1. *Value of ownership equity.* This is the estimate of the market value of owner equity in the business.
   - *Minority value of equity.* Minority owners own less than 51 percent of the equity of a firm and do not have the right to direct how the firm's assets are used. Minority owners have claims on a firm's earnings after taxes and interest and a right to vote on firm agenda items.
   - *Control premium.* When a business is sold, the buyer or buyers typically purchase full control of the firm. This gives the new

buyer the right to change the way the firm is managed, the types of products and services the firm desires to produce, and the number of employees that are required. In return for the right to make these and other decisions, a buyer will pay a premium above the minority equity value of the firm. This premium is not a constant percentage. It varies with the level of interest rates, the riskiness of the firm, and the long-term growth of the firm's earnings.

2. *Company debts (book value).* This book-value concept from the tax return balance sheet is the closest estimate of the market value of the company's debt that the Valuation GURU can make with the information provided.

Caution: The terms and conditions of any business loans should be reviewed by the company's accountant or by the owner(s) to determine whether there are any prepayment penalties or other charges that would make the market value of the company's debts different from the book value. Any differences found should be included in the preceding estimate to refine the valuation of the company.

WHAT ARE THE VALUATION MULTIPLES FOR THE EARTHRIGHT GROUP?

The Valuation GURU estimates that the value-to-revenue multiple for The EarthRight Group is 1.20 and that the value-to-earnings multiple is 15.74 as of January 1, 2001, as shown in Figure 6A-3.

FIGURE 6A-3   The EarthRight Group—Valuation multiples.

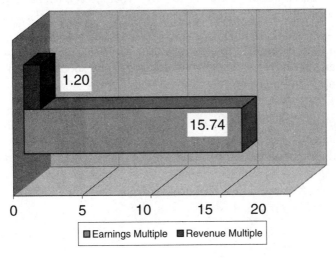

What Business Owners Need to Know about
Industry Valuation Multiples

1. *Beware of the industry valuation multiples.* These industry valuation multiples are used by business brokers and investment bankers to provide owners with a quick and supposedly costless way to find out the value of their companies. For example, a broker may tell a landscaping business owner that landscaping businesses typically sell for one times revenue.

2. *Typical concerns with industry valuation multiples.* Industry valuation estimates generally are based on the company sales experiences of, at worst, a single broker and, at best, a number of brokers. For most industries, there are no consistently reliable data sources where transaction data on the prices and terms of privately held businesses can be found. There are many factors in these sales, such as how quickly the owner needs to sell and the financing of the business before and after the sale, that have a significant impact on the actual price and hence the valuation multiple. Decisions owners make based on the valuation, such as selling a business, should be made on more solid evidence.

   • *Is this an average business for this industry?* An owner applying an industry multiple to her business should wonder whether her business is likely to have a value right at the average or median level. If a business is more productive and efficient than most, then that business should be worth a higher multiple.

   • *Problems with earnings-based multiples.* Valuation multiples based on earnings are particularly troublesome because the ways privately held companies report earnings vary significantly. Industry valuation estimates tend to be based on transactions over a long period of time, yet business valuations change frequently as interest rates change and as perceptions about industry growth opportunities and industry risk change.

   • *Valuation multiples are rarely used for the benefit of the current owner.* Business brokers and investment bankers have a natural incentive to encourage a quick transaction so that they maximize their compensation for the amount of work they do. By encouraging business owners and business buyers to rely on these industry valuation multiples, brokers reinforce the "value" of their role and justify their sizable commission.

How Can bizownerHQ Valuation Multiples Be Used?

1. *Valuation multiples can be useful shorthand tools.* The bizownerHQ company-specific valuation multiples are useful shorthand tools for understanding the current valuation of a company and how that valuation may vary in the short run from changes in revenue or earnings. For example, a business with a company-specific valuation-to-revenue multiple of six can estimate that if the company can increase revenues by $50,000, then the company should be worth approximately $300,000 more. (This assumes that the company is able to generate higher earnings and cash flow after investments at the same rate as before.)

   - *Business owners should know that company-specific valuation multiples will change as interest rates and economic conditions change.* For example, as a general rule, when the Federal Reserve increases interest rates in the U.S. economy by pushing up the federal funds rate, the valuation of all U.S. companies will decline somewhat.

2. *Valuation multiples vary within industry and over time.* There is generally a wide difference in the revenue and earnings growths of companies in the same industry. Companies with higher growth in revenue and earnings typically will have higher multiples than companies in their industry with lower revenue and earnings.

   - *Owners need to be aware of this potential valuation range within their industry.* They should evaluate potential risks and rewards that go along with a more aggressive growth strategy. They also should review whether a more aggressive growth strategy might lead to less control for the owner. For example, borrowing money for expansion from a bank increases the influence of the bank on the company's decisions.

EARTHRIGHT'S VALUE MAXIMIZER REPORT FOR JW SHAH

INCREASING VALUE: GROWTH

The Valuation GURU estimates that the fair market total value of The EarthRight Group could increase from $722,027 to $779,394 if EarthRight can move to a higher revenue and earnings growth path. In this case, EarthRight's earnings multiple will increase from 15.74 to 16.99. The

Valuation GURU has conducted a "what if" analysis for EarthRight using an alternative set of industry segment growth rates. These results, shown in Figure 6A-4, highlight the contribution that the industry growth segment projections make to the estimation of the sources of value for this company. Interest-rate assumptions are the same in the two projections.

FIGURE 6A-4   The EarthRight Group—Increasing value: Growth.

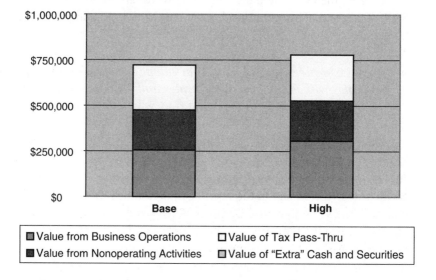

1. *Value payback from growth.* Growing a company's revenue and operating profit margins significantly over time is challenging and risky. However, if the results are successful, there is a powerful value payback, as shown in Figure 6A-4. Typical strategies used by smaller, privately held businesses to achieve higher levels of growth and earnings and thus higher valuations include

    • *Market expansion.* Many successful companies grow at above-average rates for their industry by investing in expanding their markets, the number and quality of sales or distribution channels, and broadening their product or service range.

    • *Acquisition.* Companies should consider potential acquisitions as a means of increasing revenues and increasing margins. Acquiring a competitor provides both increased revenues and the opportunity to improve operating and administrative efficiencies. Some companies expand "vertically" by acquiring their suppliers and/or their distributors. This strategic plan is generally more relevant in manufacturing than in services or retail businesses. We recommend using the Valuation GURU to help in determining the purchase price of a serious acquisition candidate.

- *Productivity improvements.* Investments to reduce cost, improve service, minimize product or service problems, and speed up new product or service innovations are also approaches many companies use to grow at above-average rates for their industry.
- *Repositioning assets.* If market or productivity growth opportunities exist for a business, then the owner(s) should consider liquidating the assets that generate nonoperating income and investing those proceeds into operating business expansion.

Risks and Trade-offs

Owners of privately held businesses and professional practices have a significant advantage over the CEOs of publicly traded companies: These owners do not have to meet outsider expectations for growth in revenues and earnings beyond being able to pay their bills and make any loan payments due. In other words, owners do not get fired for choosing to balance increasing value of the business with, for example, their comfort level with their control over the company or the time they choose to spend with their families.

With these ways to increase value, there are also serious risks involved, including the possible failure of the business, for example, if an acquisition does not work out or the expansion into new markets fails.

- There are important trade-offs owners must consider with these strategies to increase value. Success in pursuing these strategies almost certainly will involve the owner delegating more responsibility to others in the organization.
- Making an acquisition work is often as challenging from the employee perspective of integrating the different company cultures as it can be in the marketplace with customers of the acquired companies.
- Borrowing money to fund productivity-improving investments will give bankers or other financing groups more say in the management of the business if there are problems in meeting the expected benefits from these investments.

GURU Alert

Business owners and owners of professional practices should consult with their management teams, families, accountants, and attorneys before making decisions on whether and how to concentrate efforts on increasing the value of the business above its current trajectory.

INCREASING VALUE: BALANCE SHEET

With lower than average use of debt, EarthRight should consider taking on more debt. The company's capital structure is shown in Figure 6A-5 in comparison with a firm with 50 percent of its capital coming from debt. The loan proceeds can be used either for investment in the company or for diversifying the owner's assets. The Valuation GURU recommends that EarthRight should review its financial structure to see whether changing the level of debt may increase the value of the firm. Debt financing is cheaper than equity financing for an established business. Adding debt will lower the overall cost of capital, which should lead to a higher valuation estimate.

FIGURE 6A-5   The EarthRight Group—Increasing value: Balance sheet.

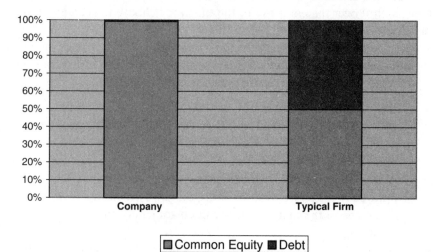

Risks and Trade-offs

A privately held company's balance sheet often holds an unexplored opportunity for increasing the value of the business. Moving the company's debt-to-equity ratio toward the industry average may increase the value of the company by more than the cost of the change. Before making a decision to change the capital structure, an owner should discuss the cost and benefits of this action with an accountant or financial advisor.

1. *Companies with lower than industry average debt.* For established businesses, the cost of borrowing money from banks is generally much lower than the cost of raising money through selling some portion of equity to outside investors. The Valuation GURU's estimate of a company's value uses the weighted average cost of capital for the company to "discount" the expected future free cash flows. When a company with lower than industry average debt increases its debt closer to the industry average, the weighted average cost of capital will generally go down. For example, take a company that is 100 percent equity financed and therefore has no debt. The cost of equity capital is 25 percent. Its weighted average cost of capital today is 25 percent; that is, it has only equity in the cost-of-capital calculation. After discounting the future cash flows of the business by 25 percent, the valuation today is $2.5 million. If this company borrows $200,000 from a bank at 10 percent interest, then the company's new weighted average cost of capital is 23.8 percent [(200,000/2,500,000) × 10% + (2,300,000/2,500,000) × 25 percent]. Discounting the same cash flows by this new weighted average cost of capital produces a new valuation figure of $2,626,050. The owner can use the $200,000 to diversify her investment portfolio or invest it in the business to gain more earnings growth.

2. *Companies with average to above-average debt relative to the industry.* Established businesses that already have debt-to-equity ratios above the average for their industry typically are charged a substantially higher interest rate for their loans by banks than companies in the same industry with average and lower than average debt-to-equity ratios. Banks justify this higher rate of interest based on their experience of a higher risk of a loan default for a company with an above-average debt-to-equity ratio. If a firm with above-average debt for its industry decided to borrow additional funds, its interest rate likely would increase sufficiently to effectively increase its weighted average cost of capital. This, in turn, would reduce the valuation of the company. The Valuation GURU's estimate of a company's value uses the weighted average cost of capital for the company to "discount" the expected future free cash flows. When a company with higher than industry average debt reduces its borrowings and thus lowers its debt-

to-equity ratio to average or below average for the industry, the valuation of the company may increase. This occurs because its weighted average cost of capital declines, reflecting that the firm is less likely to go bankrupt. Lower risk translates into a lower cost of capital, which means higher company value.

INCREASING VALUE: EXIT PLANNING

Preserving the Tax Pass-Thru

A buyer for this company that can take advantage of the tax pass-thru benefits should place a higher value on the company than a C Corporation buyer. Preserving the tax pass-thru benefit is worth $245,799, as shown in Figure 6A-6.

FIGURE 6A-6   The EarthRight Group—Increasing value: Exit planning.

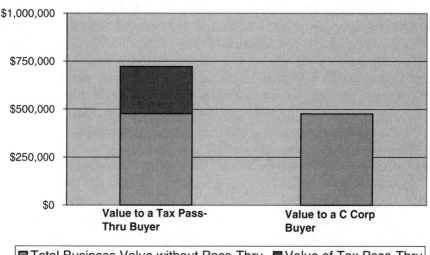

Companies that can take advantage of the tax pass-thru include

- S Corporations (companies that elect Subchapter S status)
- Partnerships
- "Lilacs" (limited liability corporations)
- Sole proprietorships

INCREASING VALUE: FINDING A STRATEGIC BUYER

Finding a strategic buyer could increase the value of EarthRight from $722,027 to $902,534, as shown in Figure 6A-7.

FIGURE 6A-7   The EarthRight Group—Increasing value: Finding a strategic buyer.

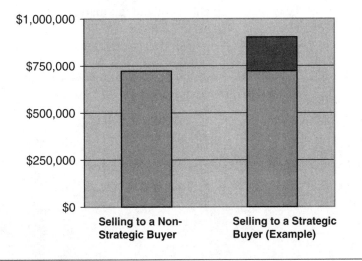

- ■ Strategic Buyer Premium (Example)   □ Total Business Value with Tax Pass-Thru

1. *Definition.* A strategic buyer is one that will evaluate this business from the perspective of either combining it with other similar businesses, that is, a roll-up, or creating an additional synergy value through distribution improvements, market reach, or fixed cost savings.
2. *Potential benefit.* If a strategic buyer can be found, he likely will pay a higher price than a nonstrategic buyer for control of a company. In this example, bizownerHQ has used a hypothetical estimate of 25 percent as an additional premium a strategic buyer might pay.
3. *Potential concern.* A strategic buyer also may be a C Corp that cannot take advantage of the tax pass-thru benefits, so losing the tax pass-thru value can reduce the strategic buyer benefit.

Caution: There will not be a strategic buyer for every business owner looking to transition out of his business. Many businesses will be too small or too personalized to fit within another company. However, bizownerHQ encourages owners to consider seriously a wide range of strategic buyer possibilities as part of the exit strategy planning. The payoff from selling to a strategic buyer can be substantial.

INCREASING VALUE: AVOIDING A COMMISSION ON THE SALE

For EarthRight, the savings from avoiding a typical business broker commission would be approximately $72,000 using 10 percent of the sale price as an estimate of the commission and using the fair market value as an estimate of the sale price, as shown in Figure 6A-8.

FIGURE 6A-8   The EarthRight Group—Increasing value: Avoiding a commission on the sale.

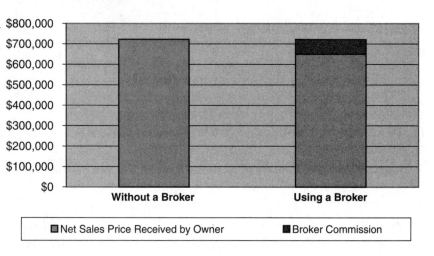

1. *Doing it yourself.* Owners actively involved in exit-strategy planning are less likely to need a business broker or investment banker to assist in a sales transaction. Finding your own strategic or nonstrategic buyer should eliminate the need to use brokers or bankers.
2. *Potential benefit.* Eliminating these participants can save a significant amount of money. Business brokers and investment bankers typically take a sizable percentage of the gross sales price of a business.

Risks and Trade-offs

1. *Assemble an experienced team of professionals.* If you choose to plan and implement an exit strategy without using a business broker or investment banker and their network of professional advisors, you

should retain at least an attorney and an accountant, both of whom are experienced in business sales. You are likely to sell only one business in your lifetime, so you should have the support of professionals who do it regularly.

2. *Time involved in exit-strategy planning may detract from running the business.* Business owners who cannot find time or who do not feel experienced enough to conduct this kind of exit-strategy planning may need to work with a business broker or investment banker. bizownerHQ recommends that these owners use the Valuation GURU reports and the other information at our Web site to "level the playing field" in these discussions. In addition, a business owner should consider

- Asking for unbundled prices for the services offered
- Using an independent attorney and/or accountant to review all broker or banker recommendations
- Negotiating a lower commission for a completed sale if you are not using all the services included in the bundle
- Limiting the length of time of a listing agreement so that you can make a change if not satisfied with the broker's marketing efforts

INCREASING VALUE: SHIFTING FROM TAXES PAID TO VALUE RECEIVED

Shifting to a value-maximizing strategy potentially could increase the value of EarthRight by $787,174, as shown in Figure 6A-9.

FIGURE 6A-9   The EarthRight Group—Increasing value: Shifting from taxes paid to value received.

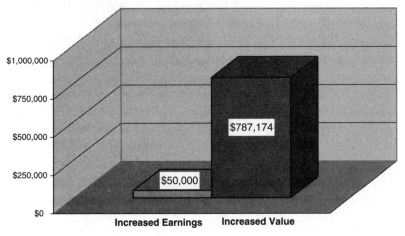

1. *A dollar saved on taxes can cost $$$ in lost value.* Owners of privately held businesses and professional practices typically put a top priority on legal tax minimization in their business decision making. However, as an owner begins to consider her eventual exit from the business, these tax-minimization activities make it difficult to demonstrate to potential buyers the "true" value of the business.

2. *Time for transition.* bizownerHQ recommends that owners change to a value-maximizing focus at least a few years before their desired exit date or change in control.

3. *Potential benefit.* Using the earnings valuation multiple for EarthRight, the potential value benefit from reporting higher earnings is shown in Figure 6A-9. The amount of increased earnings, $50,000, in Figure 6A-9 is a hypothetical example of what a firm of this size may be able to report as higher earnings.

Value-Maximization Advice

1. *Depersonalize.* Owners of privately held businesses tend to be part of every aspect of their businesses. They often have relationships with customers and suppliers. Their personal finances are somewhat intertwined with the business. These situations generally make it difficult for a potential buyer to see the full value of the company. bizownerHQ recommends that owners plan and implement steps to

   - *Delegate.* Build up the management team so that the business can run day to day without substantial involvement from the owner(s).
   - *Disentangle.* Separate owner personal finances from the business.

2. *Streamline.* Owners of privately held businesses generally have a free hand in determining who to hire and how much to pay them. In many small firms, family, relatives, or friends help with the business and are on the payroll. In planning for certain types of exit strategies, owners need to estimate to what extent all these employees are needed for the ongoing operations and how close to market value their salaries are. Moving whichever of these related employees out of the corporation ahead of when a sale or other type of transition is planned makes sense if those employees do not fit into the ongoing operation of the firm.

3. *Document.* Many privately held businesses run at such a fast and rapidly changing pace that the systems for cost accounting and customer management that are prevalent in public companies often are not

implemented or are there but out of date. Having up-to-date customer and cost-management systems is essential to developing a case for strong future revenue and earnings growth.

4. *Balance sheet "housecleaning."* Privately held businesses generally have little impetus to keep their balance sheets as cleaned up as public companies that must file detailed statements with state and federal agencies. Uncollected receivables, disputed payables, and other liabilities are among the items most often found on small business balance sheets long after they should have been removed. bizownerHQ recommends that owners plan and implement steps to

- Conduct a thorough internal review of the company's balance sheet and clean out inactive items.

- Have an independent accountant conduct a thorough audit of the business and implement as much as possible his recommendations.

Caution: Be sure to get an estimate of the cost of this audit prior to authorizing it so that you can judge whether the potential increase to the value of the business is likely to be greater than the cost of the audit.

GURU FYI
A Facilities "Housecleaning" May Increase Value!

Just as real estate agents recommend that home owners spruce up their houses and clean out their closets, basements, and garages before listing the house for sale, most businesses will benefit from a thorough cleaning of the premises and throwing out (or storing off-site) accumulated materials from many years.

VALUE SNAPSHOTS REPORT: VALUE OF EARTHRIGHT AS A NEESI ACQUISITION

WHAT IS THE EARTHRIGHT GROUP WORTH?

The Valuation GURU estimates that the fair market total value of The EarthRight Group is $1,218,505 as of January 1, 2001, based on the business tax return information entered. Please review the bizownerHQ key assumptions to make sure that they apply to this business.

The Valuation GURU builds up the fair market total value of a business by estimating value separately by source, as shown in Figure 6A-10.

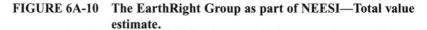

FIGURE 6A-10   The EarthRight Group as part of NEESI—Total value estimate.

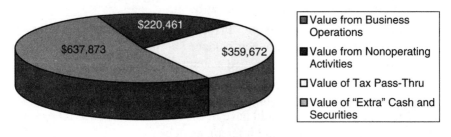

1. *Value from business operations.* Generally, the primary source of value in a business is based on the cash flows from the earnings of the business operations, that is, the products or services the company sells, less the cash needed for investments in operations. The Valuation GURU uses a sophisticated proprietary approach to forecasting the revenues and adjusted earnings of the business operations and then calculates the present value of those future anticipated earnings to determine the value shown in Figure 6A-10.

2. *Value from nonoperating activities.* Many businesses have other sources of income, such as rental income from buildings or licensing income, that are generated outside the normal business operations. While these cash flows have value, they are not given the same valuation treatment as income from business operations, reflecting that buyers often will not value these nonoperating cash flows as highly as those from operating activities. The Valuation GURU, following standard practices, calculates the present value of the current income flow to the business owner(s).

3. *Value of tax pass-thru.* Companies, that are not C Corporations filing an 1120 Tax Form have a tax advantage: Any earnings that the company reports are not taxed at the corporate level and are "passed through" to the owner's individual tax return. The Valuation GURU shows this value separately so that an owner can determine the likely reduction in value that would occur if the business were sold to a C Corporation rather than to a corporation that can take advantage of the tax pass-thru, such as an S Corporation, partnership, or sole proprietorship (all other elements of the deal being equal).

4. *Value of extra cash and securities.* The final source of value that the Valuation GURU analyzes is whether the company has on its balance sheet a level of cash and marketable securities above what is consid-

ered necessary to fund working capital. The Valuation GURU draws on financial analysis research across thousands of companies for a revenue-based factor to estimate the working capital needs of a company. If the cash and securities on the balance sheet are greater than this estimate, the Valuation GURU makes an adjustment to the fair market total valuation to reflect this extra difference.

DEFINITIONS

1. *Fair market value.* The price at which the property would change hands between a willing buyer and a willing seller when the former is not under any compulsion to buy and the latter is not under any compulsion to sell, both parties having reasonable knowledge of relevant facts (Internal Revenue Service Revenue Rule 59-60, 1959-1, C.B. 237).
2. *Fair market total value.* The sum of the fair market values of the cash flows from business operations, nonoperating activities, and the tax pass-thru *plus* the value of the current dollar amount of the extra company cash and marketable securities, if any.

bizownerHQ KEY ASSUMPTIONS

1. *Company growth rate forecasts.* Revenue and cash flows for EarthRight are projected to grow at rates consistent with the baseline or average-performing growth segment of companies in this industry.
2. *No greater use of assets.* The assets of EarthRight, including production equipment, technology, patents, intangible assets, or real estate used by the company, have no greater value as stand-alone assets than they have as profit-generating assets for this business.

GURU Alert

Please review with your accountant or other business professional whether these assumptions are correct for your business before using this valuation as input to decision making.

WHAT IS THE OWNERSHIP EQUITY IN EARTHRIGHT WORTH?

The estimated value of the ownership equity in EarthRight is $1,212,905. This is the amount the owners would receive if the company were sold today for the fair market total value of $1,218,505 minus an estimate of the amount necessary to pay off company debts and long-term liabilities, as shown in Figure 6A-11. Ownership equity is equal to the firm's minority interest value, $992,223, plus a control premium of $220,681, the amount necessary to obtain full control of the firm.

FIGURE 6A-11   The EarthRight Group as part of NEESI—Total ownership value.

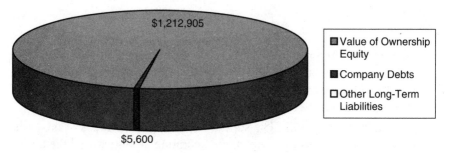

The Valuation GURU separates business value into its ownership components, as shown in Figure 6A-11.

1. *Value of ownership equity.* This is the estimate of the market value of owner equity in the business.

   • *Minority value of equity.* Minority owners own less than 51 percent of the equity of the firm and do not have the right to direct how the firm's assets are used. Minority owners have claims on a firm's earnings after taxes and interest and a right to vote on firm agenda items.

   • *Control premium.* When a business is sold, the buyer or buyers typically purchase full control of the firm. This gives the new buyers the right to change the way the firm is managed, the types of products and services the firm desires to produce, and the number of employees that are required. In return for the right to make these and other decisions, a buyer will pay a premium above the minority equity value of the firm. This premium is not a constant percentage. It varies with the level of interest rates, the riskiness of the firm, and the long-term growth of the firm's earnings.

2. *Company debts (book value).* This book-value concept from the tax return balance sheet is the closest estimate of the market value of the company's debt that the Valuation GURU can make with the information provided.

Caution: The terms and conditions of any business loans should be reviewed by the company's accountant or by the owner(s) to determine whether there are any prepayment penalties or other charges that would make the market value of the company's debts different from the book value. Any differences found should be included in the preceding estimate to refine the valuation of the company.

WHAT ARE THE VALUATION MULTIPLES FOR EARTHRIGHT?

The Valuation GURU estimates that the value-to-revenue multiple for EarthRight is 2.02 and that the value-to-earnings multiple is 12.71 as of January 1, 2001, as shown in Figure 6A-12.

FIGURE 6A-12   The EarthRight Group as part of NEESI—Valuation multiples.

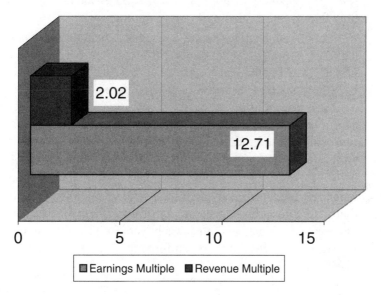

What Business Owners Need to Know about Industry Valuation Multiples

1. *Beware of the industry valuation multiples.* These industry valuation multiples are used by business brokers and investment bankers to provide owners with a quick and supposedly costless way to find out the value of their company. For example, a broker might tell a landscaping business owner that landscaping businesses typically sell for one times revenue.

2. *Typical concerns with industry valuation multiples.* Industry valuation estimates generally are based on the company sales experiences of, at worst, a single broker and, at best, a number of brokers. For most industries, there are no consistently reliable data sources where transaction data on the prices and terms of privately held businesses can be found. There are many factors in these sales, such as how quickly the owner needs to sell and the financing of the business before and after the sale, that have significant impact on the actual price and hence the valuation multiple. Decisions owners make based on the valuation, such as selling a business, should be made upon more solid evidence.

- *Is this an average business for this industry?* An owner applying an industry multiple to her business should wonder whether her business is likely to have a value right at the average or median level. If a business is more productive and efficient than most, then that business should be worth a higher multiple.

- *Problems with earnings-based multiples.* Valuation multiples based on earnings are particularly troublesome because the ways privately held companies report earnings vary significantly. Industry valuation estimates tend to be based on transactions over a long period of time, yet business valuations change frequently as interest rates change and as perceptions about industry growth opportunities and industry risk change.

- *Valuation multiples are rarely used for the benefit of the current owner.* Business brokers and investment bankers have a natural incentive to encourage a quick transaction so that they maximize their compensation for the amount of work they do. By encouraging business owners and business buyers to rely on these industry valuation multiples, brokers reinforce the "value" of their role and justify their sizable commission.

HOW CAN bizownerHQ VALUATION MULTIPLES BE USED?

1. *Valuation multiples can be useful shorthand tools.* The bizownerHQ company-specific valuation multiples are useful shorthand tools for understanding the current valuation of a company and how that valuation might vary in the short run from changes in revenue or earnings. For example, a business with a company-specific valuation-to-revenue multiple of six can estimate that if the company can increase revenues by $50,000, then the company should be worth approximately $300,000 more. (This assumes that the company is able to generate

higher earnings and cash flow after investments at the same rate as before.)

- *Business owners should know that company-specific valuation multiples will change as interest rates and economic conditions change.* For example, as a general rule, when the Federal Reserve increases interest rates in the U.S. economy by pushing up the federal funds rate, the valuation of all U.S. companies will decline somewhat.

2. *Valuation multiples vary within industries and over time.* There is generally a wide difference in the revenue and earnings of growths of companies in the same industry. Companies with higher growths in revenue and earnings typically will have a higher multiple than companies in their industry with lower revenue and earnings.

- *Owners need to be aware of this potential valuation range within their industries.* They should evaluate potential risks and rewards that go along with a more aggressive growth strategy. They also should review whether a more aggressive growth strategy might lead to less control for the owner. For example, borrowing money for expansion from a bank increases the influence of the bank on the company's decisions.

7

VALUATION FOR SELLING OR BUYING A BUSINESS— REDUX

CASE BACKGROUND

O'TOOLE INSURANCE AGENCY—REDUX

In Chapter 3 we presented the case of the unsuccessful sale by Brendan O'Toole of the O'Toole Insurance Agency to Jill Snyder. The process was long and costly (not to mention stressful) to Brendan and Jill, and in the end, the business was not sold. Let us look at how this case might have played out if both Brendan and Jill had better information and better advice.

Brendan—Redux

When Brendan first met with his attorney, Ed Callahan, Ed admitted that he had not yet been a primary advisor in the sale of a business. Ed suggested that they ask Ralph Jordan, a partially retired attorney with direct experience in many business sale transactions, to be their advisor. To Brendan's surprise, Ed even offered to split the cost of having Ralph involved. Ed felt that he should learn more on the topic of valuation because Brendan was the first of many of his clients who would be dealing with this issue in the next 10 years.

Ralph agreed to participate as an advisor to Brendan O'Toole on the sale of his business and to educate Ed on both the strategies involved and the transaction details. Ralph reminded Ed that like all things in law, "the devil is in the details."

Ralph's Recommendations

After reviewing the O'Toole financials, the Continental appraisal, Brendan's initial thoughts about financing the sale to another independent agent, and the building's rent projections, Ralph provided his initial conclusions to Brendan:

1. Be prepared to sell the building separately from the insurance agency. There is only a small chance that one buyer could be found for both. Have a serious real estate appraiser value the building. Ralph felt that the Continental estimate was questionable.
2. Have the CPA restate the business financials to disentangle owner personal spending decisions from the ongoing business. The CPA should be very clear about what gets changed in this review. This is not the place to raise buyer concerns with the authenticity of the O'Toole Insurance Agency books. Once the earnings are right, getting an up-to-date valuation of the ongoing business should not be a problem.
3. Do not plan to finance the deal. A qualified candidate should be able to get a bank loan directly to fund an ongoing business or, if not, then a bank loan with a U.S. Small Business Administration (SBA) guarantee. Given Brendan's age and health, he needs to diversify his assets quickly, most of which are tied up in this business.

The Real Estate Rewards

Brendan and the rest of his team of advisors went to work immediately on Ralph's recommendations. The real estate appraisal indeed was a pleasant surprise. The appraiser found recent comparables of similar buildings in Akron, and he prepared a discounted cash flow approach using projected rents, including an estimate of what O'Toole Insurance Agency should be paying in rent ($150,000 per year). Both methods produced valuation estimates in the range of $2 million to $2.1 million, a significant increase over the prior methods, which estimated that the building was worth $1.4 million.

Restating the Agency Financials

Second, Brendan's CPA, Jim Casey, restated the financial statements of the agency to reflect operating results under an arm's-length management. Specific assumptions included that the agency would pay Brendan a salary similar to that of the managers of insurance agencies in Ohio of similar size and revenue, automobile expense would be restated to a national average, all relatives would be removed from the payroll, and they would eliminate all expenses associated with the Akron Country Club—replacing them with insurance industry reasonable expenses for marketing and entertainment. The restated financial statements would assume that the agency did not own any real estate and paid $150,000 per year in rent. This produced a taxable income number of roughly $260,000. Jim applied the "eight times earnings" value to this new earnings number to come up with a value for the ongoing insurance agency business of $2.08 million, although Ralph cautioned him that any potential buyer would be quick to question the basis of this estimate. Ralph suggested that they use this as a starting point offer. Both would wait to see what potential buyers would say and whether they would be willing to shell out the money for a full-scale valuation.

Financing the Potential Deal

Third, Brendan, Jim, and Ed met with representatives of his current bank and a large regional bank in the Midwest about financing of the deal based on the business. They came away confident that the business would be able to borrow the necessary funds to finance a phased buyout of Brendan's ownership position.

Moving Forward

Having completed this preparation according to Ralph's recommendations, Brendan was ready to meet with Jill Snyder and any other potential buyer that might appear. Brendan met Jill to explore the idea of buying his agency only and outlined a possible phaseout deal with financing provided by a bank. Brendan did not yet quote a number for what he expected to sell the business but said that he was sure that they could reach agreement on a fair price. Jill was excited about this concept and called Brendan the next morning to express her serious interest, after she had talked with her family about the idea. She then asked him what the price would be. Brendan responded with $2.08 million, the estimate that Jim had developed using the eight times restated earnings. Jill asked for the basis of this estimate, and Brendan said that their accountants should meet to go over the restated books and the valuation estimate.

Jill's Concerns

Recalling her first meeting with Janice Smith, Jill was concerned about the sale price number and wanted to know what Brendan meant by "restated financials." Janice understood Jill's concerns and reassured her that she would go over any restatements with a fine-tooth comb, but Janice was not surprised at all that Brendan had to restate. Almost all business owners have their personal finances intertwined to some degree with their businesses.

Janice also mentioned that 2 weeks earlier she had attended a conference on "The Impact of the Internet on Accounting Practices" sponsored by the Ohio Society of CPAs. Janice told Jill that she had learned about a site that valued small businesses. She said that perhaps this Web site might produce a valuation estimate of the O'Toole Insurance Agency that Jill could understand and be comfortable with.

The CPAs Meet

Jim had closely followed Ralph's instructions to document clearly the restatements and the basis for making them. Janice was surprised to find nothing to object to in this effort until she heard Jim's eight times adjusted earnings multiple. Janice knew that valuation multiples often were suspect. She asked Jim about how recent the transactions were that made up the multiple, whether this was a median or an average multiple, and what was the standard deviation of the data. Jim at this point could only fall back on Ralph's suggestion and stated that they would be happy to receive an offer from Jill. All the underlying data were available; now it was really up to Jill to value the business.

This is exactly what Janice and Jill did later that night by going to the bizownerHQ.com Web site. Janice reviewed the data and made a few adjustments to map the restated financial statement data into the Valuation GURU's tax form data-entry module. Soon they had their result. Readers can find the restated O'Toole tax return used as the company financial inputs to the Valuation GURU and the "Valuation Snapshots report" from bizownerHQ in Appendix 7A.

JILL'S COUNTEROFFER

The Valuation GURU valued the O'Toole Insurance Agency at $1,788,136. This result, while "in the ballpark" of $2.08 million, was almost $300,000 less and got Jill's attention. Over the next week, Jill and her family advisors met with Janice and went over the tax return and valuation report. Janice reported that the adjustments to the tax return to estimate the agency's financial results without the building were reasonable. She also explained the valuation methodology from bizownerHQ.com, which used a discounted free cash flow approach. Jill and her family were convinced that the valuation estimate was reasonable, certainly a number that could serve as the basis for further negotiations.

After this careful deliberation, Jill met with Brendan at his office and made an offer to buy the O'Toole Insurance Agency for $1.8 million, contingent on getting bank financing for the deal. She provided him with a copy of the bizownerHQ reports as the rationale for her proposal.

Brendan met with his advisors to review the valuation report and the revised tax return. Ralph noted that this valuation was based on their own financial restatements. Unless they came up with something in the Valuation GURU calculations or valuation factors that could be questioned, the valuation looked like the real deal. Jim's multiple-based valuation did not hold up to this. And given what Brendan should get for the building, he was still way ahead of what those other valuations claimed his business was worth! This ended the discussion of the price, and they turned to laying out what paperwork would be needed to complete the sale.

On March 5, 2001, Brendan O'Toole and Jill Snyder agreed on the sale of the O'Toole Insurance Agency for $1.8 million without the building. Brendan paid attorney fees ($2800) and accountant fees ($2200) for a total of $5000. Jill paid attorney fees ($1000) and accountant fees ($2100), as well as the $600 paid to bizownerHQ for the valuation report, for a total of $3700. The two parties in this alternative ending spent $8700 in fees for a successful transaction, in contrast to the $40,880 in fees paid for an unsuccessful transaction in the original ending. The process in this alternative ending also was much quicker and a lot less stressful.

The transfer would take place over the 3-year period that they had discussed earlier. Jill Snyder was thrilled and relished her new role as a part, soon to be majority, owner and member of the board of directors of the O'Toole Insurance Agency.

LESSONS LEARNED

This example illustrates how better information, advice, and communication can simplify the business transition process, reduce the transactions costs, and improve the outcome for the seller and buyer. However, we must emphasize that this example is still the exception. The O'Toole outcome in Chapter 3 is the norm. It is estimated that in recent years only 1 in 5 businesses listed for sale has sold.[1] Improving the effectiveness and efficiency of the business transition process should be an important objective in light of the coming business transition tidal wave.

There are many business opportunities for business and financial services providers to profit from streamlining the existing business transition and business life events (BLEs) management processes. Take buy-sell agreements funded by insurance, for example, which virtually every expert

---

[1]Tom West, *2002 Business Reference Guide*, 12th ed. Concord, MA: Business Brokerage Press, 2002.

in this area agrees should be in place and up-to-date for an established, multiple-owner company, such as Barton and Schuler profiled in Chapter 4. It likely could take months and cost thousands of dollars for Barton and Schuler to put in place their buy-sell agreement, separate from the cost of the insurance. The high cost and long time frame are prime reasons why more multiple-owner businesses do not have these in place. The two prime cost and time culprits in this area are business valuations and overly complex legal agreements. Typically, the firm needs a current business valuation to base the amounts of insurance coverage needed to buy each co-owner's share. As we have shown, there are ways to make the business valuation process more timely and cost-effective.

On the legal side of the buy-sell agreement process, there are several different ways to structure these agreements for a company. From our market research with owners, we have found that the typical buy-sell legal agreement is well over 50 pages long and is written in language virtually incomprehensible to owners. It takes significant legal time to put these together and then more time to explain them to the owners, both exercises which are prime contributors to the high process cost. This appears to be an area where standardization, expert systems, and the use of consumer-friendly language could achieve significant improvements in time, cost, and customer satisfaction.

For the specific lessons learned in this chapter, we contrast some of the lessons learned in the unsuccessful O'Toole outcome in Chapter 3.

Business owners should know that

1. *Selling a privately held business does not have to be an expensive and time-consuming activity.* Selling a business almost always will be a challenge, but the better prepared owners are, the more likely they will be successful. One way is to be on the watch for people in the same or related industries who want to own their own business. Another way is to start the disentangling process of the owner's personal financials from the business financials at least 3 years prior to selling. Having a clean set of financials lowers the cost for buyers to evaluate a firm.

2. *Having advisors who have experience in business sales transactions is likely to be critical to a successful outcome.* When an owner encounters a BLE, such as selling the business, he often does not know what he does not know. In Brendan's case, Ralph's suggestion of getting a bank to provide financing for the deal is clearly the right way to go, given Brendan's age and health situation. In addition to searching for accountants and lawyers with the right experience, owners should consider networking with retired owners in their industries.

They have at least gone through it once, and they also may know of advisors with the right kind of experience.

3. ***Determining the value of a privately held business does not have to be a complex activity.*** Business owners armed with the knowledge from this book should know what questions to ask about the earnings- or revenue-multiples approach (ERMA) valuation multiples that they are given for their industry to determine whether these multiples can be used with confidence. They also know the basics of discounted cash flow valuation, where they need to focus on the three core factors, a baseline level of earnings, an earnings projection, and a discount rate that reflects the risk attributes of the business. If they cannot get straight answers from a valuation person on the factors used to calculate valuation results, they should take their business elsewhere.

4. ***Determining the value of a privately held business does not have to be an expensive and time-consuming process.*** There are a growing number of alternatives to traditional valuations. There are valuation software packages that perform all the necessary calculations once the user provides all the external inputs. There are valuation firms offering more standardized approaches to valuation, although some use only the ERMA method, where publicly traded companies provide the company comparables. For many small businesses, the public company counterparts in their industry are dramatically different types of firms and do not represent meaningful comparables for valuation purposes. Finally, there is bizownerHQ, where we have reengineered traditional valuation processes to make reliable valuations affordable.

MORE ON VALUATION METHODS

WHICH IS THE BEST?
In estimating the fair market value of a business, bizownerHQ.com uses the discounted free cash flow approach (DFCFA) as its primary methodology for two reasons. First, we believe that of the three basic valuation methods outlined earlier, the DFCFA is conceptually stronger than the ERMA or the asset-based approach (ABA) in that it does not require the arbitrary assumptions and estimates common to these methods. The DFCFA is a conceptually stronger method because it is based on a logical hypothesis—the value of a financial asset is the present value of the future cash flows to be gained from owning that asset.

The second reason for our preference for the DFCFA over the ERMA or the ABA is empirical. The question of valuation methodology has been the subject of considerable academic research. The question researchers address is simply which valuation methodology provides the most accurate estimates of actual value. One important academic research paper by Steven N. Kaplan of the University of Chicago and Richard S. Ruback of Harvard Business School states the following:

> Investment bankers and dealmakers typically price acquisitions, leveraged buyouts, IPOs, and other transactions using multiples of current earnings or cash flow for comparable companies or transactions. For example, if a company for sale has $100 million of current earnings before interest, tax, and depreciation, and the standard multiple for similar companies is five times EBITDA, and then the price of the company would be estimated at $500 million. . . . As we report in this article, our study provides evidence of a strong relationship between market values of transactions in our sample and the discounted value of their cash flow forecasts. . . . Although some of the "comparable" or "multiple" methods performed as well on an average basis, the discounted cash flow methods were more reliable in the sense that the discounted cash flow estimates were clustered more tightly around the actual values.[2]

These findings suggest that simply multiplying a firm's current revenue or earnings by what one believes is a "comparable revenue and/or earnings transaction multiple" to obtain an estimate of the firm's value is not prudent and in the end is not supported by the available academic research. One also must keep in mind that Kaplan and Ruback's study used data on public company transactions. Valuation of private firms using private company comparable multiples is likely to be even more error-prone than the company sample used by Kaplan and Ruback. The reasons are

1. *Private companies that are directly comparable to the private company to be valued are often very difficult, if not impossible, to find.* Hence one is often forced to use what we call proxy comparables. Using these proxy multiples assumes that the private firm to be valued has the same cash flow growth potential and the ratio of debt to equity as the proxy firm. Also, what is even more unlikely, the firm to be valued has the cash flow and/or the capital structure of the median of a set of proxy firms. Any real similarity between the firm to be valued and the proxy firm would occur only coincidentally. Thus, for example, multiplying the median proxy revenue or EBITDA (earnings before interest,

---

[2]Steven N. Kaplan and Richard Ruback, "The Market Pricing of Cash Flow Forecasts: Discounted Cash Flow vs. the Method of Comparables," *Journal of Applied Corporate Finance* (Winter):45, 1996.

tax, depreciation, and amortization) multiple by a firm's last-year revenue and/or EBITDA values, respectively, will result in a value that may be too low or too high and in any case is not correct.

2. *Suitable comparable transactions may not be available at the time the private firm in question is being valued.* Applying the median multiple for transactions that happened as recently as 3 months ago may not be appropriate. For example, if discount rates at the valuation date are different from those that existed when the comparable transactions took place, the multiples also will be different. If the current discount rate was 1 percent lower today than when the median for the comparable transactions took place, applying the multiples for the comparable transactions would result in a value that is far lower than it should be.

3. *Often the appraiser is forced to use the guideline company method.* Again, the multiples used are for proxy public companies. These guideline firms are typically in the same aggregate industry sector, usually two- or perhaps three-digit Standard Industrial Classification (SIC). Even if more detailed industry classifications are available, the guideline firms are placed in these classifications by their primary SIC code. This would not be a problem except for the fact that most public companies are in multiple SIC codes, and the primary one, which is determined by the firm's SIC that makes up the lion's share of its revenue, may not be the SIC that accounts for the lion's share of the firm's cash flow.

A good example of this disconnect is the case of IBM. It is classified as a computer equipment company and is in the computer equipment SIC. However, an increasing bulk of its revenues and cash flow comes from consulting and lease financing. Should IBM be considered a computer manufacturing firm or a consulting firm? Hence, applying IBM's multiple to a pure computer equipment firm would result in a valuation that does not fully reflect the economics and industry dynamics of the computer equipment industry. This problem is worsened when an analyst considers using the median multiple from standard industry groupings, such as those used by Standard & Poor's or *Fortune* magazine. Using a proxy median multiple based on an industry classification is a problem because these industry groupings reflect many diverse industry subsegments. Thus, while guideline company multiples have the advantage of always being up to date, analysts should consider carefully whether the degree of industry diversity within the grouping makes the multiple unreliable for valuation.

Appendix 7A

O'TOOLE INSURANCE AGENCY: (RESTATED) VALUATION INPUTS AND OUTPUTS

Partial 2000 Tax Return
Valuation Snapshots Report

O'Toole Insurance Agency Tax Return, page 1.

Form **1120S**	**U.S. Income Tax Return for an S Corporation**	OMB No. 1545-0130
Department of the Treasury Internal Revenue Service	► Do not file this form unless the corporation has timely filed Form 2553 to elect to be an S corporation. ► See separate instructions.	**20**00

For calendar year 2000, or tax year beginning _____ , 2000, and ending _____ , 20 ____

A Effective date of election as an S corporation	Use IRS label. Other-wise, print or type.	Name **O Toole Insurance Agency**		C Employer identification number
B Business code no. (see pages 29–31) **524210**		Number, street, and room or suite no. (If a P.O. box, see page 11 of the instructions.)		D Date incorporated
		City or town, state, and ZIP code **Akron, OH**		E Total assets (see page 11) $

F Check applicable boxes: (1) ☐ Initial return (2) ☐ Final return (3) ☐ Change in address (4) ☐ Amended return

G Enter number of shareholders in the corporation at end of the tax year . . . . ►

Caution: *Include only trade or business income and expenses on lines 1a through 21. See page 11 of the instructions for more information.*

Income

1a	Gross receipts or sales	1,102,472 00	b Less returns and allowances	c Bal ► **1c**	1,102,472	00
2	Cost of goods sold (Schedule A, line 8)	**2**	433,991	00
3	Gross profit. Subtract line 2 from line 1c	**3**	668,481	00
4	Net gain (loss) from Form 4797, Part II, line 18 (attach Form 4797)	**4**		
5	Other income (loss) (attach schedule)	**5**		
6	**Total income (loss).** Combine lines 3 through 5 . . . . ►	**6**	668,481	00

Deductions (see page 12 of the instructions for limitations)

7	Compensation of officers	**7**	100,000	00
8	Salaries and wages (less employment credits)	**8**	73,456	00
9	Repairs and maintenance	**9**	3,267	00
10	Bad debts	**10**	2,345	00
11	Rents	**11**	150,000	00
12	Taxes and licenses	**12**	3,412	00
13	Interest	**13**	1,981	00
14a	Depreciation (if required, attach Form 4562)	**14a**		
b	Depreciation claimed on Schedule A and elsewhere on return .	**14b**		
c	Subtract line 14b from line 14a	**14c**		
15	Depletion (**Do not deduct oil and gas depletion.**)	**15**		
16	Advertising	**16**	3,654	00
17	Pension, profit-sharing, etc., plans	**17**	21,987	00
18	Employee benefit programs	**18**	21,786	00
19	Other deductions (attach schedule)	**19**	21,897	00
20	**Total deductions.** Add the amounts shown in the far right column for lines 7 through 19 . ►	**20**	403,785	00
21	Ordinary income (loss) from trade or business activities. Subtract line 20 from line 6	**21**	264,696	00

Tax and Payments

22	Tax: a Excess net passive income tax (attach schedule) . . .	**22a**		
b	Tax from Schedule D (Form 1120S)	**22b**		
c	Add lines 22a and 22b (see page 15 of the instructions for additional taxes)	**22c**	
23	Payments: a 2000 estimated tax payments and amount applied from 1999 return	**23a**		
b	Tax deposited with Form 7004	**23b**		
c	Credit for Federal tax paid on fuels (attach Form 4136)	**23c**		
d	Add lines 23a through 23c	**23d**	
24	Estimated tax penalty. Check if Form 2220 is attached . . . . . . ► ☐	**24**	
25	**Tax due.** If the total of lines 22c and 24 is larger than line 23d, enter amount owed. See page 4 of the instructions for depository method of payment . . . . ►	**25**	
26	**Overpayment.** If line 23d is larger than the total of lines 22c and 24, enter amount overpaid ►	**26**	
27	Enter amount of line 26 you want: Credited to 2001 estimated tax ►	Refunded ►	**27**	

Sign Here

Under penalties of perjury, I declare that I have examined this return, including accompanying schedules and statements, and to the best of my knowledge and belief, it is true, correct, and complete. Declaration of preparer (other than taxpayer) is based on all information of which preparer has any knowledge.

► _____ | _____ ► _____
Signature of officer | Date | Title

Paid Preparer's Use Only

Preparer's signature ►	Date	Check if self-employed ☐	Preparer's SSN or PTIN
Firm's name (or yours if self-employed), address, and ZIP code ►		EIN	
		Phone no. ( )	

For Paperwork Reduction Act Notice, see the separate instructions. Cat. No. 11510H Form **1120S** (2000)

O'Toole Insurance Agency Tax Return, page 4.

Form 1120S (2000)   Page **4**

Schedule L   Balance Sheets per Books

		Beginning of tax year		End of tax year	
	Assets	(a)	(b)	(c)	(d)
1	Cash		19,734		21,897
2a	Trade notes and accounts receivable . .	21,897		21,879	
b	Less allowance for bad debts	3,000	18,897	3,100	18,776
3	Inventories		2,765		2,854
4	U.S. Government obligations				
5	Tax-exempt securities				
6	Other current assets (attach schedule) .				
7	Loans to shareholders				
8	Mortgage and real estate loans . . .				
9	Other investments (attach schedule) . .				
10a	Buildings and other depreciable assets .	37,654		39,876	
b	Less accumulated depreciation . . .	12,098	25,556	12,897	26,979
11a	Depletable assets				
b	Less accumulated depletion.				
12	Land (net of any amortization)				
13a	Intangible assets (amortizable only) . .				
b	Less accumulated amortization. . . .				
14	Other assets (attach schedule)		48,143		49,765
15	Total assets		115,095		120,271
	Liabilities and Shareholders' Equity				
16	Accounts payable		34,432		35,129
17	Mortgages, notes, bonds payable in less than 1 year				
18	Other current liabilities (attach schedule).		21,987		22,345
19	Loans from shareholders.				
20	Mortgages, notes, bonds payable in 1 year or more				
21	Other liabilities (attach schedule) . . .		2,676		2,987
22	Capital stock		30,000		30,000
23	Additional paid-in capital.				
24	Retained earnings		26,543		29,810
25	Adjustments to shareholders' equity (attach schedule)				
26	Less cost of treasury stock		( )		( )
27	Total liabilities and shareholders' equity . .		115,638		120,271

Schedule M-1   Reconciliation of Income (Loss) per Books With Income (Loss) per Return (You are not required to complete this schedule if the total assets on line 15, column (d), of Schedule L are less than $25,000.)

1	Net income (loss) per books.		5	Income recorded on books this year not included on Schedule K, lines 1 through 6 (itemize):	
2	Income included on Schedule K, lines 1 through 6, not recorded on books this year (itemize):		a	Tax-exempt interest $	
	....			....	
3	Expenses recorded on books this year not included on Schedule K, lines 1 through 11a, 15f, and 16b (itemize):		6	Deductions included on Schedule K, lines 1 through 11a, 15f, and 16b, not charged against book income this year (itemize):	
a	Depreciation $		a	Depreciation $	
b	Travel and entertainment $			....	
	....		7	Add lines 5 and 6.	
4	Add lines 1 through 3		8	Income (loss) (Schedule K, line 23). Line 4 less line 7	

Schedule M-2   Analysis of Accumulated Adjustments Account, Other Adjustments Account, and Shareholders' Undistributed Taxable Income Previously Taxed (see page 27 of the instructions)

		(a) Accumulated adjustments account	(b) Other adjustments account	(c) Shareholders' undistributed taxable income previously taxed
1	Balance at beginning of tax year . . .			
2	Ordinary income from page 1, line 21. .			
3	Other additions			
4	Loss from page 1, line 21	( )		
5	Other reductions	( )	( )	
6	Combine lines 1 through 5			
7	Distributions other than dividend distributions.			
8	Balance at end of tax year. Subtract line 7 from line 6			

Form **1120S** (2000)

VALUATION SNAPSHOTS REPORT

WHAT IS THE O'TOOLE INSURANCE AGENCY WORTH?

The Valuation GURU estimates that the fair market total value of O'Toole
Insurance Agency is $1,788,136 as of January 1, 2001, based on the busi-
ness tax return information entered. Please review the bizownerHQ key
assumptions to make sure that they apply to this business.

The Valuation GURU builds up the fair market total value of a business
by estimating value separately by source, as shown in Figure 7A-1.

FIGURE 7A-1   O'Toole Insurance Agency—Total value estimate.

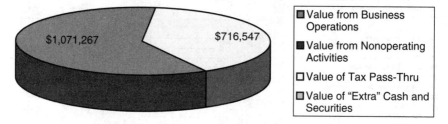

1. *Value from business operations.* Generally, the primary source of
   value in a business is based on the cash flows from the earnings of the
   business operations, that is, the products or services the company
   sells, less the cash needed for investments in operations. The
   Valuation GURU uses a sophisticated proprietary approach to forecasting the revenues and adjusted earnings of the business operations
   and then calculates the present value of those future anticipated earnings to determine the value shown in Figure 7A-1.

2. *Value from nonoperating activities.* Many businesses have other
   sources of income, such as rental income from buildings or licensing
   income, that are generated outside the normal business operations.
   While these cash flows have value, they are not given the same valuation treatment as income from business operations, reflecting that
   buyers often will not value these nonoperating cash flows as highly as
   those from operating activities. The Valuation GURU, following standard practices, calculates the present value of the current income flow
   to the business owner(s).

3. *Value of tax pass-thru.* Companies that are not C Corporations filing
   an 1120 Tax Form have a tax advantage: Any earnings that the com-

pany reports are not taxed at the corporate level and are "passed through" to the owner's individual tax return. The Valuation GURU shows this value separately so that an owner can determine the likely reduction in value that would occur if the business were sold to a C Corporation rather than to a corporation that can take advantage of the tax pass-thru, such as an S Corporation, partnership, or sole proprietorship (all other elements of the deal being equal).

4. *Value of extra cash & securities.* The final source of value that the Valuation GURU analyzes is whether the company has on its balance sheet a level of cash and marketable securities above what is considered necessary to fund working capital. The Valuation GURU draws on financial analysis research across thousands of companies for a revenue-based factor to estimate the working capital needs of a company. If the cash and securities on the balance sheet are greater than this estimate, the Valuation GURU makes an adjustment to the fair market total valuation to reflect this extra difference.

DEFINITIONS

1. *Fair market value.* The price at which the property would change hands between a willing buyer and a willing seller when the former is not under any compulsion to buy and the latter is not under any compulsion to sell, both parties having reasonable knowledge of relevant facts (Internal Revenue Service Revenue Rule 59-60, 1959-1, C.B. 237).

2. *Fair market total value.* The sum of the fair market values of the cash flows from business operations, nonoperating activities, and the tax pass-thru *plus* the value of the current dollar amount of the extra company cash and marketable securities, if any.

bizownerHQ KEY ASSUMPTIONS

1. *Company growth rate forecasts.* Revenue and cash flows for the O'Toole Insurance Agency are projected to grow at rates consistent with the baseline or average-performing growth segment of companies in this industry.

2. *No greater use of assets.* The assets of the O'Toole Insurance Agency, including production equipment, technology, patents, intangible assets, or real estate used by the company, have no greater value as stand-alone assets than they have as profit-generating assets for this business.

GURU Alert

Please review with your accountant or other business professional whether these assumptions are correct for your business before using this valuation as input to decision making.

WHAT IS THE OWNERSHIP EQUITY IN THE O'TOOLE INSURANCE AGENCY WORTH?

The estimated value of the ownership equity in the O'Toole Insurance Agency is $1,785,149. This value is equal to the firm's minority interest value, $1,406,404, plus an additional sum of $378,744 reflecting the fact that the buyer is willing to pay an additional amount to obtain full control of the firm. This increment is known as the *control premium*. This is the amount the owners would receive if the company were sold today for the fair market total value of $1,788,136 minus an estimate of the amount necessary to pay off company debts and long-term liabilities, as shown in Figure 7A-2.

FIGURE 7A-2   O'Toole Insurance Agency—Total ownership value.

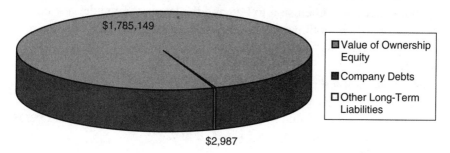

The Valuation GURU separates business value into its ownership components, as shown in Figure 7A-2.

1. *Value of ownership equity.* This is the estimate of the market value of owner equity in the business.
   - *Minority value of equity.* Minority owners own less than 51 percent of the equity of a firm and do not have the right to direct how the firm's assets are used. Minority owners have claims on a firm's earnings after taxes and interest and a right to vote on firm agenda items.

- *Control premium.* When a business is sold, the buyer or buyers typically purchase full control of the firm. This gives the new buyers the right to change the way the firm is managed, the types of products and services the firm desires to produce, and the number of employees that are required. In return for the right to make these and other decisions, a buyer will pay a premium above the minority equity value of the firm. This premium is not a constant percentage. It varies with the level of interest rates, the riskiness of the firm, and the long-term growth of the firm's earnings.

2. *Company debts (book value).* This book-value concept from the tax return balance sheet is the closest estimate of the market value of the company's debt that the Valuation GURU can make with the information provided.

Caution: The terms and conditions of any business loans should be reviewed by the company's accountant or by the owner(s) to determine whether there are any prepayment penalties or other charges that would make the market value of the company's debts different from the book value. Any differences found should be included in the preceding estimate to refine the valuation of the company.

WHAT ARE THE VALUATION MULTIPLES FOR THE O'TOOLE INSURANCE AGENCY?

The Valuation GURU estimates that the value-to-revenue multiple for the O'Toole Insurance Agency is 1.62 and that the value-to-earnings multiple is 6.76 as of January 1, 2001, as shown in Figure 7A-3.

What Business Owners Need to Know about Industry Valuation Multiples

1. *Beware of the industry valuation multiples.* These industry valuation multiples are used by business brokers and investment bankers to provide owners with a quick and supposedly costless way to find out the value of their companies. For example, a broker might tell a landscaping business owner that landscaping businesses typically sell for one times revenue.

2. *Typical concerns with industry valuation multiples.* Industry valuation estimates generally are based on the company sales experiences of, at worst, a single broker and, at best, a number of brokers. For most industries, there are no consistently reliable data sources where transaction data on the prices and terms of privately held businesses can be found. There are many factors in these sales, such as how quickly the

FIGURE 7A-3   O'Toole Insurance Agency—Valuation multiples.

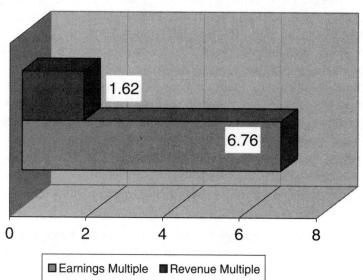

owner needs to sell and the financing of the business before and after the sale, that have significant impact on the actual price and hence the valuation multiple. Decisions owners make based on the valuation, such as selling a business, should be made on more solid evidence.

- *Is this an average business for this industry?* An owner applying an industry multiple to his business should wonder whether his business is likely to have a value right at the average or median level. If a business is more productive and efficient than most, then that business should be worth a higher multiple.

- *Problems with earnings-based multiples.* Valuation multiples based on earnings are particularly troublesome because the ways privately held companies report earnings vary significantly. Industry valuation estimates tend to be based on transactions over a long period of time, yet business valuations change frequently as interest rates change and as perceptions about industry growth opportunities and industry risk change.

- *Valuation multiples are rarely used for the benefit of the current owner.* Business brokers and investment bankers have a natural incentive to encourage a quick transaction so that they maximize their compensation for the amount of work they do. By encouraging business owners and business buyers to rely on these industry valuation multiples, brokers reinforce the "value" of their role and justify their sizable commission.

HOW CAN bizownerHQ VALUATION MULTIPLES BE USED?

1. *Valuation multiples can be useful shorthand tools.* The bizownerHQ company-specific valuation multiples are useful shorthand tools for understanding the current valuation of a company and how that valuation might vary in the short run from changes in revenue or earnings. For example, a business with a company-specific valuation-to-revenue multiple of six can estimate that if the company can increase revenues by $50,000, then the company should be worth approximately $300,000 more. (This assumes that the company is able to generate higher earnings and cash flow after investments at the same rate as before.)

   - **Business owners should know that company-specific valuation multiples will change as interest rates and economic conditions change.** For example, as a general rule, when the Federal Reserve increases interest rates in the U.S. economy by pushing up the federal funds rate, the valuation of all U.S. companies will decline somewhat.

2. *Valuation multiples vary within industries and over time.* There is generally a wide difference in the revenue and earnings of growths of companies in the same industry. Companies with higher growth in revenue and earnings typically will have a higher multiple than companies in their industry with lower revenue and earnings.

   - *Owners need to be aware of this potential valuation range within their industry.* They should evaluate potential risks and rewards that go along with a more aggressive growth strategy. They also should review whether a more aggressive growth strategy might lead to less control for the owner. For example, borrowing money for expansion from a bank increases the influence of the bank on the company's decisions.

C H A P T E R

MAXIMIZING THE VALUE OF A BUSINESS

CHALLENGES FACING PRIVATE BUSINESS OWNERS

As we noted at the beginning of this book, there will be a private business transition tidal wave rolling through the U.S. economy over the next 10 years. The people starting businesses in the 1970s and 1980s who launched the entrepreneurial boom have begun to retire, and over the next decade, an unprecedented number of businesses will go through some form of ownership transition.

Our research shows that most of these owners have done little to prepare for their transition as yet. So far, most have avoided, where possible, managing the life events of their business. Most of these businesses are run more from a tax-minimization perspective than a value-maximizing strategy. The support structure for owners managing their business life events (BLEs) is inefficient and expensive, which does not bode well for how this support structure will handle a many-times increase in volume of businesses to be sold or otherwise transitioned.

As we have shown through the case studies of this book, planning ahead for business transition and being prepared for a wide range of challenges will pay enormous dividends to owners. In this chapter we will focus on helping owners to maximize the value in their businesses, including both the whys and the hows. The hows include

- How can I increase firm value by moving to a higher profit growth path?
- How can I increase the value of my firm through refinancing?
- How can I increase the diversification of my net worth when the value of my business is by far the largest asset?
- How do I determine the price I should pay for a target acquisition and ensure that I am maximizing the value of the newly combined entity?

PRIVATE BUSINESSES SHOULD JOIN THE "VALUE REVOLUTION"

The commonly stated goal of a publicly traded business is the maximization of stockholder wealth, that is, maximization of the value of the firm. The acceptance of this objective by boards of directors and managers of publicly traded businesses gives their firms a tangible goal against which operating decisions can be evaluated. For example, will investment spending on a new factory lead to an increase in the value of the firm and, therefore, the wealth of its stockholders? Or will it lead to overcapacity, a decline in prices, and reduced earnings? Boards of directors are increasingly attentive to holding management accountable for the results of their plans. The turnover rates for CEOs of public firms have risen as a result.

For private businesses, where ownership and management generally are one and the same, we recommend that value maximization be adopted as a core management strategy but that its implementation must be adapted to fit the different ownership circumstances and ownership transition plans. Owners will not and should not "fire themselves" if they do not meet their value-maximizing targets. However, they should recognize the strong correlation between value-maximizing activities and recommended actions for owners planning to sell or otherwise transition out of their businesses.

Incorporating value maximization into the small, private business sector will help both business owners, who will be able to sell their businesses for more money, and the overall economy as private businesses become even more efficient.

Adapting the Time Dimension of Value Maximization

For most private businesses, the most relevant time dimension for measuring changes in value is annual. The combination of audited annual financial statements and tax returns provides the accuracy and detail in the information necessary for valuing a business.

Adapting the Uses of Value Maximization

Boards of directors of public companies use the value yardstick to evaluate CEOs and their management teams. Similarly, owners of private businesses can use value-maximization measurement to help determine how well their key managers are suited to replace the current owner(s).

By setting a value-maximizing goal for management teams rather than a tax-minimization goal, the owner or owners are providing their managers with a new and different challenge. This alternative goal will provide feedback on how well the managers as a group and individually react to significant change. The owner or owners also have to decide how much they will step back to let their managers make the decisions. This has the potential side benefit of making the business less dependent on an owner or owners who will be leaving at some point in the future.

Owners who will be selling their firms outright and do not have a management team also benefit from using a value-maximizing strategy, beyond the obvious benefit of a higher price when they sell if they are successful. Often owners of what are typically smaller, established businesses, such as retail shops, restaurants, and professional practices, do not get much feedback on how well they are doing in running their business strategically. The first step in this process is to set value-maximizing goals and develop realistic plans for achieving those goals. The second step is to track how well the business is performing against those goals on an annual basis. In this way, owners can get concrete, actionable feedback on their businesses.

MEASURING VALUE

Better, faster, and cheaper ways to value a private business will be essential to the adoption and adaptation of value maximization to private businesses. Business owners need to know both the fair market value of their businesses and the potential for a strategic buyer premium. The Valuation GURU is making it easier and cost-effective for private businesses to obtain this information on a regular basis, and over time, other expert-system valuation capabilities will emerge that will further expand the market and meet the rising tidal wave of business transitions that will occur over the next decade. As this sector grows, valuing a private business will become a standard rather than an extraordinary event.

There will always be a role for the local valuation consultant, who can provide specialized, in-depth coverage of special circumstances and testimony in legal and arbitration settings. There is also a role for business consultants, who can help owners implement value-maximizing strategies. However, both valuation and business consultants will need to use these new valuation expert systems and databases to deliver their services in a more timely and cost-effective manner.

INCREASING VALUE THROUGH EARNINGS GROWTH

Owners intuitively understand that if a firm can raise its profit level and sustain this higher profit into the future, then the firm will be more valuable to a prospective buyer. While this is generally true, greater earnings growth will only result in greater business value if this greater growth does not subject the firm to proportionately greater risk (remember Figures 2-3 and 2-4, which showed that moderately increasing earnings in an environment of higher risk can lead to lower rather than higher value). For most private businesses, however, raising the earnings growth bar does not mean taking greater risk but merely executing current operations more effectively. A business owner can create value through

1. Managing the internal activities of the firm more efficiently
2. Changing the firm's capital structure to lower the cost of capital
3. Acquiring other firms

MANAGING THE FIRM MORE EFFICIENTLY

This means reducing the costs of operating a business. The easiest way to do this is by reducing working capital requirements. *Working capital* is money needed to pay bills as they come due. It covers the gap between when the business collects from its customers and when it has to pay its employees and suppliers. For most businesses, the following are the primary ways to reduce the company's need for working capital:

1. *Reduce inventory levels.* To lower these costs, the owner must try to better match production levels to customer demand. The portion of goods produced but not sold goes into inventory. Since these goods were not sold, the firm does not receive revenue for them but must pay employees and others supplying the time and materials to produce them. In this situation, the owner is forced to borrow money for a short period of time to pay for these inputs before the outputs are sold. By matching production to purchases, owners can reduce reliance on borrowed money and thus reduce interest expense associated with goods produced but not sold.

2. *Increase collections.* Once goods are sold, payment for them generally lags behind, unless the payment is made in cash or with a credit card at the time of sale. Suppose that a lawyer bills her only client $1000. The client pays the bill at the end of 2 months. In the mean time, the

lawyer needs to pay her monthly rent of $1000. Where does she get the money? She borrows it. When she receives the $1000 from the client, she repays the $1000 plus the interest she owes. If the lawyer increased her collections, that is, has the client pay her in 1 week and not 2 months, the lawyer would receive the cash sooner, reduce her need for credit, and pay less interest.

3. *Increase the time its takes to pay suppliers.* This effectively allows the owner to keep the cash received from customers for a longer period of time before paying suppliers what he owes them. In this case, the suppliers are providing credit without an associated interest expense.

The Artful Lighting Example

Artful Lighting is a lighting and fixture wholesaler. Artful sells to department stores and retail lighting stores. Revenue in 2000 was $3,121,000. Before-tax profits were $400,000. Total working capital requirements represented about 15 percent of sales. The Valuation GURU indicated that the value of Artful was about $3 million.

The owners of Artful Lighting wondered what they could do to get on a higher profit growth path without making a major investment. Their accountant recommended that they focus on reducing the ratio of working capital to sales from its current level of 15 percent to 10 percent over the next several years. To accomplish this reduction in the working-capital-to-sales ratio, Artful Lighting would have to change some of its traditional practices. The company's proposed tactics to accomplish this goal are to

1. Focus more of its sales efforts on the retail lighting stores that tend to pay their bills more quickly than the department stores
2. Limit selling to one department store chain that is a potential bankruptcy candidate and is a notoriously slow payer
3. Expand efforts to sell returned, undamaged merchandise through Internet auction sites such as eBay
4. Improve supply chain use by segmenting its parts inventory by turnover rates and significantly reducing over time the amount of low-turnover parts inventory held by the company

As the company moves to this lower ratio, earnings growth likely will rise above what the company had expected prior to making any changes in its working capital practices. Rerunning the Valuation GURU with this higher earnings path resulted in the valuation of Artful Lighting increasing to $3.4 million. This $400,000 increase did not require any significant investment to achieve this result. It is predicated on management running the business smarter.

INCREASING VALUE THROUGH FINANCIAL LEVERAGE

In general, businesses are financed with a combination of equity and debt. Equity is a security, which represents the ownership of the business, but this security has no guarantee of a dividend payment. Dividends are only paid when a company's board of directors determines that there is sufficient capital in the business to support the dividend payment. Because dividend payments to equity holders are both voluntary and changeable, financial analysts call equity a *variable-payment security*. On the other hand, debt is a fixed-payment contractual obligation of the firm to a creditor. The relative amounts of debt and equity used to finance a business are called its *capital structure*. The use of debt financing is often called *financial leverage* because the business is bringing in fixed-payment debt financing. The hope is that the debt financing can be invested in activities that will generate a return greater than the required debt payments, and in this way, the return to the equity holder will be increased (i.e., leveraged).

The relationship between financial leverage and firm value is a contentious and unsettled area that has received considerable attention from financial academics and practitioners. Although there is disagreement on many points, we can make some general observations about this topic. We encourage business owners to give the capital structure of their businesses the serious thought we believe it deserves.

Financial Leverage in a C-Type Corporation

The strongest statement that can be made about debt financing is that if a business is a taxable entity (e.g., a C Corporation), then the tax law of the United States gives a business owner a strong incentive to use debt. Here is an example that shows why. Todd owns Todd's Dental Supply, a C Corporation. Current annual sales are $500,000, and pretax profits (profit before taxes and any interest expense) are $150,000. Todd is the only investor in the firm. Table 8-1 shows the financial results under a no debt scenario and a 10 percent debt scenario, where Todd provides $100,000 of the necessary financing to his company as a loan that pays interest of 10 percent.

The basic point of Table 8-1 is that if Todd's Dental Supply is all equity financed, then the firm has $105,000 in net income that Todd, as the owner, could take as dividends. If the firm is financed with $100,000 of debt with interest payable at 10 percent, then the net income is reduced to $98,000, which Todd could take as dividends. However, Todd also would receive $10,000 in interest income from his $100,000 debt investment in the firm. With debt financing, Todd would be paid $108,000 for his investments in the firm, as opposed to $105,000 if the firm were all equity financed.

TABLE 8-1   Todd's Dental Supply Under Two Capital Structure Scenarios

Capital Structure Scenarios

Key Financial Concepts	No Debt	10% Debt
Sales	$500,000	$500,000
Operating expenses	$350,000	$350,000
Interest expense	$0	$ 10,000
Taxable income	$150,000	$140,000
Tax (30%)	$ 45,000	$ 42,000
Net income	$105,000	$ 98,000
Payments to Todd		
Dividends	$105,000	$ 98,000
Interest income	$0	$ 10,000
Total payments to Todd	$105,000	$108,000

Where does this extra $3000 come from? The answer is simple. For tax purposes, interest on debt is considered a tax-deductible expense. Without debt, Todd's Dental Supply pays $45,000 in taxes; with debt, it pays $42,000 in taxes. The total value of Todd's Dental Supply (i.e., the value of all equity and debt) is greater if the firm uses debt financing. This is so because corporate tax payments are lower, and payments to equity and debt investors are higher.

Financial Leverage in a Tax Pass-Thru Type of Entity

In the case of a nontaxable business, such as a partnership or an S Corporation, the value-enhancing effect of debt financing is less clear than in the taxable case. Since a partnership and an S Corporation do not pay taxes, the tax deductibility of interest expense is not relevant. If value is to be increased by using debt for these firms, it must come from the fact that the debt financing costs less than equity financing.

As we have previously noted, the market for equity capital for a privately held small business is illiquid and inefficient. For this reason, the equity of these firms is more expensive than the comparable equity of publicly traded firms. Although small, private businesses do not have access to the public debt markets (i.e., the public bond market), their situation with debt is improved because of the existence of commercial banks that make loans to these businesses. There are many commercial banks that compete to serve the small business segment, so a small business owner has the ability to acquire debt financing at rates that are closer (than for equity financing) to that of publicly traded firms. Government programs, such as the Small Business Administration (SBA) Loan Guarantee Program, further improve this situation. Qualifying businesses can obtain loans from commercial banks that are guaranteed by the U.S. government through the SBA. In these cases, the cost of debt financing is artificially lower than it would otherwise be.

Rod's Dental Supply Example

The owner of the private, tax pass-thru type of firm may be able to increase his wealth through refinancing the assets of the company. Here is how. Let's now look at Rod's Dental Supply, Inc., which is an S Corporation. Current annual sales are $500,000, and pretax profits (profit before taxes and any interest expense) are $150,000. Rod's salary is consistent with dental supply industry benchmarks.

The firm currently has no debt. For estate-tax purposes, Rod valued his business at $750,000, using a five times earnings multiple. Rod wanted to raise $375,000 in cash, or 50 percent of what he believed the firm was worth. He thought that the best way to do this was to borrow through the SBA loan program against the earning power of the business. Before the bank agreed to loan Rod the $375,000, the loan officer told Rod that the bank needed to do an arm's-length valuation of the firm. The bank valued the firm at $1 million to Rod's surprise and delight. Table 8-2 shows how the $1 million valuation was determined using a simple rule of thumb that divides cash flow by the cost of capital.

The bank's valuation was higher than Rod's estimate because the firm's cost of capital declined from 20 to 15 percent. This is so because the bank did the following calculations. Rod's loan request amounted to 50 percent of the value of the firm, as it is currently financed. Based on the firm's credit history, the SBA guarantee, and the growth in pretax cash flow, the bank was willing to loan Rod $375,000 over a 10-year period at 10 percent. Since half the firm was financed with equity at a rate of 20 percent and the remainder financed with debt at 10 percent, the firm's cost of capital was reduced to 15 percent, or the average of the cost of debt and the cost of equity. Since the pretax cash flow of the firm remains at $150,000, a lower discount rate translates into higher value.

TABLE 8-2   Valuation of Rod's Dental Supply Before and After Debt Financing

Cash Flow for Rod's Dental Supply	Cost of Capital Before Debt Financing	Cost of Capital After Debt Financing	Value of the Firm Before Debt Financing	Value of Firm After Debt Financing
$150,000	20%	15%	$750,000	$1,000,000
Before interest and taxes			Column 1 divided by column 2	Column 1 divided by column 3

The Wealth Effect of Financial Leverage

To see why Rod is really better off after the financing than before, we need only consider how his wealth has changed. Prior to the financing, all of Rod's wealth was tied up in his business. If he sold his business, he would have received $750,000 in cash. However, a new buyer would not likely purchase Rod's business with 100 percent of the buyer's own money. The buyer would have borrowed part of the purchase price rather than tying up wealth in this business. Thus, if this financing split is optimal for a new buyer, it also should be optimal for Rod as long as the cash flows of the business are adequate to pay the interest on the debt.

Figure 8-1 shows the level of Rod's wealth before borrowing the $375,000 increased, as well as its distribution. Prior to the financing, 100 percent of Rod's wealth was represented by his business. Afterwards, business ownership represented 62.5 percent and cash represented 37.5 percent.

FIGURE 8-1   Rod's assets before and after loan.

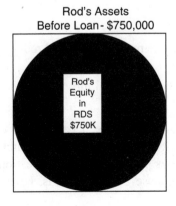
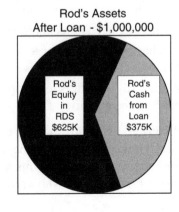

DIVERSIFICATION RESULTS IN LESS RISK

Rod, like many owners of established businesses, had all his wealth tied up in his dental supply business. While the return on the dental supply business is quite high, it is also quite risky; a point that is often overlooked when one runs a successful business. The risk emerges because the success of the business often depends on the health and well-being of the owner(s) or on other attributes unique to the firm. In Rod's case, he could become unexpectedly injured and not able to manage the business. The firm might be subject to a legal judgment that exceeds the firm's insurance liability coverage so that the excess would have to be paid out of firm earnings. These are only two of many possibilities. The point is that when these events occur, the firm's ability to meet client needs may be hampered. If Rod cannot deliver dental equipment and supplies to his customers when they need them, they look to other suppliers. They may never come back, particularly if Rod's competitors meet their needs as well as Rod does.

Prior to refinancing, Rod was not very well diversified—all his wealth was tied up in his business. After refinancing, Rod's portfolio was far less risky because almost 38 percent of it was held in cash, an asset that has no risk. The upshot, however, of this diversification is that this now lower-risk portfolio also has a lower return because the ownership of the business, which has a very high return, is now combined with an asset—cash—that has a very low return.

Rod's objective is to reinvest these cash proceeds into other high-return investments without increasing the risk of the overall portfolio. Rod realizes that he will need help from his financial advisor to achieve this.

INCREASING VALUE THROUGH ACQUISITION

Public firms purchase other public and private firms all the time. The reasons for these purchases differ. These reasons include

- Entering new domestic and foreign markets
- Expanding niche product lines
- Purchasing needed technology
- Purchasing a competitor to both increase market share and reduce fixed costs per dollar of revenue
- Buying key suppliers to ensure access to a critical input needed to produce the acquiring firm's product and service

Whatever the motivation, acquisitions are made because it is often cheaper to buy an existing business than it is to build one from scratch.

This is true for private firms as well as public firms. The question for owners of private firms who seek to purchase another firm is, How do I determine how much to pay for a target firm? The maximum price an acquirer would pay for a target can be stated as follows:

Maximum value of an acquisition candidate (target firm) to an acquiring firm = value of the target as an ongoing business + incremental value the acquiring firm expects to create after it purchases the target firm

The Valuation GURU can be used to calculate the value of a target firm as an ongoing operation, and it can be used to calculate the incremental value created as result of the combination. The price that an acquirer should be willing to pay is between the value of the firm as an ongoing business and its maximum value. There are a number of factors that will determine where along this range of values the actual sale price will land. These include

- *Experience in building value by acquisition.* For example, a company that is "rolling up" many similar businesses, such as insurance agencies or veterinary practices, should have a high degree of certainty about its ability to increase the value of the next acquired firm.
- *Presence of multiple buyers.* The larger the number of potential buyers, the greater is the likelihood that the successful acquirer will have to pay a price close to the maximum value.

AN ALTERNATIVE ENDING TO THE EARTHRIGHT CASE

In Chapter 6, NEESI, a public company, acquired The EarthRight Group, a private company. In this case, JW Shah of NEESI used the Valuation GURU to analyze the incremental value that NEESI would gain from acquiring EarthRight. JW's scenario for EarthRight included pushing it to the high-growth path for earnings in its sector and adding $50,000 to pretax earnings. This adjustment to earnings was based on an assumption that EarthRight's expenses could be reduced by a net of $50,000, due to costs that would be unnecessary once EarthRight was part of NEESI. As we noted, JW also believed that there were additional financial benefits to the acquisition. As a rational businessperson, he only wanted to offer a price sufficient to win over the owners of EarthRight, not a price that reflected the full incremental value that NEESI expected to gain.

This same logic applies to a private company acquiring another private company. In the EarthRight case, there also was the possibility of selling the firm to another environmental consulting partnership or S Corporation. We shall now explore what could have happened if another firm interested in EarthRight had come along at the same time.

The Winter Environmental Consulting Group

John Winter, president of the Winter Environmental Consulting Group, in Newton, Massachusetts, also heard of the Milton divorce case and its potential impact on The EarthRight Group. The Winter Group, an S Corporation with 10 owner-officers of the firm and revenues just under $3 million, frequently competes with EarthRight for residential jobs. John knew and respected all three partners of EarthRight. He believed that they would fit right into the collegial, partnership-like atmosphere at the Winter Group. He asked Laura Simon if EarthRight would be open to an offer from the Winter Group, and after checking with her partners, she responded with a very positive yes. After John faxed Laura a signed confidentiality agreement, she sent over a copy of the Valuation GURU "Snapshots" and "Maximizer" (see Appendix 6A) for EarthRight as a stand-alone business. As John reviewed the material, he considered how much incremental value EarthRight might bring.

Sources of Incremental Value

In professional services businesses, revenue comes from billable hours. The billability and the rates of EarthRight's partners were at the same levels as Winter's officers, so John could not count on incremental value from revenue efficiency gains. Consequently, for his valuation of EarthRight, he chose the baseline industry growth path.

On the expense side, the opportunities were much more positive. The Winter Group had extra office space, so the company could absorb three additional senior people and two clerical people with no increase in its occupancy costs. EarthRight had already found that its landlord was willing to let the company out of its lease with no penalties because there was a dental practice looking for space in that building and willing to pay higher rent. EarthRight's rent expenses of $25,000 should be saved by this move, plus at least $4000 in utilities and other occupancy-related costs.

The Winter Group also had an opening for a clerical staffer because one of its employees had resigned recently. The Winter Group considered itself a leader in using office technology to get the most productivity from its staff. If the EarthRight staff joined the Winter Group, John planned not to fill the clerical vacancy. He was confident that putting the two EarthRight clerical people into his more productive clerical environment would allow him to cover the vacancy and the needs of the three new partners. Not filling this vacancy would save $30,000 in salaries and another $4500 in benefits.

Finally, similar to what JW of NEESI estimated, there are duplicate association memberships, insurance policies, auditing costs, and other expenses. John's estimate of this amount was $25,000, rather than the $50,000 estimated by JW. Table 8-3 summarizes the full savings estimated by John Winter.

TABLE 8-3   Sources of Incremental Value to the Winter Group from EarthRight Acquisition

Expense Gains	Annual Savings
Rent savings	$25,000
Other occupancy savings	$ 4,000
Clerical position, salary	$30,000
Clerical position, benefits	$ 4,500
Other duplicative expenses	$25,000
Total expense gains	$88,500

John already knew that the Winter Group had an advantage over NEESI's situation because the Winter Group would retain the tax pass-thru status of EarthRight's earnings. He also knew that there would be no business broker commissions paid for a Winter Group acquisition of EarthRight.

Now John wanted to see how much additional value would be created as a result of these expense savings. He went to the bizownerHQ.com Web site and set up his own account and entered the EarthRight tax return. He than reran the Valuation GURU, adding $88,500 to the "Other Adjustments" line. The reader can see the EarthRight tax return in Appendix 6A and the "Valuation Snapshots report" for EarthRight as part of the Winter Group in Appendix 8A.

The Maximum Amount of Incremental Value

The $88,500 that John added to EarthRight's earnings increases the value of EarthRight from $722,027 as a stand-alone business to $1,391,455, given the special circumstances arising from an acquisition by the Winter Group. This is the maximum price that the Winter Group should pay for EarthRight. This is an illustration of how significantly the value of a business can change when there is a buyer positioned to generate higher earnings through cost savings or revenue enhancements. These results are compared with the NEESI maximum incremental value in Table 8-4.

TABLE 8-4   Comparison of NEESI and Winter Group Value Analyses

Potential Acquisition Alternatives	NEESI	Winter Group
Fair market value for EarthRight	$ 722,027	$ 722,027
Maximum pretax price for acquisition	$1,438,060	$1,391,455
Rationale for incremental value	Move to high growth for earnings + $75,000 expense savings	Stay at baseline growth for earnings + $88,500 expense savings
Minus adjustment for tax pass-thru status	$413,844	$0
Equals maximum price for acquisition	$1,024,216	$1,391,455
Minus incremental value retained by acquirer	$ 164,216	$ 531,455
Equals purchase price offered	$ 860,000	$ 860,000
Final bid—EarthRight goes with Winter Group	$1,000,000	$1,100,000

John Winter believed that all he had to do was match the NEESI offer in order to win EarthRight because moving to the Winter Group required the least amount of change for Randy, Robin, and Laura. His initial offer of $860,000 that matched the NEESI offer used only a small part of the incremental value that Winter Group estimated was available from this acquisition. This offer left over $530,000 in value retained by the Winter Group. John was certain that JW Shah of NEESI also had additional incremental value from this acquisition in his back pocket. As shown in Table 8-4, JW had over $160,000 in incremental value to NEESI after his offer of $860,000. Thus John expected that competition between NEESI and the Winter Group would push up the eventual successful offer for EarthRight Consulting, which it did. After a few weeks of going back and forth between NEESI and the Winter Group, EarthRight was sold to the Winter Group for $1.1 million, more than the maximum value to the NEESI group but still within the value created by the combination with the Winters Group.

Business owners should know that not all businesses will find a strategic buyer, or more than one, who will offer a premium over the stand-alone value of the business. However, all established business owners who plan on their businesses continuing should allocate some amount of time and resources to investigate whether there are potential strategic buyers for the business. In this chapter's "Backgrounder" we look at new ways to find buyers for a business.

Business owners should know that sometimes the strategic buyer with the most to gain may be a competitor who only wants customer lists or contracts so that it can serve them with its products and people. Owners have to determine what is the right mix of financial rewards and good feelings about the future of the business and their former employees.

Finally, *business owners should know that they are not alone in finding the exit planning, working through valuation scenarios, and other BLE management issues among the hardest tasks in their business lives.* Based on our survey research and confidential interviews, few owners have "gotten off easily" in their business transitions despite what many boast in public. With the coming business transition tidal wave, we expect that many of these challenges will intensify. We strongly encourage owners to begin the hard work of exit planning and BLE management sooner rather than later!

BACKGROUNDER

NEW AVENUES FOR SELLING A BUSINESS

Being able to sell one's business may sound like a pipe dream to many smaller business owners, and until recently, it was. Consider Sam Kazanjian, a 55-year-old owner of a vending machine business. He thinks of his business as a means to support himself and his family. When the time comes to retire, he plans to do what others in his industry have done: close the business, sell the assets (i.e., vending machines), and move on.

Sam recently has become more curious about selling the entire business. However, Sam is concerned that costs associated with selling the ongoing business may wipe out any potential gain above what just an outright equipment sale would bring. For example, before setting a price for the business, Sam would need to have the business valued. He knows other business owners who have paid as much as $25,000 for a business valuation. Then there is the business broker commission. For a smaller business, this could be 10 percent or more of the selling price. As Sam ticks off these potential costs in his head, he can understand why so many owners in the past have just taken the liquidation route.

Business owners should know that there are a growing number of alternatives to these high-cost services for selling a business. As the transaction costs for selling a business decline, more and more businesses that generate profits will be worth selling as ongoing entities.

Since Sam's business generates cash above and beyond expenses, including Sam's salary, it is likely to be valuable to somebody else. Sam can extricate himself from the business in a number of ways. The exit strategies include

1. Outright sale
2. Family member buyout
3. Partner purchase
4. Establishing an employee stock ownership plan (ESOP)
5. Liquidating the assets of the business

The first four strategies, in which the business continues after the initial owner exits, have the potential to be financed with borrowed money.

One day Dave Asarto, one of Sam's customers, mentioned that his brother, Bob, was looking to buy a vending machine business. Sam agreed to meet with Bob. After discussions and a review of Sam's financials and business tax returns, Bob made the following offer to Sam:

1. The vending machine business is worth $100,000 as an ongoing business.
2. Bob will buy the business outright, paying $50,000 in cash to Sam and giving Sam a note for the remaining $50,000.
3. The note term is 5 years with an interest rate that is 4 percent above prime.
4. The $50,000 loan principal is paid back in equal installments beginning 1 year from the date of the sale.
5. Interest payments begin 1 year after the date of the sale.

After considering the offer, Sam decided not to accept. While Sam was glad to see that someone was willing to pay more than the liquidation value of his vending machines, he was concerned about two aspects of the deal. First, Sam did not want to finance any part of the sale. Second, Sam was not sure whether the $100,000 price was high enough. Sam realized that the best way to get a higher price was to make the sale of the business known to a larger number of potential buyers. Unfortunately, this thinking took Sam back into two things he did not want to do: pay a lot of money for a valuation and/or pay a sizable commission to a broker. He mentioned these frustrations to his son, Arnie, a graduate student and an avid Internet surfer.

Arnie told Sam that there must be Internet sites to help small business owners sell their businesses. Arnie first went to *www.business.gov*, an SBA site with links to resources on the Web, and then onto the SCORE site (*www.score.org*). SCORE is the Service Corps of Retired Executives, a program that provides free consulting help for small business owners. The SCORE site had a listing for a business valuation site and several sites for listing a business for sale. Within a few hours, Sam accomplished the following:

1. He got an accurate valuation ($250,000) of his business from www.bizownerHQ.com.

2. He reviewed the customized valuation report on maximizing the value of his business from www.bizownerHQ.com.

3. He made a preliminary assessment of a listing-for-sale price ($300,000) and his bottom-line price ($250,000).

4. He reviewed several business-for-sale sites.

Armed with this information, Sam called his accountant and his lawyer to go over this information and his thoughts. Both advisors gave their approval after reviewing the reports and rationale for setting the price at $300,000.

Listing a Business for Sale on the Internet

Sam also outlined his plans for reaching the largest number of potential buyers through the Internet. From his site review, he had concluded that the Internet has changed the rules governing the sale of private businesses and that both buyers and sellers potentially can benefit. The way this actually works is quite straightforward, but Sam realized that posting his business for sale on the Web might not create a significant benefit to him.

There are two types of Web posting models. The first type includes business brokers using the Web to post businesses as a way to reach a wider audience. The owner needs to be aware that dealing through brokers always results in some commission-based costs and that these costs are not necessarily reduced because of Web access. The business broker typically will package a set of services including a business valuation intended to provide information to the buyer and raise his comfort level about the proposed transaction and associated financing.

The second type of business posting Web sites focuses on facilitating transactions and does not charge a commission when a transaction is completed. These Web sites focus on making any transaction as transparent as possible by unbundling the various services for which a seller-owner typically pays. An owner can have the business valued for a modest fee and then post the business for sale for free. Buyers can avail themselves of the same resources and feel comfortable that the firm does not collect any commission-based fees from any of the parties. While this environment does not remove selling costs totally, it does remove broker commissions, which represent a large percentage of selling costs. Lower costs show up as higher net proceeds for the seller and a lower price for the buyer. Figures 8-2 and 8-3 show the benefits the Internet offers business owners.

FIGURE 8-2   Old model: Net proceeds to seller are too low and price buyer
pays is too high.

FIGURE 8-3   New model: Net proceeds to seller increase and price buyer
pays is lower; both buyer and seller benefit from reduced
transactions costs.

Sam found a buyer for his business through an Internet listing. Posting
the business allowed Sam to achieve far greater reach than he could if he had
tried to promote the business in any other way. Sam found a buyer willing to
purchase the business. Although the sale price was less than $300,000, his
proceeds, after accounting for transactions costs, were greater, $280,000
($290,000 − $10,000), than they would have been if the business had been

sold through a business broker. After transactions costs, Sam would have only retained $270,000. The buyer also benefited from this transaction because Sam now could afford to pass on some of his savings to the buyer in the form of a reduced price—$290,000, a $10,000 savings from what the business would have cost through a traditional business broker.

The result is that the Internet platform can and will force those involved in a private business transaction to, in effect, unbundle their services and price each separately. This makes the business selling process far more transparent because buyers of these services know what they are paying for. They can make a reasoned determination whether the value received is worth the price. By allowing buyers and sellers of businesses to shop for various services, the market for them is likely to be more competitive, which in the end will drive down prices and increase the value of what is offered. Finally, the volume of transactions is likely to increase as both buyers and sellers of businesses are forced to meet market-imposed disclosure standards arising out of increased transparency. This development has important advantages for potential buyers and sellers, such as

1. More capital will enter the private market.
2. Raising capital will be less onerous and expensive.

With the coming business transition tidal wave, improving efficiency and cost-effectiveness in all aspects of selling and buying a business will be important for business sellers and buyers, as well as for the U.S. economy as a whole.

Appendix 8A
THE EARTHRIGHT GROUP: VALUATION OUTPUTS

Valuation Snapshots Report: EarthRight as a Winter Group Acquisition

VALUATION SNAPSHOTS REPORT: EARTHRIGHT AS A WINTER GROUP ACQUISITION

WHAT IS THE EARTHRIGHT GROUP WORTH?

The Valuation GURU estimates that the fair market total value of The EarthRight Group is $1,391,455 as of January 1, 2001, based on the business tax return information entered. Please review the bizownerHQ key assumptions to make sure that they apply to this business.

The Valuation GURU builds up the fair market total value of a business by estimating value separately by source, as shown in Figure 8A-1.

FIGURE 8A-1 The EarthRight Group as part of the Winter Group—Total value estimate.

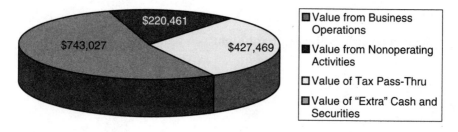

■	Value from Business Operations
■	Value from Nonoperating Activities
☐	Value of Tax Pass-Thru
■	Value of "Extra" Cash and Securities

$220,461

$743,027

$427,469

1. *Value from business operations.* Generally, the primary source of value in a business is based on the cash flows from the earnings of the business operations, that is, the products or services the company sells, less the cash needed for investments in operations. The Valuation GURU uses a sophisticated proprietary approach to forecasting the revenues and adjusted earnings of the business operations and then calculates the present value of those future anticipated earnings to determine the value shown in Figure 8A-1.

2. *Value from nonoperating activities.* Many businesses have other sources of income, such as rental income from buildings or licensing income, that are generated outside the normal business operations. While these cash flows have value, they are not given the same valuation treatment as income from business operations, reflecting that buyers often will not value these nonoperating cash flows as highly as those from operating activities. The Valuation GURU, following standard practices, calculates the present value of the current income flow to the business owner(s).

3. *Value of tax pass-thru.* Companies, that are not C corporations filing an 1120 Tax Form have a tax advantage: Any earnings that the company reports are not taxed at the corporate level and are "passed through" to the owner's individual tax return. The Valuation GURU shows this value separately so that an owner can determine the likely reduction in value that would occur if the business were sold to a C Corporation rather than to a corporation that can take advantage of the tax pass-thru, such as an S Corporation, partnership, or sole proprietorship (all other elements of the deal being equal).

4. *Value of extra cash and securities.* The final source of value that the Valuation GURU analyzes is whether the company has on its balance sheet a level of cash and marketable securities above what is considered necessary to fund working capital. The Valuation GURU draws on financial analysis research across thousands of companies for a revenue-based factor to estimate the working capital needs of a company. If the cash and securities on the balance sheet are greater than this estimate, the Valuation GURU makes an adjustment to the fair market total valuation to reflect this extra difference.

DEFINITIONS

1. *Fair market total value.* The price at which the property would change hands between a willing buyer and a willing seller when the former is not under any compulsion to buy and the latter is not under any compulsion to sell, both parties having reasonable knowledge of relevant facts (Internal Revenue Service Revenue Rule 59-60, 1959-1, C.B. 237).

2. *Fair market total value.* The sum of the fair market values of the cash flows from business operations, nonoperating activities, and the tax pass-thru *plus* the value of the current dollar amount of the extra company cash and marketable securities, if any.

bizownerHQ KEY ASSUMPTIONS

1. *Company growth rate forecasts.* Revenue and cash flows for EarthRight are projected to grow at rates consistent with the baseline or average-performing growth segment of companies in this industry.

2. *No greater use of assets.* The assets of EarthRight, including production equipment, technology, patents, intangible assets, or real estate used by the company, have no greater value as stand-alone assets than they have as profit-generating assets for this business.

GURU Alert

Please review with your accountant or other business professional whether these assumptions are correct for your business before using this valuation as input to decision making.

WHAT IS THE OWNERSHIP EQUITY IN EARTHRIGHT WORTH?

The estimated value of the ownership equity in EarthRight is $1,385,855. This is the amount the owners would receive if the company were sold today for the fair market total value of $1,391,455 minus an estimate of the amount necessary to pay off company debts and long-term liabilities, as shown in Figure 8A-2. Ownership equity is equal to the firm's minority interest value, $1,133,707, plus a control premium of $252,149, the amount necessary to obtain full control of the firm.

FIGURE 8A-2   **The EarthRight Group as part of the Winter Group—Total ownership value.**

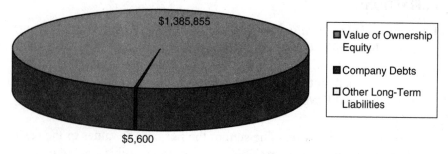

The Valuation GURU separates business value into its ownership components, as shown in Figure 8A-2.

1. *Value of ownership equity.* This is an estimate of the market value of owner equity in the business.
   - *Minority value of equity.* Minority owners own less than 51 percent of the equity of a firm and do not have the right to direct how the firm's assets are used. Minority owners have claims on a firm's earnings after taxes and interest and a right to vote on firm agenda items.

- *Control premium.* When a business is sold, the buyer or buyers typically purchase full control of the firm. This gives the new buyers the right to change the way the firm is managed, the types of products and services the firm desires to produce, and the number of employees that are required. In return for the right to make these and other decisions, a buyer will pay a premium above the minority equity value of the firm. This premium is not a constant percentage. It varies with the level of interest rates, the riskiness of the firm, and the long-term growth of the firm's earnings.

2. *Company debts (book value).* This book-value concept from the tax return balance sheet is the closest estimate of the market value of the company's debt that the Valuation GURU can make with the information provided.

Caution: The terms and conditions of any business loans should be reviewed by the company's accountant or by the owner(s) to determine whether there are any prepayment penalties or other charges that would make the market value of the company's debts different from the book value. Any differences found should be included in the preceding estimate to refine the valuation of the company.

WHAT ARE THE VALUATION MULTIPLES FOR EARTHRIGHT?
The Valuation GURU estimates that the value-to-revenue multiple for EarthRight is 2.31 and that the value-to-earnings multiple is 10.36 as of January 1, 2001, as shown in Figure 8A-3.

What Business Owners Need to Know about Industry Valuation Multiples

1. *Beware of the industry valuation multiples.* These industry valuation multiples are used by business brokers and investment bankers to provide owners with a quick and supposedly costless way to find out the value of their companies. For example, a broker might tell a landscaping business owner that landscaping businesses typically sell for one times revenue.

2. *Typical concerns with industry valuation multiples.* Industry valuation estimates generally are based on the company sales experiences of, at worst, a single broker and, at best, a number of brokers. For most industries, there are no consistently reliable data sources where transaction data on the prices and terms of privately held businesses can be

**FIGURE 8A-3   The EarthRight Group as part of the Winter Group—
Valuation multiples.**

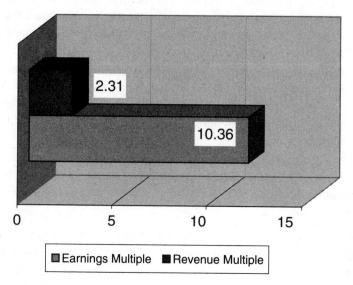

found. There are many factors in these sales, such as how quickly the owner needs to sell and the financing of the business before and after the sale, that have significant impact on the actual price and hence the valuation multiple. Decisions owners make based on the valuation, such as selling a business, should be made on more solid evidence.

- *Is this an average business for this industry?* An owner applying an industry multiple to her business should wonder whether her business is likely to have a value right at the average or median level. If a business is more productive and efficient than most, then that business should be worth a higher multiple.

- *Problems with earnings-based multiples.* Valuation multiples based on earnings are particularly troublesome because how privately held companies report earnings varies significantly. Industry valuation estimates tend to be based on transactions over a long period of time, yet business valuations change frequently as interest rates change and as perceptions about industry growth opportunities and industry risk change.

- *Valuation multiples are rarely used for the benefit of the current owner.* Business brokers and investment bankers have a natural incentive to encourage a quick transaction so that they maximize their compensation for the amount of work they do. By encouraging business owners and business buyers to rely on these industry valuation multiples, brokers reinforce the "value" of their role and justify their sizable commission.

How Can bizownerHQ Valuation Multiples Be Used?

1. *Valuation multiples can be useful shorthand tools.* The bizownerHQ company-specific valuation multiples are useful shorthand tools for understanding the current valuation of a company and how that valuation might vary in the short run from changes in revenue or earnings. For example, a business with a company-specific valuation-to-revenue multiple of six can estimate that if the company can increase revenues by $50,000, then the company should be worth approximately $300,000 more. (This assumes that the company is able to generate higher earnings and cash flow after investments at the same rate as before.)

   - ***Business owners should know that company-specific valuation multiples will change as interest rates and economic conditions change.*** For example, as a general rule, when the Federal Reserve increases interest rates in the U.S. economy by pushing up the federal funds rate, the valuation of all U.S. companies will decline somewhat.

2. *Valuation multiples vary within industries and over time.* There is generally a wide difference in the revenue and earnings growths of companies in the same industry. Companies with higher growth in revenue and earnings typically will have a higher multiple than companies in their industry with lower revenue and earnings.

   - *Owners need to be aware of this potential valuation range within their industry.* They should evaluate potential risks and rewards that go along with a more aggressive growth strategy. They also should review whether a more aggressive growth strategy might lead to less control for the owner. For example, borrowing money for expansion from a bank increases the influence of the bank on the company's decisions.

INDEX

ABOUT THE AUTHORS

STANLEY J. FELDMAN, PH.D.

Stan is an expert in the theory and practice of private business valuation and financing. In addition, he is one of the most experienced industry forecasters in the United States. As chairman of bizownerHQ, he has overall responsibility for bizownerHQ's valuation expert system and the industry-forecasting databases that support this system.

Stan is associate professor of finance at Bentley College in Waltham, MA. For the last 10 years, he has consulted on complex business valuation situations. From 1980 to 1989, Stan developed the industry-forecasting services at DRI/McGraw-Hill, rising to senior vice president of industry information services. Dr. Feldman has a Ph.D. in economics from New York University.

TIMOTHY G. SULLIVAN, PH.D.

Tim is a professor of finance at Bentley College in Waltham, MA. Tim has over 25 years' experience teaching undergraduate and graduate finance courses in which business valuation is a major topic. He has written numerous articles and monographs for both the academic and professional finance communities. He holds an M.B.A. and a Ph.D. in finance from the Eli Broad Graduate School of Management of Michigan State University.

ROGER M. WINSBY

Roger has developed an in-depth understanding of American business owners from directing several major market research studies for financial services companies. He also has hands-on experience in running a small business. As president of bizownerHQ, he has overall responsibility for bizownerHQ's marketing, technology, and business operations. From 1994 to 1998, he was chief operating officer and executive vice president for Chadwick Martin Bailey, a market research firm. Previously, he served as group vice president for U.S. sales, marketing, and consulting of DRI/McGraw-Hill.